Global TV

Global TV

New Media and the Cold War,
1946–69

JAMES SCHWOCH

University of Illinois Press
URBANA AND CHICAGO

Library of Congress Cataloging-in-Publication Data

Schwoch, James
Global TV : new media and the Cold War, 1946–69 /
James Schwoch.
p.   cm.
Includes bibliographical references and index.
ISBN-13 978-0-252-03374-2 (cloth : alk. paper)
ISBN-10 0-252-03374-4 (cloth : alk. paper)
ISBN-13 978-0-252-07569-8 (pbk. : alk. paper)
ISBN-10 0-252-07569-2 (pbk. : alk. paper)
1. Television broadcasting—United States—History.
2. Television in propaganda—United States.
3. Television broadcasting of news—United States.
4. Cold War.
I. Title.
PN1992.3.U5S32   2008
070.1'95—dc22   2008019204

For all our friends from Finland

From the formalized government-to-government communications of the classical past, we have now witnessed the advent of epistolary diplomacy, electronic diplomacy, summit diplomacy, and unofficial diplomacy—not to mention undiplomatic diplomacy.
—Mansfield Sprague to Dwight Eisenhower, January 1961

Contents

Illustrations follow pages 76 and 138

Acknowledgments

So many people and so many institutions supported my research over the past decade that I consider myself a fortunate scholar whose greatest challenge is not in finding collegiality with this project, but rather in remembering its infinite varieties. Without the advice and labor of a multitude of people whose names I largely do not know—the archivists, cataloguers, indexers, librarians, and similar staff of the National Archives, the Hoover, Truman, Eisenhower, Kennedy, and Johnson presidential libraries, the Wisconsin Historical Society, the Ford Foundation archives, and the British Public Records Office, I never would have found, read, and written about the documents used in this study. Fellowships, grants, and financial support from the Center for Strategic and International Studies, the Ford Foundation, the National Science Foundation, the Fulbright Commissions of Germany and of Finland, and the Ameritech Foundation enhanced my ability to conduct research. Visiting professorships at the University of Jyvaskyla and University of Helsinki, near the start and then near the end of this project, stimulated my insights.

Many universities, scholarly organizations, and agencies were gracious hosts as I presented portions, versions, and musings from this project, including the German Historical Institute, the Newberry Library, the Renvall Institute, New York University, University of Texas, Pritzker Military Library, University of Wisconsin, National War College, Carnegie-Mellon University, Florida Atlantic University, the International Telecommunications Union, Macalester College, Rutgers University, Stockholm University, Tartu University, Woodrow Wilson International Center for Scholars, Chicago Council on Foreign Relations, Center for Twentieth Century Studies, Dartmouth College, Massachusetts Institute of Technology, and Brown University. The

Association for Cultural Studies, the Society for Cinema and Media Studies, the Society for the History of American Foreign Relations, the International Studies Association, the International Communication Association, the National Communication Association, the Modern Language Association, and the International Association of Mass Communication Research all welcomed me as a presenter at one or more of their annual conferences. I received so many good ideas and helpful comments from participants at all these venues that I can scarcely imagine how this book could ever have been completed without their feedback and encouragement.

A world of friends and colleagues always knew I would finish this project—although I occasionally forgot I would—and their solidarity was inspirational. Thanks to, in no particular order, Lisa Parks, Anna McCarthy, Jen Light, John Durham Peters, Janet Staiger, Charles Whitney, Ellen Wartella, John Hartley, Michael Curtin, Michelle Hilmes, Julie D'Acci, Shanti Kumar, Mark Williams, Mary Desjardins, David Hounshell, Vanessa Schwartz, Susan Smulyan, John Caldwell, Hamid Naficy, Susan Reilly, Michael Hofmann, David Chioni Moore, Kathleen Woodward, Raili Põldsaar, Markku Henriksson, Mikko Saikku, Esa Väliverronen, Ullamaija Kivikuru, Ritva Levo-Henriksson, Yonca Ermutlu, Helena Tapper, Terhi Rantanen, Raimo Salokangas, Ulla Eckmann-Salokangas, Kaarle Nordenstreng, Terhi Mölsä, Barbara Ischinger, Thomas Doherty, Richard John, Douglas Gomery, Daniel Headrick, Slava Gerovitch, James Der Derian, Tetsuo Arima, Tom Will, William Uricchio, Sasha Torres, Tim Anderson, David Culbert, Nicholas Cull, Michael Kackman, Jonathan Winkler, Michael Krysko, Jeremi Suri, David Nickles, David William Cohen, Bruce Cumings, Ken Abbott, Charles Ragin, Jane Guyer, Micaela DiLeonardo, Carl Petry, Frank Safford, John Bushnell, Ken Alder, Robert Launay, Jack Doppelt, Ben Schneider, Brian Hanson, Ed Gibson, Judy Gibson, Michael Loriaux, Theodore and Louann Van Zelst, James Pritzker, Ambassador Leonard Marks, Ambassador Diana Dougan, William Garrison, Barry Fulton, Wilson Dizard, Erik Peterson, Kevin Hartman, Robert Pepper, and William L. Bird. A special thanks to everyone at the Tabard Inn.

Joan Catapano, Copenhaver Cumpston, Sara Luttfring, Angela Burton, and Joseph Peeples at the University of Illinois Press were terrific, and I give thanks to two anonymous reviewers for their thoughtful encouragements. I will always be grateful for the copyediting by Karen Hallman, who improved this book immeasurably; thanks to Susan Cohen for the index. Finally, Mimi and Travis showed interest, patience, and understanding of a magnitude beyond my comprehension, which made me feel awfully special and important when I really needed a boost—and I needed a boost pretty much each and every day for the ten years it took to bring this project to completion.

Abbreviations

AEC	Atomic Energy Commission
AID	U.S. Agency for International Development
AM	amplitude modulation; the first common bandwidth of radio broadcasting; precedes FM and is not in VHF bandwidth of electromagnetic spectrum; also known as medium wave
ARPA	Advanced Research Projects Agency
AT&T	American Telephone and Telegraph
BBC	British Broadcasting Corporation
CBC	Canadian Broadcasting Corporation
CBS	Columbia Broadcasting System
CENIS	Center for International Studies, MIT
CIA	Central Intelligence Agency
COMSAT	Communications Satellite Corporation
DARPA	Defense Advanced Research Projects Agency
DEW Line	Distant Early Warning RADAR Line of NORAD
DNA	deoxyribonucleic acid
DTRA	Defense Threat Reduction Agency
ECA	Economic Cooperation Administration (Marshall Plan)
ELEINT	Electronic intelligence, including traffic analysis, chatter, data collection of electronic information; see also HUMINT, PHOTOINT, SIGINT
EMP	electromagnetic pulse
ESSR	Estonian Soviet Socialist Republic (Estonia)
FBIS	Foreign Broadcasting Intelligence Service
FCC	Federal Communications Commission
FFA	Ford Foundation Archives, New York City
FM	frequency modulation; a common bandwidth for radio broadcasting; in VHF bandwidth of electromagnetic spectrum

FO	Foreign Office, United Kingdom (see also PRO-UK)
FRG	Federal Republic of Germany (West Germany)
GDR	German Democratic Republic (East Germany)
HDTV	high-definition television; also refers to technical standards for same
HICOG	Office of the U.S. High Commissioner for (occupied) Germany
HUMINT	human intelligence, or data collection for intelligence by humans; see also ELEINT, PHOTOINT, SIGINT
IBI	International Broadcast Institute; same organization as International Radio and Television Institute
IBM	International Business Machines
ICBM	Intercontinental Ballistic Missile
IGY	International Geophysical Year, 1956–58
IIA	International Information Activities division of the U.S. State Department (existed prior to formation of USIA)
INTELSAT	International Telecommunications Satellite Corporation (also International Telecommunications Satellite Organization)
IRTI	International Radio and Television Institute; also known in Ford Foundation documents as International Broadcast Institute
ITSO	International Telecommunications Satellite Organization (INTELSAT)
ITU	International Telecommunications Union
LEO	low-earth orbit (of satellites)
MIT	Massachusetts Institute of Technology
NARA	National Archives and Records Administration, Washington, D.C.
NARCOM	North Atlantic Relay Communications System
NAS	National Academy of Sciences
NASA	National Aeronautics and Space Administration
NASC	National Aeronautics and Space Council
NBC	National Broadcasting Corporation
NET	National Educational Television
NORAD	North American Aerospace Defense Command
NSC	National Security Council
NSF	National Science Foundation
NSSDC	National Space Science Data Center
NTSC	National Technical Standards Committee (set USA TV technical standards, some other nations also use NTSC standards); also USA TV technical standards
NTV	Nippon Television Network
OCB	Operations Coordinating Board
OMGUS	U.S. Office of Military Government for (occupied) Germany
OSS	Office of Strategic Services
OWI	Office of War Information

PAL	phased alternation line; UK TV technical standards, and TV technical standards of many other nations
PHOTOINT	photographic and image-based intelligence and data collection; see also ELEINT, HUMINT, SIGINT
PRO-UK	British Public Records Office
PSB	Psychological Strategy Board
RADAR	Radiolocation and Direction system
RAMAC	IBM 305 computer
RAND	Research and Development Corporation
RCA	Radio Corporation of America
RG	record group (from NARA)
RIAS	Radio in the American Sector of Berlin
SCORE	Signal Communication by Orbiting Relay Equipment
SECAM	sequential color with memory; TV technical standards of France and many other nations
SHSW	State Historical Society of Wisconsin (Wisconsin Historical Society)
SIGINT	signals intelligence; cryptanalysis, cryptography and code breaking; see also ELEINT, HUMINT, PHOTOINT
SMOF	Staff Member and Office Files
TV	television
UHF	ultrahigh frequency; a section of the electromagnetic spectrum with many applications, including some TV channels
U.K.	United Kingdom
UN	United Nations
UNESCO	United Nations Educational, Scientific, and Cultural Organization
UPU	Universal Postal Union
U.S.	United States
USA	United States of America
USAID	U.S. Agency for International Development
USIA	United States Information Agency
USSR	Union of Soviet Socialist Republics
VHF	very high frequency; a section of the electromagnetic spectrum with a variety of applications, including some TV channels
VOA	Voice of America
WHCF	White House Central Files

Global TV

Introduction

The July 1969 Apollo 11 moon mission marked two new moments. First and best known is the moon landing of American astronauts, from Neil Armstrong's one small step to Buzz Aldrin's magnificent desolation. Second, the mission was the televisual inauguration of an American-led global satellite network. Just nineteen days before mission launch, the final International Telecommunications Satellite Corporation (INTELSAT) satellite needed for live worldwide television (TV) networking became operational over the Indian Ocean, meaning that American television coverage of Apollo 11 could be globally distributed as it happened, live via INTELSAT, to all of the national TV networks of the world. Many of those networks chose to take the INTELSAT feed and telecast the moon landing over their own national networks. Virtually every nation in the world telecast at least some of the Apollo 11 moon mission. Although television was, among other things, international (intentionally or not) from its inception, and although throughout the Cold War, the United States of America, the Union of Socialist Soviet Republics, the United Kingdom, and other nations strove to expand the global reach of their own television services, the 1969 moon landing was not only the culmination of the superpower space race and a global triumph for American science, it was also a global triumph for American television.

This book narrates how American television during the Cold War began its global quest in very ad hoc and circumstantial ways, without a grand design or much thought from policy makers and strategic thinkers in the late 1940s and early 1950s. The story proceeds through the rise of Cold War tensions, propaganda battles of the superpowers, competition in science and technology, the growth of television in other nations, global electronic information networks, early forays into information diplomacy, and the growing importance of consumer culture on both sides of the Iron Curtain. Finally, in the 1960s, efforts by American diplomats and policymakers, encouraged by a durable network of communications researchers and media experts, conceptually positioned television on a list of signifiers of "world citizenship." In addition to television, this list included environmental issues, Antarctica, the International Geophysical Year (IGY), open science, outer space, public opinion polling, and on the darker side, weapons of mass destruction. Even though the new discourse of world citizenship was rooted in earlier conceptualizations and articulations around issues of security, this initial Cold War discourse of security did show signs of change and mutation. In this regard, the global Cold War story of American television also reveals origins of an American articulation and operationalization of a particular discourse about globalization. Thus, this book reveals both common ground and distinction between global Cold War discourses about security and globalization, demonstrating that global dissemination of American television with other new electronic information networks is interlaced with these discursive formations.

This book therefore tells a Cold War story. Centrally based on archival research, this project takes up relationships between television, telecommunications, and Cold War diplomacy during the formative period of global television growth. It considers well-known agencies of American foreign relations, such as the State Department and the United States Information Agency (USIA), as well as lesser-known but important entities such as the Psychological Strategy Board (PSB) and the Operations Coordinating Board (OCB). The book also pays close attention to the military, the intelligence community, and the White House. Beyond the government agencies of American Cold War foreign relations, this project is also concerned with the interplay between these agencies and the worlds of foundations, universities, and media/public relations (or Madison Avenue). Activities of many European and Asian nations and institutions are also key aspects of the overall narrative. This study tells the global story of the rise of television from a new communications technology to the dominant form of global media.

The architects and carpenters of global television from the Cold War era were a mixed, diverse, and often obscure lot. Although some clearly centered their actions on television, many others had different projects: psychological warfare, mass education, business expansion, computers and information technologies, superpower diplomacy, national security, East-West strategic relations, consumer society, and modernization, to name a few. All, in their own ways, worked on global TV, knowingly or not. The thematic chapters of this book use quotes, statements, and phrases from the wide range of individuals who worked on global TV; each narrative chapter is titled with a phrase taken out of the past. As such, these individuals herein speak in their own words via the medium of the archives, exemplifying their thoughts, perceptions, and actions about global television and the global pursuit of other new electronic communication technologies during the Cold War.

Although the globalization of television is a major question in twenty-first century media research, this book is at the same time a story set in middle of the twentieth century. Although the historical events and contours explored in this project took place within the past fifty or so years—the temporal equivalent of petty cash, by history's reckoning—the twenty-first century world of television, electronic information networks, and American diplomacy is in many ways millennially distant from the period of the Cold War. Since the fall of the Berlin Wall in 1989, the number of television sets in the world more than doubled, surpassing 1 billion sets in use in 1994. Most of this growth is outside of North America, Western Europe, and Japan. One implication of this unprecedented growth in the number of TV sets is that the traditional understanding of television as a phenomenon of the world's most advanced industrialized societies is now an outmoded concept. No longer a luxury, not even a signifier of middle-class consumer aspirations, now television hovers close to the baseline of human existence. In terms of everyday life on earth, television is now more likely to be an everyday experience than the automobile. The traditional national networks of the industrialized world have seen significant erosion of market share and audiences. Finally, conventional over-the-air (terrestrial) broadcasting itself is now only one of a wide array of global electronic visual media technologies. While the total hours of television programming across the planet grow at a rapid pace, occupying more and more bandwidth, that same growth is ultimately challenged by other information flows in cyberspace occupying even more bandwidth. The television of the Cold War era is in fact a relic. Electronic information networks have undergone a similar shift of quantum proportions since the Cold War era.[1]

Why, then, a book about television, electronic information networks, and Cold War diplomacy? Doubtless, there are a host of social critics, do-gooders, and esthetes who would gladly applaud were television dumped into the dustbin of history, never to be seen or heard from again. A new generation of policymakers for telecommunication issues, honed on the good, the bad, and the ugly of markets rather than governments as engines of change, would find the Cold War era of telecommunications quaint. Despite latent nostalgia and occasional rhetoric otherwise, a diplomat worthy of a Foggy Bottom office who would advocate a retrograde return to Cold War diplomatic practices as in the strategic interests of twenty-first century America seems impossible to find (in the public glare of the spotlight, at any rate).

Therefore, this book is not prescriptive; its narrative is not designed to chart a new course for television, for telecommunications, or for diplomacy in the twenty-first century. Rather, the goal is to provide a richly detailed history, including new narrative threads, of the rise of television during the Cold War to its position as a medium of global influence and to show how global television was significantly shaped by the theory and practice of Cold War geopolitics. Despite a number of well-crafted studies (see the notes and bibliography) there is still a vast amount of information regarding the Cold War history of television and electronic information networks that is under-researched and little-known. These knowledge gaps are particularly glaring in historical questions concerning international and global developments in television and telecommunications during the Cold War period, especially before the 1970s. However, this book also has value for current affairs, in that another goal of this book is to provide a sort of map: not so much a map of where we are heading, but rather a map showing how we got here. This map is important, because our contemporary world of satellites, cyberspace, and multimedia, as shown in the various chapters of this book, is firmly rooted in the global growth of Cold War television and other new electronic communication technologies of the era.

Even though global television has changed significantly, particularly since the fall of the Berlin Wall, the world still lives with much of the historical residue of Cold War television. This residue is now visible because the world of Cold War television is in retreat toward abandonment. Yet it is that retreat that allows for global Cold War television to now be more accurately seen while it fades away. In his study of Hong Kong culture written on the eve of Hong Kong's absorption into mainland China, Ackbar Abbas argued that Hong Kong's disappearance into the mainland was a not a moment of déjà vu, but rather a moment of *déjà disparu:* just as Hong Kong was about to disappear, Hong Kong could finally be seen for what it was.[2] A sense of *déjà disparu* also inhabits this study: the present historical moment of the early twenty-first century, when contemporary global television is becoming something quite different from global television during the Cold War, is also the moment when Cold War television can be seen in *déjà disparu,* a vision realized through the residue left by its own retreat, abandonment, and eventual disappearance. This book is, in this sense, the history of a disappearing global television, finally visible for what it was, seen by tracing through the archive of its own residue.

Tensions, Resolutions, and Extraterritorialities

The Cold War tensions and resolutions of the two superpowers as they nego-tiated security and globalization in a growing world of global television and electronic information networks were more often than not manifest beyond the borders, landmasses, and other traditional defining characteristics of nation-states. These extraterritorialities, or spaces beyond the traditionally understood borders and perimeters of nation-states, emerged continuously throughout the era in context with global television and electronic infor-mation networks. International agreements regarding the electromagnetic spectrum and International Telecommunications Union (ITU) membership, TV in postwar Germany, and the growing spectrum demands for the strategic defense needs of the superpowers turned the electromagnetic spectrum into one of the first Cold War extraterritorialities regarding global TV and elec-tronic information networks. Cold War tensions and resolutions regarding the extraterritoriality of the electromagnetic spectrum were later followed by similar tensions and resolutions in additional extraterritorialities: Antarctica; ocean floors and undersea cables; the magnetosphere and Van Allen belts; the geosynchronous orbit and outer space; above-ground and high-altitude atomic weapons testing; atmospheric and oceanic purity along with conserva-tion of wildlife and natural resources (now known as environmental issues); concepts of world citizenship; the global spread of science and technology; differing visions of consumer culture; very early ideas about cyberspace and what is now known as the Internet; and the moon. All of these extraterritori-alities became grounds for perceiving, intensifying, and eventually diffusing superpower tensions and resolutions concerning the global growth of televi-sion and electronic information networks during the Cold War.

From an American perspective, the interplay of extraterritorialities with global television and electronic information networks was first conceptual-ized as a security issue. Arguments, positions, rhetoric, and discourse invari-ably began with an articulation of security concerns. If one were to analyze what went on in this period of study strictly and exclusively from the point of view of the intended actions of the principal dramatis personae—or to borrow a methodological thought from literary studies, analyze strictly along the lines of authorial intent—one would place concerns over East-West or superpower security as the central motivating factor for all actions. To push this further for a moment, one might even say that a globalization thesis is inaccurate, because based on available evidence, it is not clear that outcome is what the actors strictly intended.

Globalization was, in the main, not the conscious or articulated intent, particularly the exact articulation of the term *globalization,* of most of the principal actors. Globalization was not a term in common use during the period of this study.[3] One might even go so far as to say that these actors globalized television in a manner akin to what we now think of today as a globalization process without fully realizing that is what they were doing, or put another way, they placed television on a path toward globalization before the existence of such a path was generally realized and articulated with that specific word. However, globalize they did, and over time articulated a particular discourse about globalization. Although the word *globalization* was not in common use by the dramatis personae at that time, *globalization* can be used retrospectively to help describe, analyze, and understand the actions, ideologies, and discourse of these individuals; that part of the analysis is an analysis transcending the strict limits of intent. To infer and analyze beyond the strict limits of intent is part of scholarship.

However, intent is important. Knowing the intent of the principal actors in any historical analysis—at least trying to know it as best as the available evidence permits—is crucial to understanding the past and is another important part of scholarship. The (possibly subconscious) collective globalization of television and electronic information networks during this period must be understood and analyzed in conjunction with understanding and analyzing the (clearly conscious) collective intent regarding issues of global security in a Cold War world. Although the globalization of television was the prime outcome of the period from 1946 to 1969, the pursuit of East-West security in relation to global television growth from 1946 to 1969 was the prime motivator of actions. The principal actors set out at the beginning of the Cold War with the intent of anchoring the global growth of television and electronic information networks into ideas, concepts, doctrines, and policies regarding global security in the Cold War, and for the most part, they succeeded in this task. However, over time, a slow recognition emerged that "security" might not be the best or most efficacious vision for understanding global television and other new electronic communication technologies in the contexts of tensions, resolutions, and extraterritorialities. With this slow recognition, global television and electronic information networks were nudged along the newly emergent path of globalization. Regarding intents and outcomes, globalization and security are thus inextricably conjoined in this study, centrally so by the tensions and resolutions of various extraterritorialities.

Methodologies in Action:
Cold War Communications Research

For American diplomats, policymakers, researchers, experts, and other such individuals during the period of this study, concerns and thoughts about the global growth of American television and other new communications technologies moved from peripheral concerns in the aftermath of the Second World War, to concerns at the core of American foreign policy in the 1950s and 1960s. This shift regarding television and other new global electronic communication technologies from the periphery to the core of strategic vision involved exploring conceptual parameters from security to globalization. The shift also entailed a wide range of what might be called *applied methodologies* in considering global media and world public opinion. This was not so much a case of deep exploratory studies into basic methodological questions concerning media and communications research, but rather a wide range of cases where differing methodologies for media and communications research were employed, albeit almost always haphazardly and, in terms of rigor, on shaky ground, but such methodological practices are evident nevertheless. As is discussed in several of the following chapters, those who worked on global TV wrestled (often with limited results) with methodologies akin to textual analysis, attitudinal analysis, behavioral sciences, political economy, geopolitics, cultural analysis, and even a crude form of semiotics.

In short, the intellectual and methodological search by policymakers, diplomats, business leaders, entrepreneurs, foundations, and the researchers who worked with them for ways to understand global television and global electronic communication technologies in both traditional and extraterritorial geopolitical settings was wide and vast. Their efforts and techniques put too much emphasis on immediate applicability and not enough emphasis on results that could hold up to rigorous scrutiny over the long term. These methodological forays also represented, albeit often in a crude and ham-handed fashion, many of the methodologies and approaches to social, political, and cultural analysis prevalent in both the social sciences and the humanities during the Cold War era. Despite the significant shortcomings of their efforts, it can nevertheless be said that both policymakers and researchers of the era were influenced by methodological assumptions and scientific methods of the time, indeed had a hand in shaping those methods, even if the results of applying such methods can now be seen as falling short of the mark.

Simply put, social science- and humanities-based research, shaped by Cold War convictions, did make an imprint on perceptions and decisions regarding global television and new electronic communication technologies, even if that imprint was not always inlaid with the quality and care the social scientists and humanists would have preferred. These methodologies in action supported decisions and policies, but they also displayed attitudes, beliefs, and perceptions of the methodologists, policymakers, and their cohorts. So methodologies in action regarding communication research and Cold War geopolitics exemplify decisions and attitudes, actions and perceptions. Even though this book *is* about what American policymakers were doing in the Cold War world of global television and electronic information networks, just as accurately this book is also about what those policymakers *thought* they were doing in the Cold War world of global television and electronic information networks. Thus, from both the discursive positions of security and globalization, projecting America's global image via television and electronic information networks during the Cold War was a process shaped and informed by both actions and perceptions.

Finally, I have often thought while writing this book about a great Cold War science breakthrough—deoxyribonucleic acid (DNA) and the double helix—as a metaphor or analogy for understanding two superpowers locked in a spiral of response and counterresponse. Cold War television and globalization, emerging and growing together in a world defined by superpower geopolitics, are also recognizable through the metaphor of the double helix: television and globalization spiraled around each other as both emerged and grew in a Cold War world. This book tells the story of television and globalization as a double helix.

Chapter Organization

This project is organized into eight thematic chapters contained between an introduction and epilogue, along with several illustrations, maps, and photographs. The book may also be seen as a manuscript in two strands, with the first strand (chapters 1, 2, 3, and 4) more focused on questions of discourse, policy, ideology, and geopolitics. The second strand (chapters 5, 6, 7, and 8) is more focused on questions regarding new technologies of global electronic communications media. This separation into two strands is not strict and absolute. The strands are complementary, not distinct. The two strands inform each other; they spiral and link together in many ways.

After the introduction, chapters 1 and 2 take up the reorganization of the ITU with the first major question of Cold War television, television in Berlin and occupied Germany. Beginning with postwar conferences stemming from the Yalta and Potsdam meetings, these chapters examine the global telecommunications strategies of the emergent superpowers, as well as tactics and actions in occupied Germany. This includes discussions of the incorporation of the ITU into the United Nations (UN) system, the subsequent engagement of the ITU with the newly independent nations of the world, and the problems arising from the expulsion of Germany from the ITU during the Second World War. This discussion of the ITU and postwar European TV frequency assignments lays an extraterritorial context for understanding the specific challenges of postwar TV and global electronic communication technologies in occupied Germany. The chapters also take up the reintroduction of television services in Germany, and the emergence of Berlin as one of the first sites of superpower conflict in the Cold War global media sphere. Berlin TV helped shape the early emergence of a televisual Iron Curtain in occupied Germany, along the border of the Soviet zone, and in places such as Finland and Austria. Thus, these two chapters center on the first important national territory for questions of Cold War global television (Germany) and by extension anchors the study in Europe, probably the most important region for understanding and analyzing the early dynamics of Cold War global television. Finally, these chapters also argue for the importance of the Allied occupation of Germany in setting a trajectory not only for the future of the ITU, but also for the initial development of television in Cold War Europe on a very confined track, heavily influenced by concepts of East-West security and structured to create the conditions for three types of European audiences. Two types, the Western (capitalist) audience and the Eastern (Communist) audience, were for the most part contained and isolated from each other. A third audience was an audience of combined citizens from both sides of the Iron Curtain who lived in range of TV signals from both East and West. Examples of this third audience include greater Berlin, the four occupation zones of Germany, Finland-Estonia (ESSR), and eventually, the audiences along the border of the Iron Curtain. The first era of Cold War TV growth in Europe, in both technology and programming, was often contested in the extraterritorial space of this third audience. Archival materials are primarily drawn from State Department and related records at the National Archives, and from the Public Records Office of the UK (PRO-UK).

Chapter 3 examines the institutionalization of psychological warfare by the U.S. government, including the emergence of the Central Intelligence Agency (CIA) and PSB; the need to distinguish between overt and covert propaganda practices; the problematic place of the State Department; and the eventual emergence of the OCB and USIA. The so-called War of Words between the superpowers as well as the rise of global public opinion polling as an instrument of American global security, and the impact of this rise on American science and technology policy and planning, are central themes. This chapter discusses the institutional growth of American psychological warfare as well as a growing interest in the global growth of mass media through several government agencies, such as the CIA, PSB, OCB, USIA, National Science Foundation (NSF), and National Security Council (NSC). Additionally, the chapter further explores linkages between diplomacy, media studies, and science studies, centrally through investigating the shaping of science policy as a forum for projecting the global image of America in the 1950s and 1960s. The chapter ends with a thorough discussion of Eisenhower's Presidential Committee for Information Activities Abroad, known as the Sprague Committee. This committee, meeting from 1959 to 1961 with Ford Foundation officer Waldemar Nielsen as research director, C. D. Jackson of *Time-Life* as a key member, and Ithiel de Sola Pool of the Massachusetts Institute of Technology (MIT) as a consultant, developed an across-the-board plan to link American science policy, global public opinion, and psychological warfare. The Sprague Committee argued for using all available mass media, global public opinion polling, and existing and emerging global electronic communications technologies, such as television, to promote a positive global image of American science and technology as a means to enhance the global image of America through funding a wide range of "feasible" American-directed science projects that had proven popular in world public opinion. Archival materials are mainly drawn from the National Archives and presidential libraries. The central focus, although not exclusive focus, of this chapter is U.S. government agencies and operations.

Chapter 4 is in many ways a companion to chapter 3, but follows similar themes through nongovernmental institutions, including universities, Madison Avenue, and philanthropy. Of particular interest is the seminal role played by the Ford Foundation during this period, as well as the impact international communications research and media studies research had within the foundation at a major period of the foundation's own transformation to, at that time, the largest philanthropic organization in the world. The Ford Foundation's role as the major philanthropist of early international communications research, its intimate links with RAND (Research and Development Corporation) and the U.S. government, and the transition of many former World War II and postwar public information officers—several of whom previously served in occupied Germany—into senior management officers at the Ford Foundation are among the major themes in the first half of this chapter. The chapter also lays groundwork for the discursive transformation from East-West security toward globalization by analyzing various Ford Foundation projects dealing with the global growth of television in the late

1950s and 1960s. In addition to early research funding at MIT and Stanford, of particular interest in the 1960s is the role of the Ford Foundation in establishing the Presidential Freedom Awards (first conceived as a global TV propaganda event and an American counterweight to the Lenin Prize) and the efforts by the foundation to establish an International Broadcasting Institute in the 1960s. During this latter initiative and particularly at a Ford-sponsored conference on global television held at Bellagio in 1966, the discursive transformation from security to globalization is described and analyzed in detail. Two discursive communities, a discursive community centered on security and later, a discursive community centered on globalization, are eventually knitted together, particularly by the incredibly durable network of experts represented in the advisors, consultants, funded researchers, task forces, and conferences sponsored by the Ford Foundation and other private philanthropic efforts. Archival materials are mainly drawn from the Ford Foundation Archives and the Kennedy and Johnson libraries.

Chapter 5 opens the second thematic strand as the first of four chapters looking at technological transformations in global television and other new electronic communications technologies of the era. This chapter centers on failed efforts in the 1950s to build international and intercontinental TV networks and opens the discussion of the American Cold War quest to bridge the Atlantic Ocean with live (rather than taped or filmed) television. This included elaborate plans to rim the world's oceans (and connect islands) with microwave relay towers. The quest to bridge the Atlantic via some sort of means of electronic communications is an enduring narrative at the very heart of media history. Whether it be Cyrus Field laying the transatlantic cable in the 1850s and 1860s, Gugliemo Marconi transmitting the letter "S" via wireless from Cornwall to Newfoundland in 1901, the 1912 saga of the *Titanic,* or recent efforts in successfully transmitting via the Internet 2.8 gigabits per second from Chicago to Amsterdam in 2002 (then a new world record for bit volume per second across the Atlantic),[4] the achievement of transatlantic electronic communications is the enduring great quest of each new form of electronic communications networking technology. So there is another installment of an enduring story here: Cold War television and telecommunication's holy grail of the transatlantic crossing. Building on themes introduced in the previous strand, this chapter pushes more centrally into questions regarding new communications technologies and Cold War military technologies. This chapter, therefore, explores several issues: "new media technologies" circa the early 1950s; the involvement of Congress, particularly the U.S. Senate; the early linkage of television, telecommunications, and information technology to strategic security issues, particularly

RADAR (radiolocation and direction system), DEW Line (distant early warning RADAR line of NORAD), NORAD (North American Aerospace Defense Command), and homeland defense; and even early visions of global information technology "wideband linkage," as it was called then, now known as "broadband convergence" via the Internet. This chapter also returns to the question of television growth in Europe first explored in the context of occupied Germany and provides more information on television growth in the rest of the world (particularly Japan). This is done by discussing the relationships between this global microwave TV relay project and the rise of commercial television in Japan, the growth of television networks in Europe, and the emergence of television and other new electronic communications technologies as potential tools for modernization and development in the newly independent nations of the world. The importance of the coronation of Elizabeth II in 1953 as the first preplanned "global TV event" is highlighted; this includes the use of the coronation by the British cabinet and the British Broadcasting Corporation (BBC) to launch the British global TV export market, the emergence of television in Canada, and the elaborate efforts by American networks to rush film footage of the coronation to American television networks. Archival materials are mainly drawn from the Hoover Library, the Eisenhower Library, the National Archives, PRO-UK, and State Historical Society of Wisconsin.

Chapter 6 takes a detour to Moscow in the 1950s and opens with the story of the IBM 305 computer popularly known as RAMAC, the computer-cum-diplomat. Installed by IBM for the 1959 USIA Moscow Exhibition, RAMAC was preprogrammed to answer over 3,000 questions about America. The RAMAC story illustrates the increasing importance of computer technologies in the Cold War; the interface between computers and public relations; and allows for discussion of the importance of USIA exhibitions, of which the 1959 Moscow Exhibition was the most important during the Cold War. Additionally, the discussion of RAMAC allows for further exploration of the uses of new electronic communication technologies to promote the global image of America in one of the first organized applications of what now falls within the rubric of "information diplomacy." This chapter is more focused on a single event than are other chapters. However, the event in and of itself was of extreme importance in Cold War public diplomacy and, among other things, helps mark the ongoing transition of a superpower rhetorical shift in psychological warfare away from extremely strident tones toward a mutually recognized strategy stressing competing visions of science and technology. Additionally, the 1959 exhibition was an important moment for Cold War television, as American-style closed-circuit color television was distributed throughout the exhibition grounds. These closed-circuit broadcasts and the reactions of Soviet audiences provided many insights into questions of American and Soviet culture, including consumer society, race relations, and leisure activities. Using the 1959 exhibition as a springboard, this chapter also gives additional background and detail on television in Moscow and the Union of Soviet Socialist Republics (USSR) during the 1950s. Archival materials are largely drawn from USIA records of the 1959 Moscow Exhibition and State Department reports about television in Moscow and the USSR. These State Department records offer a detailed discussion of Moscow television in the 1950s, largely told from the perspective of several foreign-service officers in the American embassy in Moscow, who in the early 1950s sent many detailed reports and descriptions about Moscow television programs back to Washington.

Chapter 7 opens with the inauguration of live all-Europe television from the Soviet Union, networking with the help of the BBC, in April 1961. The first live all-Europe TV event was coverage of the Soviet celebrations of Yuri Gagarin's pioneering spaceflight. This Soviet all-Europe live telecast across the Iron Curtain predates by sixteen months the first live transmission of American television to European audiences across the Atlantic Ocean relayed by the Telstar satellite in July 1962. From an American perspective, all of Europe was viewing Soviet space accomplishments and celebrations live on their own national TV networks, but American space accomplishments were relegated to the delays of transatlantic film newsreel exchanges. Therefore, in the arena of global public opinion regarding science, technology, and the image of America, live transatlantic television was an incredibly important goal for American interests. The narrative then turns to American efforts to bring live television across the Atlantic Ocean to Europe, first accomplished with Telstar in 1962. The development of Telstar is set in distinction to concurrent developments in military communications technology, as well as high-altitude nuclear weapons testing, which proved to be a threat to Telstar and all other orbiting satellites.

Chapter 8, the final thematic chapter, makes the transition from Telstar to the emergence of the Communications Satellite Corporation (COMSAT) and the International Telecommunications Satellite Consortium (now the International Telecommunications Satellite Organization or ITSO, but best known by the acronym for its satellite services, INTELSAT). This chapter discusses the American quest for a single global satellite system in the name of world citizenship and concludes the main narrative of the book with the 1969 moon landing. This chapter also brings forward the full transformation into a discourse of globalization, with American science and communication satellites as major signifiers of that discourse. Included is a discussion of COMSAT, INTELSAT, and other new communications technologies as signifiers of world peace in contradistinction to weapons of mass destruction, military communications, and disarmament problems as signifiers of world conflict.

The epilogue offers observations on television, new electronic communication technologies, geopolitics, diplomacy, and the Cold War discursive transformation from security to globalization from the retrospective position of the early twenty-first century. Acronyms used in the text and notes are defined in the front matter, and the notes use an abridged citation system for published works; see the bibliography for a full citation of those works. Now, allow me to begin my story of electronic information networks, global television, and the Cold War with this short prewar prelude.

* * *

In April 1935, the League of Nations hosted in Nice their first conference about international television as a part of its International Institute of Educational Cinematography. Max Jordan of the National Broadcasting Company (NBC) reported that the rivalries between the film and broadcast industries were typically obvious, but that the stronger tendency was a consensus among various national broadcast groups that common technical standards for international TV were highly desirable "to avoid a confusion of the sort that has been experienced as long as there was no international regulation of radio waves." Regarding global TV, Jordan concluded, "As a whole the Nice meeting was valuable for the purpose of establishing preliminary contacts between the interested parties, but it was generally realized that the time for practical cooperation has not yet come."[5] NBC sent C. W. Farrier on a fact-finding mission exploring European television in 1937, who found national rivalries were already becoming bitter and that television in Europe "is no place for an amateur." Farrier also learned that the Philips Company, heavily involved in building up TV service in the Netherlands, believed the future of European television was to be found in America: "They feel that program material is much more plentiful in America than in Europe, and thus if television is used on the continent for broadcasting service, the major portion of the material must be recordings from America."[6] By September 1938, NBC saw Germany as the leading TV nation of Europe, having built new TV studios, transmitters, and forged plans for national networking through coaxial cable. Thomas Hutchinson reported that "the German government believes that television will play a very important part in the dissemination of news and they are doing all they can to put it into actual service as quickly as possible."[7] One year later, the darkness of war fell across everything in Europe, including television.

PART 1

The First Strand

1. "A Facet of East-West Problems"

While President Harry Truman considered the final phase of the war in the Pacific in July 1945, one of the many memos crossing his desk that summer analyzing the postwar world advised, "it is *essential* that some action be taken without further delay in the interests of promoting American diplomatic, military and commercial interests in international communications."[1] These issues first came to the foreground in the ITU and in Allied-occupied Germany.

Most mainstream and conventional historical accounts examining the conditions needed in postwar Germany before television—and all broadcasting—could return to German society center on a shared vision of the occupying powers. This shared vision included a decentralized national system, re-education and the fostering of civic society, press freedom, and a full rejection of the broadcast propaganda and similar media practices of the Third Reich. Although these goals were largely accomplished, particularly for what became West Germany, the actions and decisions of the occupying powers surrounding the accomplishment of these goals helped create the conditions for another, unstated vision held by only one of the occupying powers: a powerful presence in European telecommunications policy and significant control of frequencies and bandwidth in the European region of the electromagnetic spectrum for the United States.

Therefore, another discreet condition that needed to be addressed before television could return to postwar Germany was the relative lack of American influence on European telecommunications and broadcasting. The return of broadcasting and television to German society not only was done in a manner to promote and foster the shared vision of the occupying powers regarding such issues as decentralization and the fostering of civic society, but just as importantly took place along a highly particular trajectory that had the end result of the United States enjoying, for the first time in the history of global electronic communications, a highly influential position regarding European telecommunications strategy coincident with the rise of the Cold War. Though it is no secret that American influence over global telecommunications strategy and practice expanded rapidly as a result of the outcome of the Second World War, decisions and policies crafted in conjunction with the occupation of Germany and the incorporation of the ITU into the UN were crucial to the final outcome: not just the return of television and broadcasting to German society, but also the dominance of global Cold War telecommunications by the United States.

The ITU, the UN, and Rising Cold War Tensions

As a consequence of the Second World War, Germany was temporarily expelled from the ITU, the oldest global regulatory body in the world. The ITU dates to 1865, when various European nations first met and faced common problems in the international transmission and reception of telegraph messages. The ITU became the global forum for settling accounting and billing rates for international telecommunications, for technical standardization and compatibility of telecommunications equipment across national boundaries, and for global dialogue on the development and dissemination of new electronic communications technologies. Folded into the UN in 1946, the ITU remains the most important global regulatory and technical body for global telecommunications policy. Among the key functions of the ITU is to allocate new spectrum, frequencies, and bandwidths for a wide range of telecommunications services, including television broadcast frequencies, to member nation-states. To avoid unintentional spectrum-sharing interference, this is by necessity a global process. As of 2006, the ITU has 190 nation-state members.

The temporary expulsion by the ITU of the two major Axis belligerents—Germany and Japan—proved to have profound ramifications on postwar telecommunications growth in both nations. Even though Japan was readmitted by 1949, various political, cultural, and geostrategic issues effectively kept Germany formally out of the ITU until 1953, and then initially saw only the admittance of the Federal Republic (West Germany). This meant that from 1945 to 1953, Germany essentially had no official ITU representation, but was instead de facto represented by the United States as its surrogate. Germany thus faced incredible difficulties in actually securing frequencies from the ITU for television broadcasting precisely at the period when postwar European television was experiencing its first major growth cycle. Yet television did eventually emerge in what became West and East Germany, in part due to the foreign policy of the United States and despite the foreign policy of the other three occupying powers (France, United Kingdom, Union of Soviet Socialist Republics), all of whom had their own reasons for opposing West German postwar television. Germans themselves also played an important role in promoting the growth of German television during the Cold War, and the Soviets played a significant role in shaping television in East Germany.

In addition to the Germany membership question regarding the ITU, the ITU itself underwent a remarkable metamorphosis during this same period. This metamorphosis is highlighted by the ITU Atlantic City Conference of 1947, the first global ITU conference held after the Second World War and the first ITU conference of any sort held in nearly a decade. Prior to the war, the ITU had largely been a small coterie of industrialized nations who, as either de jure or de facto imperial powers, set policy for themselves and for a colonial world. The 1947 conference was the first ITU conference to have delegations from the newly independent, or postcolonial, nations of the world, which changed the ITU considerably. Furthermore, during the period of conference planning (1945–47), the Cold War escalated. This meant that the 1947 conference was one of the first global conferences of any sort to experience the "legitimate" versus "puppet" government debate, with raging battles over "who should be seated" about such nations as Korea, Vietnam, Laos, the Baltics, Eastern Europe, and, at one point, even San Marino.

Into this maelstrom came the Germany question, with the United States doing everything it could to secure as many frequencies of all types, including television, for West Germany to (1) use broadcasting to rebuild German civic society, (2) secure frequencies for anti-Communist radio stations such as Radio Free Europe, Radio Liberty, or RIAS (Radio in the American Sector of Berlin), as well as clandestine and so-called "black" propaganda stations, and (3) occupy as much spectrum space and as many frequencies as possible to thwart Soviet militarization of the European spectrum and frequency system. Among other things, television and RADAR occupied similar areas of the spectrum and every ITU-approved television frequency in West Germany increased the difficulties of East German/Soviet military communications. The same was true in reverse from the Soviet viewpoint, and the Soviets went so far as to reassign unused spectrum space from east of the Ural Mountains in its occupied zone of Germany (which created massive interference and totally flew in the face of ITU principles). France and the United Kingdom were initially less interested in the geostrategic issues but very interested in trying to divert German TV frequencies for use in their own nations.

Even though a number of scholars have looked at television in Germany prior to and during the Second World War[2] and others have examined television in West Germany[3] (and by the early 1990s, television in a unifying Europe),[4] scholarly analysis of German television and telecommunications during the occupation period has apparently received less attention to date.[5] Additionally, as Jessica C. E. Gienow-Hecht argues, most of this research has yet to integrate political, economic, and military issues with issues of culture, technology, education, and the pursuit of everyday life.[6] Walter LaFeber commented it is "surprising that historians of U.S. foreign relations have done relatively little with technology."[7]

The first four decades of twentieth-century American telecommunications policy were marked by successful leadership in determining and charting the uses of the electromagnetic spectrum throughout the entire Western Hemisphere.[8] The immediate postwar period and the rise of the Cold War mark the era when the United States expanded its influence in telecommunications policy and spectrum planning to a level of global strategy. In essence, telecommunications and the electromagnetic spectrum in the postwar period are areas where American foreign policy and security issues became not only concerns of trade and commercial expansion, but also topics indicative of postwar views regarding security, military strength, and strategic global power. In the 1960s and 1970s, these concerns would become manifest in areas such as aerospace, satellite development and deployment for observation, surveillance, and strategic arms treaty verifications. However, postwar telecommunications policy at a global level, and the relationship of European TV spectrum planning to U.S. security and strategic interests, are as illuminating in understanding the historical background to such issues as Cold War security and contemporary space policy as the more commonly recognized historical influences such as missile systems, disarmament, and strategic weapons. The immediate postwar arenas in which these new telecommunications and spectrum concerns would first become evident were twofold: new multilateral and international forums such as the UN, and European political, economic, and cultural reconstruction.

During the nineteenth century, the United States was not a regular participant in ITU activities, and truth be told, the United States was not at the center of global electronic communications. The First World War was a learning experience for the United States in the need for a central role in global communications,[9] and the 1920s marked the decade in which the United States, largely through leadership in radio technology, moved to occupy a major position in global electronic communications. Hosting an ITU conference for the first time in 1927 (with Washington, D.C. the host city), the United States succeeded in convincing the rest of the world to adopt a basic principle for new technological developments to guide global spectrum management, a principle that still is in place today.[10] By the end of the Second World War, American policymakers fully realized the importance of telecommunications, electronic networks, and spectrum planning to build a postwar world consistent with the new visions of American security and strategic interests, which meant that significant changes needed to be rapidly introduced into postwar telecommunications policy and spectrum planning at global levels. A domination of the spectrum-planning process in the Western Hemisphere alone would no longer suffice. The new strategic issues of the spectrum included the following: global electronic surveillance and global military expansion; reforming the ITU, particularly in light of eventual membership of newly independent postwar states; instituting the global registration of frequency users; coordinating the global expansion of commercial or consumer services such as broadcasting (both radio and television), with broadcasting expansion tied to the expansion of the American broadcast and electronics industries; shaping the expansion of global spectrum use for new electronic communication technologies; and the postwar telecommunications reconstruction of Europe, and to a somewhat lesser extent, Asia (particularly Korea and Japan).

The linkages between electronic communications of all sorts and a robust military were learned anew in the Second World War. Strength in aviation was particularly dependent on vast amounts of spectrum bandwidth for command and control with airborne units, air-ground-sea troop coordination, RADAR, and air traffic control. In addition, the art and practice of cryptography had advanced tremendously, and the value of ongoing cryptography, particularly in signals intelligence or electronic intelligence (ELEINT—interception of electronic communications for decoding, traffic analysis, and similar tactics) became recognized as paramount for postwar security. Photo intelligence or PHOTINT in the postwar era, in the 1940s and 1950s completely through ground-based and aerial rather than satellite photography, was also a goal.[11]

A problem existed for accurate global electronic surveillance, and this was the lack of a global system of frequency registration. Although the ITU agreed in 1927 to set aside certain bandwidths for certain services, it had not yet required that actual users of frequencies within those designated bandwidths register their use with their national regulatory agency and, via that agency, the ITU. Prior to the war, this had not been much of a problem. However, the vast expansion of spectrum uses during the war had brought a host of new users and a confusing situation as to "who" was occupying "what" frequency. Problems such as frequency registration led to a series of "mutually beneficial" informal meetings in the last days of the war between the United States, the United Kingdom, and the USSR on the need for postwar international telecommunications conferences.[12] By the end of 1945, the United States looked for a global telecommunications conference as soon as possible. Secretary of State James Byrnes advised Ambassador Averill Harriman that the need to discuss global frequency registration and allocations was urgent so the "post-war activities of many services may be established on a sound basis" and suggested the need for a preliminary conference among the United States, USSR, China, France, and the United Kingdom, adding "it is considered almost imperative that USSR participate in this preparatory meeting."[13]

After several delays, the USSR hosted a five-power preliminary telecommunications conference at Moscow in September 1946. Considered "exploratory" in nature, the 1946 Moscow conference called for a worldwide telecommunications conference as soon as possible, and proposed that the ITU become incorporated into the UN.[14] American and Soviet delegates found themselves in general agreement at the Moscow conference, with both delegations favoring the integration of the ITU into the UN and the hosting of the next ITU worldwide conference in the United States (China agreed). France and the United Kingdom pressed for continuing the more or less established practice of holding meetings in Europe and retaining the ITU in Switzerland. A sticking point was the inclusion of Spain, then prohibited from UN participation because of actions of the Franco government. Even though the United States agreed to refuse to recognize Spain as an ITU member after the ITU joined the UN, the status of who was and was not an ITU member, particularly in regard to the supposed autonomous status of Soviet republics, remained an ambiguous question after the Moscow conference. This question expanded in significance between 1946 and 1947.

Overall, the American and Soviet delegations at the 1946 Moscow conference enjoyed amicable and productive relations. U.S. Delegation Chair Francis Colt de Wolf noted in his final report that the Moscow conference was "somewhat modeled" on Dumbarton Oaks and the subsequent agreements that led to the formation of the UN. Unlike other international agreements such as those in aviation, USSR participation in global telecommunications agreements was more than desirable: it was "absolutely essential" to avoid worldwide spectrum-sharing interference and other problems. De Wolf also praised Assistant People's Commissar for Communications A. D. Fortushekno, the head of the Soviet delegation, for Soviet willingness to "work in close cooperation" with the American delegation. Few if any 1946 participants realized this would be one of the last telecommunications conferences to experience such levels of Soviet-American friendship for many years.[15] It is likely that both the United States and the USSR wanted the ITU to join the UN because they saw the incorporation of the ITU into the UN as a way of weakening European influence in ITU decisions as well as a way of better securing their own postwar telecommunications concerns. The United States and the USSR had both been relative latecomers to the ITU, and although the United States had seen success in spectrum policy dating back to the 1920s, both superpowers recognized that European nations still had a large measure of control over ITU decisions. The Soviets, in particular, had always been heretofore marginalized at ITU meetings.

Doubtless, both nations saw incorporation of the ITU into the UN system as in their strategic interests. These concerns were more common than one might at first assume. Both the Americans and Soviets wanted greater control of the spectrum, not only within their immediate geographical spheres but also at global levels. Both had particular ideas about the reconstruction of postwar Germany, including the new role for telecommunications and broadcasting in Germany. In fact, the two views on Germany became diametrically opposed, but both needed a large measure of control over European telecommunications policy to successfully pursue those independent visions. Both wanted global frequency registration, and both would experience significant postwar domestic growth in telecommunications services. So it is not so unusual that the very first postwar telecommunications conference would see a high degree of harmony among the two emergent superpowers as they worked to secure strategic positions for the future. The subsequent conferences would now see those superpowers in conflict.

In 1947, the United States hosted the first worldwide telecommunications conference to be held in fifteen years, with a venue of Atlantic City, New Jersey. The United States and USSR agreed, based on findings at the Moscow conference, that the UN Economic and Social Council should call the conference as part of the integration of the ITU into the UN system. Exactly who should be invited remained ambiguous. Although the Moscow conference agreed to a refusal to invite Spain, defining what was, and what was not, an "inevitable" nation stirred differing opinions.[16] The Soviets argued that invitees should include "all members of the United Nations Organization, as well as all other countries, members of the International Telecommunications Union, having their own territory, permanent population, their own government, and possessing the right to establish diplomatic relations with other governments, excluding Franco Spain." Sensible on the surface, this did raise a few eyebrows, particularly regarding the status of emergent Eastern

European governments, and most certainly in regards to the supposedly constituent republics of the Union of Soviet Socialist Republics.

Although Ukraine and Byelorussia (Belarus) had been granted UN membership, other republics presented problems from the American viewpoint. The case of Estonia, Latvia, and Lithuania—now the Estonian, Latvian, and Lithuanian Soviet Socialist Republics—was one testing ground. The Soviets argued for separate delegations from each of these Soviet Baltic Republics. Turning to the Universal Postal Union (UPU) for precedent, the State Department confirmed with UPU officials in Bern, Switzerland, that on December 4, 1940, the Soviet government informed Bern that the Soviet Socialist Republics of Latvia, Lithuania, and Estonia were now part of the USSR and as such "not separately members of the Universal Postal Union" as of the dates of their entry into the USSR and asked the UPU "to make known the foregoing information to all the members of the Universal Postal Union." In January and February of 1947, however, the USSR attempted to register all twenty-one Soviet republics with the UPU, aiming to rescind the December 4, 1940, decree.[17] The State Department noted that "representation of more than three UN Soviet republics raises issues of major importance" and that the Soviet Baltics were a problem. The United States had not recognized the incorporation of Latvia, Lithuania, and Estonia into the Soviet Union, and therefore, it must approve their participation by appropriate representatives of those nations at ITU conferences. However, "those governments as at present constituted are not (repeat not) considered representatives of Latvia, Lithuania, and Estonia as individual and sovereign states. Consequently the US is under necessity of opposing their participation in ITU conferences."[18]

Thus the ITU joined the UN in conjunction with the rise of heated rhetoric over who should be seated—a question that came to pervade so many international forums during the Cold War, particularly in the 1950s and 1960s. For this conference, the debate over who was, and was not, a legitimate representative of a government included, at one point or another, a wide array of states and protostates. The occupied nations of Germany, Japan, and Korea (and to a certain extent Finland and Austria) were one category; rising nationalist movements in Vietnam and other areas posed questions of legitimacy; the soon-to-be-independent states of the former British empire raised other questions. This particular debate would not reach full fruition until subsequent ITU conferences, particularly a 1952 conference in Buenos Aires. The Atlantic City conference served as one of the first global forums that saw participation from the newly independent nations of the world. Prior ITU participation had been dependent on nations agreeing to adopt recommendations from earlier ITU conferences, but many new nations had not been politically independent at the time of the last worldwide ITU conference (convened in Madrid in 1932); conjoining the ITU with the UN basically changed ITU membership such that UN and ITU membership were now synonymous.

Atlantic City actually hosted simultaneous ITU conferences, with one devoted to general telecommunications issues, one devoted to working out a process for global frequency registration, and one devoted to the allocation and assignment of so-called "high frequency" bandwidths, which were primarily used for aviation, shortwave radio, and television. The process of global frequency registration extended well beyond the six weeks in Atlantic City, and eventually became a permanent administrative unit within the ITU. The question of television proved more difficult and would eventually be worked out on a regional basis.[19] Although frequency registration was politically benign, subsequent conferences dealing with television, particularly in Europe, became incredibly controversial. In particular, the European television question fully revealed the competing interests of the occupying powers of Germany, and it is in the context of that issue to which this chapter now turns.

ITU European Regional Conferences and Technical Standards for TV

A series of European regional conferences directly related to television issues opened in the summer of 1948. As shall be discussed, these conferences and their study groups failed to find closure on a wide range of issues, and meetings related to these initial conferences dragged on into 1953. This complicated situation essentially centered on three issues. The first was an ongoing debate over the possibility of a single universal standard for television technology. This goal failed for many reasons, and the result was three largely incompatible technical standards (which eventually became NTSC [National Technical Standards Committee] in the United States, PAL [phased alternation line] in the United Kingdom, and SECAM [sequential color with memory] in France).[20] Second, a "land rush" mentality emerged on the part of many European nations to acquire frequencies in the various bandwidths assigned for television use, which particularly threatened American military interests in Europe, the TV interests of Germany, and the radio broadcast services of the American authorities in Germany. Finally, the "zonal mentality" of Allied occupation influenced the re-emergence of German television, first with Soviet experimental TV in East Berlin and British TV in Hamburg, and an initial perceived absence of American-led TV in West Berlin and the American occupation zone.

In 1948, European nations, convening under the authority of a regional ITU meeting held in Stockholm, began what became a long series of discussions about television technical standards. Ostensibly an engineering conference, the question of technical compatibility in television standards evolved into what must have seemed an interminable series of ongoing studies that lasted into the early 1950s. The Americans, French, and British all proposed their own technical standards for consideration as a single worldwide television technical standard. Though it was conceded by delegates that there were more television stations broadcasting in the United States than any other nation that did not necessarily mean the American technical standards served the needs of Europe, and a subsequent push for regional, rather than global, standards gained momentum.[21]

The American negotiating position on European television standards had been compromised by unforeseen events and policy decisions in the American domestic television industry. In 1948, the Federal Communications Commission (FCC) issued a temporary "freeze" on the issuance of construction permits (and by extension, licenses) for new TV stations in the United States. Although the FCC originally believed the freeze was a temporary measure of a few months, the freeze lasted until 1952. Policymakers initially operated under the assumption that the freeze was temporary, but as the FCC continued to study the conditions that led to the freeze (such issues as interference from adjacent stations, the sunspot cycle, or the relative lack of available channels or frequencies in the very high frequency [VHF] bandwidth), the American negotiating position in Europe eroded and undermined the possibility of European adoption of American television technical standards. Invitations to Europeans offering opportunities to visit the United States and view American television were routinely delayed and occasionally rescinded in light of the FCC freeze.[22]

The freeze unwittingly became a significant factor in preventing American technical standards from becoming a worldwide standard for television in the postwar era. The FCC's domestic actions put Americans in the uncomfortable and compromised position of appearing internally divided and, therefore, weak on technical and engineering issues regarding global telecommunications. De Wolf lamented the FCC had been "hindered" through its very own hearings, adding that FCC representatives on the American delegation "felt they could not participate formally in the preparation of the U.S. international position on television standards inasmuch as there exists a possibility that the domestic television standards can be changed as a result of the hearings." The FCC actually withdrew its representatives from the American delegation participating in European television standard-setting discussions. De Wolf suggested Americans agree to regional standards as a last resort for Europe. The Western Hemisphere was already well along in developing American (or NTSC) television standards and this growth could not be risked on worldwide agreements, especially if those agreements took hemispheric leadership away from the United States.[23]

The ITU study of global television standards continued into 1952, with additional formal and informal meetings. By the summer of 1952, the number of different technical standards and systems were actually increasing rather than decreasing. An American representative to a 1952 television conference in Stockholm found that—depending on how one did the counting—there were plans for at least nine different standards systems either in operation or proposed for construction.[24] In an open statement, the American delegation advised conferees that American interests in television were longstanding, warned against technical decisions diminishing against enhanced international program exchange, held out American scientific research as a positive force for worldwide television, and urged delegates to "lay the groundwork for the widest possible interchange of television programs throughout the world."[25] It was not to be. Due to a number of factors—the domestic problems in American television that led to the FCC freeze, the national interests of France and the United Kingdom, the growing interest in Soviet and Eastern European television combined with the question of information flow across the Iron Curtain—all these factors undermined the American position on global television standards.

Another concern of American policymakers, evident at a 1948 ITU regional conference in Copenhagen, was the perceived threat against U.S. interests in occupied Germany. A combination of the threat from an emergent bloc of the USSR and Eastern European delegations, along with the seeming intransigence of the British and French delegations, meant the "U.S. position in broadcasting in Germany [is] seriously jeopardized [including the] OMGUS [U.S. Office of Military Government for Germany] information dissemination program, troop information program, Voice of America project, and decentralized German broadcasting."[26] Arguing that pressure on the British and French delegations against Soviet designs was indispensable, the State Department suggested as much to its Paris legation, believing "the best that can be done from the point of view of the British and French their purpose at Copenhagen is to engineer an adjournment of the Conference before any more damage is done" and admonished that "the technicians and specialists at Copenhagen are acting on narrow technical considerations rather than on broader political requirements of the situation." Warning that "the British and French, together with other Western European delegations, are now in accord with the Soviets in seeking to reduce frequencies in the U.S. zone to a minimum," the conference momentum if allowed to continue on its present course would solidify a perception by the British and French that "Germans must not retain capacity for broadcasting propaganda to outside countries." The United States stood alone against British and French protectionism in spectrum policy, stood alone against Soviet aims to "keep Western and particularly U.S.-controlled broadcasting potential at the lowest possible level" and suppress the international exchange of print materials, thus meaning "broadcasting is now our only effective instrument for reaching Eastern Zone Germans." Sufficient frequencies were needed for the American zone to promote a "vigorous reorientation program to strengthen democratic forces in Germany and to counter effectively Soviet propaganda" as well as to broadcast to U.S. troops in Germany and Europe. Even though other occupying powers could service their troops with home-based amplitude modulation (AM) or medium-wave radio broadcasts from London and Paris, the United States could not do so across the Atlantic Ocean.[27]

The U.S. Embassy in Berlin, following the advice of General Lucius Clay, believed that "thus far French and British have not viewed German frequency problem in true light as a facet of east-west problems" and reiterated the list of needs for a strong American hand in postwar German broadcasting frequencies.[28] A conversation with the French delegation confirmed this view for De Wolf: the French believed "the U.S. and Soviet claims fore-shadowed a 'radio battle' between the U.S. and Soviet Russia . . . it might prove dangerous to allocate so many wave lengths to German areas since they could be misused by a later German government."[29] One British observer later conceded, "the Germans on their side undoubtedly feel that Stockholm has cheated them of a certain proportion of their legitimate needs for television broadcasting" in Germany.[30] Again, higher-level American policymakers saw the need for consciousness-raising with various technicians and specialists from various delegations in Western Europe so that those delegations might understand they were not merely dealing with a problem of national interest, but rather dealing with a larger problem at the higher level of strategic interest and East-West security. This task of raising the bar from national to strategic issues came along with the larger problem of fully integrating the ITU into the political arena of global strategic and security issues in the context of the emergent Cold War.

By the last days of the Copenhagen conference, the British delegation had changed its position in accordance with American views. Although this improved prospects, the spectrum allocation for U.S. forces fell far short of the minimum needs for U.S. forces in Germany. Although a series of agreements

were ratified at the Copenhagen conference, many nations filed reserva-
tions, indicating the dim likelihood of strong adherence. The agreements
meant that the United States would be unable to "fulfill its commitments to
Germany," and the Soviets also objected, declaring that "if the Copenhagen
plan is not observed by other occupying powers of Germany or by Spain or
by all countries in general, the Soviet Union would feel free to take necessary
compensatory steps."[31]

As the conference wound down, Harvey Otterman, a telecommunications
specialist in the State Department, commented on the decay of American-
Soviet relations in postwar telecommunications policy, relations that had
been so promising in 1946 and 1947. The chair of the Soviet delegation at the
Moscow and Atlantic City conferences, the aforementioned Fortushenko,
had been an "exceedingly amicable and cooperative individual" who was a
strong negotiator for USSR interests, but was also capable of cooperation.
Fortushenko had so impressed the other delegates that he was elected as
chair of the new ITU Administrative Council, but was mysteriously absent
for that council's first meeting in Geneva, and had not been seen again at
international telecommunications conferences, having "completely disappeared from view . . . one of his aides at Atlantic City has also disappeared
from the telecommunication scene with obviously vague and embarrassed
explanations by the Russians." The new Russian attitude was one of "ob-
struction and delay . . . bitter speeches . . . every effort to destroy the work
. . . unpleasant nature . . . declined to pay its share of [translation] expenses
. . . disagreeable attitude . . . we not only have to be thoroughly prepared, as
we invariably are, on the substantive questions involved but must seek also
to prepare ourselves for unexpected and frequently indefinable contingen-
cies." Otterman also predicted that the subsequent complaints by the Soviets
regarding the 1947 Atlantic City conference and attendant behavior after that
conference could mean that the Soviets felt the cooperative 1946–47 period
in telecommunications policy was "a mistake. If they carry this to a logical
conclusion it would mean their unwillingness to accept [all recommendations and actions at Atlantic City]."[32] This change in Soviet attitude toward
international telecommunications agreements was not only indicative of
the rise of larger Cold War tensions, but in the specific arena of global telecommunications policy, it may also be tied to Soviets tilling the diplomatic
ground for their subsequent jamming of radio broadcasts from the West
aimed at Soviet and Eastern European listeners. In sum, the electromagnetic
spectrum and its postwar uses, particularly in Europe, became one of the
very first extraterritorial spaces of global contestation for Cold War tensions
regarding telecommunications, television, and electronic information net-

works. Contestations between the superpowers over extraterritorial spaces such as the electromagnetic spectrum would continue throughout the 1940s, 1950s, and 1960s. Eventually this contestation would extend into the oceans, Antarctica, outer space, the magnetic fields of planet Earth, and ultimately the moon. However, for the moment, European spectrum policy was the first battleground. The implications of this contestation for television in Germany and all of Europe would soon become visible.

2. "A Western Mind Would Consider This Kind of Spectacle as Stupid"

Discussing West German broadcasting in 1976, Arthur Williams recognized that "the western allies themselves often pulled in different directions and entertained several clearly contradictory views about the treatment to be meted out to the vanquished enemy."[1] Writing at a time before archival documents such as those cited herein were generally open, Williams likely had only an inkling of the depth of accuracy of his statement. For a ten-year period, the four occupying powers exerted great influence on both radio and television in Germany, and more often than not determined an individual course pursuant to their own national interest. Only over time did telecommunications and broadcast policymakers from France and the United Kingdom subscribe to the American view that telecommunications and television in Germany transcended national interests of the individual occupying powers to a higher level of East-West security and strategic relations. Eli Noam, if anything, understated the situation in his 1991 study *Television in Europe* with his comment that "German broadcasting was completely revamped by the occupying powers, each influenced by its own broadcast tradition and by a desire to provide a system for reeducation of Germany."[2]

The question of television in occupied Germany was also, at the time, a specialized issue in an extraordinarily large system of American information programs and policies for occupied Germany. When James Conant left the presidency of Harvard University in 1953 and arrived in Germany as the U.S. high commissioner and ambassador, he found the number of individuals involved in running American information programs in Germany was greater than the sum total of all his staff and faculty at Harvard.[3] The question of German television during the Cold War had a major impact on the growth

of television in Europe, as well as on both American and Soviet thinking
about the uses of television in a world increasingly charted and navigated
along the rhetorical, intellectual, and geopolitical contours of superpower
conflict and East-West security.

The Americans contemplated the return of broadcast media (in this case,
radio) to German nationals in their own zone as early as 1947, although
recognized this raised problems of ownership, decentralization, and the role
of broadcasting in building a civic society.[4] The commonly held assumption
that broadcast services in postwar Germany should be decentralized, along
with the pursuit of individual national interests, evolved into a system of
state-centered or *länder* broadcast entities, ranging from a giant broadcast
system at Hamburg to a tiny station at Bremen. Furthermore, military needs
for spectrum space and frequencies that also had broadcast implications
posed additional problems. The immediate result was a significant threat
to future spectrum space for West German television, along with the initial
development of postwar German television largely taking place in Hamburg
and the British zone, and in East Berlin and the Soviet zone.

The problems caused by wartime ITU expulsion of Germany became more
apparent to the occupying powers. The Republic of Korea was admitted to
ITU membership on November 1, 1950, with forty-seven member nations
supporting, six member nations (all from the Soviet bloc) opposing, and
Israel abstaining.[5] The American High Command in Germany supported,
in late 1950, the membership of the Federal Republic of Germany in the ITU,
noting the case was difficult in terms of protocol. Despite this advocacy,
HICOG (Office of the U.S. High Commissioner for Germany) continued
to exercise control over frequency uses in the American zone, including
broadcasting.[6] Was the best route to suggest that the Federal Republic was
in fact the prewar "Germany"? Or should the Federal Republic apply as
through the ITU provision for "appropriate protocol" whereby the appropriate governing authorities of occupied nations approved the membership?
This latter approach would not only be opposed by the Soviets, it would also
open the possibility of the German Democratic Republic (GDR) applying as
a new nation, which American delegates "would have to oppose vigorously."
Americans at Atlantic City in 1947 had specifically argued to the ITU that
"Germany" meant the "whole of Germany and not one or more of the occupied zones" and to reverse this position would be a problem.[7] Francis Colt
De Wolf recommended that the question be held off for the time being to
lay the groundwork, because eventually admitting West Germany as a new
ITU member and seeking a two-thirds majority vote presented a "far pref-
erable course. I do not believe there is much chance that Eastern Germany

could come in under the same procedure . . . it is preferable to follow this course of action rather than give a definitely twisted interpretation of the term 'Germany' and the term 'appropriate authorities.'"[8]

The Germany ITU membership question continued through 1951 and into 1952, and as postwar telecommunications growth in Europe expanded, the question became more acute. Conrad Adenauer asked that the Allied High Commission not make decisions on licensing television broadcasters in West Germany without first consulting his government, suggesting that discussions between Allied and German TV experts would not only place the question of television more directly into West German "hands" but also "enable the Federal Government to assume responsibility for compliance with the international obligations" it would assume upon re-entry into the ITU.[9] The ITU convened a regional (European) conference on assigning frequencies for radio and television broadcasting, which was held in Stockholm in May 1952. Harvey Otterman summed up the importance of this conference for American interests in Germany:[10]

> The European Regional Conference convened in Copenhagen in 1948 . . . virtually ignored the broadcast requirements not only of the Zones of Occupation in Germany but of the additional services employed in those zones as a direct result of occupation and propaganda effort. The frequencies assigned to the U.S. Zone . . . were so inadequate that the United States . . . was forced to declare at the Copenhagen Conference that it could not be bound by the terms of the Convention and it would take whatever steps it deemed appropriate to satisfy its broadcast requirements. The USSR Delegation stated in effect that if we did as we said we were going to do, that it would take countermeasures.

These U.S. and USSR declarations to "take whatever steps deemed appropriate" doomed the agreements to eventual failure. This in turn meant that European broadcasting was not bound by adherence to ITU frequency assignments, which was in all likelihood a major step in opening the door to the jamming of Western shortwave propaganda broadcasts by the USSR, because jamming was unfettered by regionwide strong adherence to ITU frequency agreements for Europe. As discussed in chapter 1, this conference showed the problems of Western European delegations promoting only their national interests rather than thinking of telecommunications and the spectrum as primarily a strategic and security issue of East-West extraterritorial tensions.

> In pursuing its plan to satisfy broadcast requirements in the Federal Republic of Germany, the U.S. embarked on a program of construction of directional antennas at considerable cost not only to the Germans but to the U.S. forces as

well to permit the sharing of frequencies assigned to other countries on a non-interference basis [which was accomplished] with a great deal of success but not without a great deal of expense and bickering. . . . The Soviets, in carrying out the intent of their declaration, have transferred frequencies assigned to the interior of the USSR to the East Zone of Germany and have and are building powerful transmitters to be used on those frequencies for the sole purpose of interfering with the broadcasts of the Federal Republic, the VOA, and RIAS. The situation in Germany is critical and becoming more so daily as the East German [USSR] transmitters go into operation.

The breakdown of international spectrum-sharing agreements in occupied Germany is remarkable. These are some of the most blatant violations of spectrum-sharing agreements anywhere in the world since the ITU instituted its first spectrum-sharing and management plan in 1927.

> The long range plan of the United States envisages the blanketing of the Federal Republic by FM transmitters[11] which would carry, for the large part, the same program of the medium wave[12] services . . . the FM services are virtually jam-proof except at the Eastern periphery of Germany . . . the Allied High Commission and the Germans, as well as the military, have agreed to an assignment plan in this band which, in addition to accommodating the German television requirements, will permit the use of radar by the U.S. Air Force on a non-interference basis. As can be imagined, the radar installations are of strategic importance . . . television is [also] of great importance to the Germans. . . . The USSR and its satellites will undoubtedly make every effort to locate on the periphery of its land mass, particularly the portion bordering the Federal Republic, Austria, France, and the low lands, transmitters which can be used for jamming and interference and propaganda purposes. A similar situation can be anticipated in Berlin.

In April 1952, the Federal Republic of Germany (hereafter FRG) was admitted as an ITU member. The ITU Administrative Council decided upon a procedure that, at least at that time, allowed for the admission of only one Germany.[13] The ITU voted against participation from the GDR in an ITU plenipotentiary conference hosted in October 1952 in Buenos Aires by about a four-to-one margin.[14]

The FRG was also invited to participate in an upcoming meeting, again in Stockholm, on VHF frequencies in Europe. To guard against the possibility that Soviet plans for the Stockholm conference may risk the point-to-point military and government radio relay systems linking Berlin with the FRG in Bonn, the Americans decided to also press for additional facilities and VHF spectrum in the region of the Harz Mountains.[15] Soviet jamming of American radio in Germany had already begun and would significantly increase. By

1953, RIAS was a target of intense jamming. A report prepared for the PSB of the State Department saw a risk to the credibility of RIAS, and even with adding more transmitters (which would undoubtedly raise further jamming by the Soviets), the question remained "whether we can afford to let RIAS deteriorate with the interpretation that the United States is losing interest in Berlin and our friends behind the curtain in East Germany." The PSB recommended that continued support of RIAS was a major psychological symbol of the free world's interest in Berlin.[16] Jamming by the USSR in East Germany had begun with the lifting of the Berlin blockade in 1949 and increased during the long proceedings of ITU conferences in Copenhagen and Stockholm. Simultaneously with the increase in jamming of American radio broadcasting, the Soviet zone began to bring television to East Berlin; in the British zone, television came to Hamburg. Thus television returned to postwar occupied Germany in a multitude of contested extraterritorial contexts: ITU membership, European frequency battles, the militarization of the electromagnetic spectrum, differences among occupying powers, and the early convergence of electronic communications and Cold War psychological warfare. British occupying administrators concerned with German television believed the issue was "primarily a German question," but the initiative should not be defaulted to the Soviets, for if that should come to pass, "it is fairly certain that without the prospect of an early Western service the novelty and entertainment value would encourage many Westerners to buy sets designed to receive the Eastern programmes. . . . The propaganda value to the East is obvious."[17]

American Strategic Interests and TV in Occupied Germany

American occupying administrators had not given much, if any, specific thought to German television prior to 1950, beyond a complete rejection of the broadcasting policies and practices of the Third Reich in favor of a decentralized and democratic system anchored on press freedom and a civic society (and that vision began with a vision for radio).[18] Noting the beginnings of television experiments in Hamburg as well as the announcement of eventual television service in East Berlin, HICOG asked the State Department if Washington had any formal policy on television, finding "television is being developed by the networks in the British and Soviet Zones and by the manufacturers in all Zones." Sensing "practically no public interest," HICOG argued, "television is an unnecessary luxury in today's Germany, particularly now, when tremendous expenditures are being made for medium wave and FM installations" and closed by requesting that the State Department provide "a clarification of the extent and source of U.S. aid envisioned for television."[19]

Despite HICOG's initial dismissal as an unnecessary luxury, American interest in German television, often expressed through RIAS, began to grow. The RIAS explored the possibility of a low-power TV transmitter for the western sector of Berlin in early 1951. In May 1951, the Economic Cooperation Administration (ECA) hosted in West Berlin a demonstration of new consumer goods, including television. Aimed at a youth audience, the closed-circuit television display was seen as an attractive lure to persuade various Communist youth organizations of the value of Western consumer culture. Several dozen public viewing receivers were also set up beyond the fairgrounds.[20] The Radio Corporation of America (RCA) followed television developments in Germany and conducted its own informal research in early 1951 after reading a short article in a New York City newspaper about the introduction of television in East Berlin. Questioning the promise of a receiving set for the equivalent of $28, RCA surreptitiously contacted an East German engineer to find out if such a thing were likely. The East German engineer replied with a long discussion of the difficulties of living in East Berlin and concluded no East German TV sets were to be had for such a low price.[21]

Work continued on the East Berlin television system throughout 1951, with studios at Adlershof, and experimental broadcasts began there in 1952.[22] Adapting German television equipment from the Third Reich era, Soviet and German engineers built large facilities and also established a television receiver manufacturing plant in the Soviet zone to supply consumers in both the Soviet zone as well as in the USSR. Although the USSR had experimented with television in the 1920s and 1930s, the Soviet zone of occupied Germany and its television manufacturing plants may have played a greater role in the growth of postwar Soviet television than has been previously understood.[23] The first American descriptions of Soviet zone television provided by RIAS observers depict a bleak televisual landscape.

> The Chief of the Radio Branch, HICOG, viewed Sovzone television in Berlin recently. He observed that it was technically very poor and that its contents bordered on inanity. One program he viewed was made up almost exclusively of still pictures. Its content was 90% anti-American hate propaganda much cruder than the usual radio counter-part, featuring pictures of hunger and unemployment in the U.S., policemen mercilessly clubbing strikers, etc. . . . anyone with a Western mind would consider this kind of spectacle as stupid and ineffective. However, from an analysis of similar Sovzone propaganda as a whole, he wonders whether people behind the Iron Curtain still react with Western minds. Eastern Germany has been under one form of totalitarian regime or another for the past 20 years.[24]

Growth continued in East Berlin TV in 1952 and 1953. In the fall of 1952, a show called *Gerhart Eisler's Ministry of Truth* premiered along with increased availability of TV sets in East German shops.[25] On December 21, 1952, in honor of Stalin's birthday, regular programming began. Soviet zone TV reached Leipzig with a transmitter in 1953, including public viewing rooms reminiscent of the Third Reich, and a second TV transmitter appeared in East Berlin in 1954. East Germans were also allowed to purchase TV sets on credit.[26] The June 1953 uprisings in East Berlin saw television become directly involved in reporting on violent conflict in the context of the Cold War, with RIAS cameras working for the American zone TV station "inside the mobs" on the first day but confined to "shots across the border" of "deserted squares and Soviet tanks" by the second day. Nevertheless, as "proof of the impact of television in a violent situation it was very significant."[27] Meanwhile, a 1953 report on East German TV as a sidebar in a global television roundup published in the American trade newsletter *Television Opportunities* found East German TV programs "not very edifying." Noting the heavy use of "ancient" Russian and Chinese films, "what was supposed to be live TV consisted of propaganda in its crudest form." Peasants were depicted as showing contempt for Western leadership, and women "were urged to learn the gentle art of stonemasonry as a gesture to father Stalin."[28]

The re-establishment of television in postwar Germany was highly fraught with the growing tensions of the Cold War. European television development and global telecommunications policy were both shaped by rising Cold War tensions. These tensions appeared everywhere, from official recognition of ITU representatives to arcane engineering debates about technical standards and frequency assignments. The 1946–54 period in particular saw constantly shifting positions of negotiations along with battles across and within various nations regarding telecommunications and television policy in postwar Europe. Certain individuals were much more willing than others to paint European telecommunications in stark Cold War terms, and over time, this particular line of rhetoric became convincing—even useful—to its audience of policymakers.

This rhetoric at times even reaches the point of possibly blurring conventional understanding of the history of postwar German television. A close reading of some of the more strident American reports out of Germany regarding television promote a perception that television growth during the period in question first proceeded on a zone-by-zone basis, with the British and Soviets leading and the Americans straggling badly in the rear. Put another way, these reports now make a researcher wonder if the perception of zone-by-zone TV development among senior policymakers in Washington was used as a bit of a red flag to capture attention and promote the particular interests of a certain group of American officials on the ground in occupied Germany, particularly individuals at places such as HICOG and RIAS. Few if any scholarly studies of German television argue that, for example, the postwar Hamburg TV station was a "British" TV station—but that is the perception of national (or perhaps "zonal") identity one retrospectively gets from reading several of these reports out of Germany and sent on to Washington.

In other words, there is little evidence to suggest that British occupying forces or German audiences actually considered the postwar Hamburg TV station to be a British station.[29] However, several reports from Americans on the ground in Germany back to senior policymakers in Washington unmistakably suggest this TV station should be considered "British" rather than "German" in its origins. This does beg the question of "who was leading who" (senior diplomats in Washington or Americans on the ground in occupied Germany?) in arguing telecommunications policy and postwar European television were now issues of East-West security rather than simply issues of national identity.[30] The restoration of German television also took place at a time when the politicization of German broadcasting along East-West lines had already emerged, unlike the case in radio, where a period of political neutrality, with varying success, was attempted during the 1945–47 period.[31] Thus RIAS officers and other leading personnel who arrived in occupied Germany during the 1948–53 period, when television got off the ground, articulated firm convictions that radio and television were manifestations of an East-West security conflict. In retrospect, both Washington and the American occupiers on the ground in Germany had their own moments of rhetorical leadership on this issue.

By 1955, a televisual manifestation of the Iron Curtain was slowly appearing across Europe. Certain populations and cities were becoming points of contestation, among them Berlin, Helsinki, and Vienna. The U.S. Information Agency (USIA) investigated the possible impact of Soviet television on "free world conditions" in December 1955 and found that "the Soviet Orbit countries are developing their television networks with a view toward reaching audiences in adjacent Free World countries wherever possible."[32] East Germany constructed a station on Mt. Broken in the Harz Mountains, close to the West German border, although USIA believed the "advanced stage of TV development" in West Germany with many hours of West German programming meant "no dilemma of either having to accept the Soviet brand of TV or none at all for some time to come" existed in West Germany. Nevertheless, there was widespread evidence of Berliners routinely watching both East and West Berlin TV programs. Furthermore, the residents of certain West German areas, such as Hof, also watched East German TV due to the lack of a reliable West German TV signal. The costs of modifying a Western TV set to receive Eastern technical standards was nominal, about ten dollars, and the sound channel could be picked up on a frequency modulation (FM) radio receiver. In 1956, many West Germans beyond the range of Eurovision program exchange broadcasts watched the 1956 Winter Olympics at Cortina over East German TV.[33]

Elsewhere in the emergent world of Iron Curtain television, the USIA reported in 1955 that TV from Tallinn (ESSR) was viewable in Helsinki, and Finland was being pressured to purchase Soviet TV sets as a result. Coincident with the inauguration of test telecasts from Tallinn on July 19 of that year, a Helsinki department store put a "big powerful American Sylvania receiver" on display as it received the Tallinn signal. This led the "Communist press" in Finland to call "vociferously for the import of Soviet sets" as they claimed Leningrad, Riga, and Tallinn were now three "eastern" TV stations serving Helsinki, "while there were no operating stations within the field of vision of a Western set."[34] Even though Finland had in 1952 agreed to Western TV technical standards and earlier in 1955 the TV Club of Helsinki had conducted low-power experimental telecasts, no regular Western TV technical standards signal was as yet receivable in Finland. Sweden had attempted a series of relay telecasts from Stockholm to Marianhamm in the Aaland Islands, but these were unsuccessful; the TV relay from Helsinki to Stockholm via the Aaland Islands would eventually be developed and, as shall be seen in chapter 7, played a significant role in live telecasts across the Iron Curtain in 1961. Further televisual border crossings from East to West were evident in the border regions of West Germany and along the Czech-Austrian border, including concerns that a new TV station in Bratislava would appeal to viewers in Vienna. For many RIAS, USIA, and Voice of America (VOA) officers, all this new activity meant European television was beginning to spin along a "Communist orbit."[35]

Romney Wheeler of NBC, reporting about European television in 1956, found that "Eastern Germany is busily pumping Communist TV programs over the border" and speculated that Soviet jamming of West German TV could happen in the near future. NBC's news director William McAndrew noted that East Germany officially began a TV network in January 1956 with nine stations operating and four more planned. The East Germans had also formed "television clubs" for mass viewing "to help fill their once nearly-empty propaganda centers. After the TV programs end, the Communists start their political discussions." The 1956 Winter Olympics had been watched via East German TV in a good number of Bavarian restaurants and beer halls, suggesting that West German audiences were susceptible to penetration by

Communist television. Adding to the Bavarian temptation of East German TV (and confirming that even fifty years ago the adult male beer-drinking viewer was a prized demographic) was "the inevitable element: most of the program announcers are women, a number of whom are quite attractive."[36]

Toward the end of the 1950s, the USSR saw television development as an antidote to lure listeners away from Western shortwave radio broadcasts.[37] By 1957, all of the Eastern European nations except Albania had either experimental or regular television broadcast services.[38] The USIA, having set up a division specifically for television in 1958, reported that by 1960 a total of 899 television stations in the world were on the air, with 189 of those in Communist nations and regions. These transmitters served an estimated 32 million homes worldwide, and over 5 million of those homes were somewhere behind the Iron Curtain. "Infiltration" of West Germany and the free world at large by Communist television was represented by, among other developments, new transmitters on the borders of East Germany and Czechoslovakia, with additional spillover from other Soviet TV stations into Norway (from Murmansk), Denmark, Finland, Sweden, Afghanistan, and Iran.[39] The USIA found that by 1960, about 36% of the West German population could receive East German television, and a new and "vicious program" called *The Black Channel* specifically critiqued West German TV. In general, the USIA warned that

> East German television is busily extending its network of stations along the East Zone borders, and increasing its anti-West German and anti-American programs. . . . A vicious program has recently appeared called "The Black Channel" in which the "star" commentator offers a critique of West German TV. The program notes stated: "The Black Channel is a series about West German television in which Karl-Eduard von Schnitzler uses actual kinescopes of this poisonous [West German] production to show up the un-German lies and provocations these epidemic-merchants propagate. The Black Channel rips the mask off them all, or rather, they rip off their masks themselves, the Adenauers, Lübkes, Oberländers and their whole brood. . . . The Black Channel is one of the most important television programs in the fight for peace, against lies and slander and for a cleaner Germany."[40]

At the same time, however, the USIA also found that East German refugees spoke of widespread viewing of West German TV and that commercials and advertising were quite popular because they depicted a consumer lifestyle and availability of goods far beyond the typical East German conditions.

In retrospect, one wonders about European television in the context of a classic American value in communications: the free flow of information.

There is good evidence to suggest that television from the Soviet zone of Germany and from areas of Eastern Europe and the USSR, in general, reached and crossed the border of the Iron Curtain before Western television reached and crossed that same border.[41] Thus, in applying the principle of free flow of information and then examining the archival residue, one concludes that in European television during the Cold War, the Soviets, rather than the Americans, were often the first to create a televisual space that encouraged the flow of television programs across borders. Of course, the programs in flow were Socialist rather than Western programs, flowing from East to West. Another example is the construction of a TV station in Tallinn. Despite hosting the 1952 Summer Olympics, television development in Finland had been limited to university tests prior to the construction of the Tallinn TV station. Anticipating in 1954 the forced importation of Soviet TV sets and the possibility of a relay transmitter on the Soviet-occupied Porkalla peninsula, the Finns moved rapidly to establish their own television service during the latter half of the 1950s.[42]

Western-inspired television programming and development in Cold War Germany and Europe began as not so much a case of the unfettered free flow of information from West to East, but rather as a strong counterbalance preventing, or discouraging, the Soviet-sourced first flow of the European television landscape. The counterflow of American values eventually proved more popular among all European audiences, whether Eastern or Western.[43] Put another way, the American value of the free flow of information regarding European television has historically contingent roots. These roots suggest that American values regarding the free flow of television in Cold War Europe began not so much as an attempt to be the first across the border of the Iron Curtain, but to counter the prior televisual crossing of that border from the East. The successful rhetoric portraying a Soviet threat in television (and other occupying powers as television concerns) during the occupation period of Germany had a greater impact on the long-term infrastructure of Cold War television in Europe than is generally realized. This suggests that the linking of global telecommunications policy and German television into an East-West security dialogue—a rhetorical linkage fostered by American foreign policy and strategic interests in global telecommunications—had as much to do with shaping the contours of postwar German television as did the professed and sincere desire by the occupying powers to totally reject the centralized broadcast practices of the Third Reich. Therefore, the question regarding what was needed before television could return to postwar Germany is not only a question about Germany: it is just as importantly a question about American foreign policy.

Looking back on the history of American foreign policy and electronic communications during the twentieth century, a trajectory can be discerned. That trajectory begins with the United States as a peripheral factor in global telecommunications policy, largely sidelined by European dominance of global telegraph and undersea cable systems. The rise of radio technology, innovations during the First World War, and a very aggressive and visionary American policy regarding global telecommunications in the 1920s and 1930s succeeded in moving the United States from the periphery to the core of global telecommunications strategy, largely by carving out a dominant sphere of influence in the Western Hemisphere.[44]

Despite this shift from the periphery to the core and dominance of the Western Hemisphere during the first four decades of the twentieth century, it is questionable whether the United States could have reached the dominant position of global telecommunications strategy it enjoyed throughout the Cold War—and still enjoys to this day—without the opportunities presented during the period of German occupation. The challenges and opportunities presented to American policymakers in both Germany and Washington during the postwar occupation period were not only met in such a way that television could return to Germany under the principles of a decentralized system of broadcasting, but also resulted in the rejection of propaganda and the promotion of a civic society for the German people. The question of postwar German television also created the initial conditions and laid the first groundwork necessary for the United States to become during the Cold War period what it remains today: the premiere architect of global telecommunications strategy. Becoming this premiere architect of global telecommunications, as well as a leading "artist" of global television, was not a foregone conclusion at the start of the Cold War. Television, in particular, was poorly understood in a global context in the aftermath of World War II, and the first organized stance regarding global television from American policymakers was to see television as a "facet of east-west problems" or as yet another component of superpower relations, strategic issues, and East-West security. This led to television being considered one of several emergent electronic communication technologies that would eventually play important roles in the brewing "War of Words" between the Americans and Soviets, but precisely how global television would become involved in psychological warfare remained a question open to much debate, study, and speculation.

3. "The Key to Many of These Countries Is Not the Mud Hut Population"

The aftermath of the Second World War saw the initial dismantling of wartime measures regarding American propaganda and information dissemination as practiced by such agencies of the Office of War Information (OWI) in response to peace, new world conditions, and the emergence of the UN.[1] Although State Department officials explored ways in which the State Department could and should continue activities of information dissemination in a postwar world, little was initially accomplished in settling questions regarding the role of propaganda and information dissemination during times of peace. Rising Cold War tensions demonstrated to American policymakers that propaganda, information dissemination, public opinion, and global attitudes were of significance, but how best to conceptualize such issues and then operationalize statecraft remained murky. For example, the value of monitoring foreign press and propaganda broadcasts had been recognized during the war, and the continuation of this practice was seen as a component of postwar intelligence. The FCC had established the Foreign Broadcasting Intelligence Service (FBIS) during the war, but intended to dismantle this service in the fall of 1945. Instead, FBIS functions were taken over by the War Department on an interim basis late in 1945 with the intention of finding an appropriate agency to carry out this task as a part of an emergent national intelligence authority.[2] The FBIS is one of several examples where federal agencies involved in wartime propaganda and information dissemination on the one hand recognized the need for their involvement during war hostilities, and at the same time questioned whether their continued involvement after the end of such hostilities still served the core mission of that given agency. Yet some sort of government involvement in said activities was definitely in the interests of postwar national security.

Project Troy, Political Warfare, and Emerging
U.S. Propaganda Agencies

Despite the uncertainties, many government agencies pressed forward with studies and operations planning regarding Cold War propaganda, information dissemination, and psychological warfare. This included (but was not limited to) actions by the military, the emergent Central Intelligence Agency (CIA), the State Department, and the White House.[3] These early activities reached beyond the confines of government to recruit and enroll a vast range of American individuals and institutions, from voluntary organizations to funding agencies to American universities. The State Department was particularly influenced by a report produced at MIT in 1951 called Project Troy.[4]

Originally commissioned by the State Department in response to Soviet jamming of Western radio broadcasts into Eastern Europe and the USSR, Project Troy took on a life of its own and became a four-volume study exploring the feasibility of collapsing the USSR through a strategy of "information overload." With public opinion and communication specialists such as Jerome Bruner, Clyde Kluckhohn, Donald Marquis, and Hans Speier on its research team, Project Troy advocated that "attempts be made to attack the Soviet Union as a system . . . and to introduce problems into the system which will induce varying degrees of paralysis."[5] The Project Troy research team labeled its strategy as "political warfare" and its approach as systemic:

> . . . the aims of an information program can be fully realized only when the many elements of our national power, political, economic, military, are wielded as an integrated effort. We therefore urge the unification of political warfare . . . an information program becomes a significant instrument in the achievement of our national objectives only when designed as one component in a political "weapon system." . . . It is within the framework of this conviction that we have closely examined several of the components of political warfare: e.g., our telecommunications system, an information program, a program for defectors, and a program designed to produce overload and delay within the enemy's administrative infrastructure.[6]

Even though the specific recommendations of Project Troy did not immediately translate into action steps for the State Department, the research design of Project Troy, particularly its broadscale planning and vision of a systematic approach, was highly influential. After receiving the Project Troy report, Undersecretary of State James Webb wrote the director of the Bureau of the Budget advocating the establishment of a Psychological Strategy Board composed of the undersecretary of State, the deputy secretary of Defense, the director of Central Intelligence, an executive director, additional appropriate representatives, and an advisor from the Joint Chiefs of Staff.[7]

The PSB was a short-lived, understaffed, yet volatile entity. Created to coordinate both information and action across a variety of government agencies, ostensibly housed in the State Department yet in reality ultimately reporting and responding to the NSC, PSB responded to perceived battlefronts in Cold War psychological warfare. At the same time, PSB recognized the deep difficulties in enacting psychological warfare for an American government that had yet to coalesce its resources from the aftermath of the Second World War into fully functioning Cold War assets. In the realm of global public opinion, PSB operated from an untested assumption that global public opinion ran counter to American interests. This led PSB to advance plans and strategies that attacked these untested assumptions about global public opinion. In short, the PSB's first general thrust was to attack on the psychological warfare front, rather than to seek ways in which to measure, gauge, and assess the various components, qualities, and aspects of that front. A "Grand Strategy for Psychological Operations" written in November 1951 by Palmer Putman for fellow PSB member and former University of North Carolina President Gordon Gray posited the key to negating Soviet threats was the destruction of Soviet power without waging general warfare. Finding a way to do this was "a nice problem—like trying to prevent a squid from squirting ink while you are destroying it." Palmer called for "the paralysis of the Soviet world by psychological judo" and advocated political and psychological warfare against the USSR as avenues to spread rumors and prey on superstitions through "balloon-borne loudspeakers; colored snow; and other manifestations."[8]

That a war of words had broken out between the superpowers was, by this time, everyday knowledge among both the elites and the masses. Typical of the fervor was the man-on-the-street letter from Joseph Ochenkowski of Northford, Connecticut, to President Truman in July 1951. Fed up with the "barrage of vituperation and lies that the Soviets are sowing on the world," Ochenkowski suggested Truman appoint a "Truth Mobilizer" as our nation's "Propaganda Chieftain" and added for good measure that in terms of the effectiveness of global communication, "we spend more on getting the word of Coca-Cola around the world than what we really stand for."[9]

If the American government had a truth mobilizer at this time, as good a candidate as any would be Assistant Secretary of State for Public Affairs Edward W. Barrett. Barrett typically appeared at public events to discuss the American response to the war of words. Appearing as the guest of the School of Speech at the Centennial Celebration of Northwestern University in October 1951, Barrett told the audience they already "knew the ruthlessness of the enemy" on this topic. On the statistical front, the Northwestern community learned that the latest U.S. intelligence estimates forecast the Soviets spending the equivalent of $928 million annually on propaganda, with the Soviet satellite states kicking in an additional $481 million per annum. These figures did not include the propaganda activities of card-carrying Communists scattered throughout the rest of the world.[10] Appearing on WGN radio two days later in an episode of *Northwestern University Reviewing Stand* with Northwestern School of Speech Dean James McBurney and Northwestern Department of Radio and Television Chair Donley Feddersen, discussion centered on radio broadcasting activities such as VOA and RIAS.[11]

Barrett, the PSB, and the Truman administration, in general, did not, in the main, show signs of placing a high premium on testing and polling global public opinion. The emphasis was on producing and promoting propaganda content, searching for systemwide approaches to fighting psychological warfare, and enlisting a vast armada of warriors to the cause. For example, Raymond Allen responded to the call in a 1952 lecture given at the Psychological Warfare Seminar of the University of North Carolina, reminding his audience that "the twentieth century world lives and breathes by communication" and social scientists, including biologists, must recognize the "dramatic speed-up in world wide communications among peoples and governments." Warning that we already know what the historian of the future "will write if the plans of the Bolsheviki succeed . . . what he is told to write and nothing more," Allen stressed cyberspectral extraterritorialities, arguing the war of words was one facet

> in the broad spectrum of many colors which characterizes the global struggle. One line in the spectrum is the electro-magnetic war which the Bolskeviki have forced upon us. Belatedly, we are recognizing this facet of the struggle as one of its most deadly salients . . . the Bolsheviki have made shrewd use of what little is known of the biology of communication. They have aggressively and to a purpose narrowed the range of information reaching their captives and behind their slick-sided prison walls. These walls, as you know, are partly electro-magnetic walls—other parts are barbed wire and guns. Thus they hope to evolve robots who respond as one man to the word from the Kremlin.[12]

Additionally, PSB, following the model of the MIT Troy Project, undertook a series of studies toward action plans in various nations and regions of the world. For example, a 1953 plan for goals in Vietnam, Cambodia, and Laos cast the task in terms of psychological objectives "to the crystallization of national and military political forces (in the area) to a more effective free world support for these forces and to the ensuing denial of those countries to Soviet bloc orbit."[13] The plan called for the following actions:

- Identify targets of psychological strategy in France and Indochina
- Encourage aggressive and adequate military operations to restore "the free world power position" in Indochina
- Find French Army officers receptive to a new tactical approach
- Elicit increased interest in unconventional warfare in the French and American press
- Publish articles on the "uneconomic aspect of modern colonialism" in *Foreign Affairs*
- Build a sense of "true nationalism favorably disposed" to France and the free world
- Stress the historic menace of China
- Deprive the Vietminh of its rice supply
- Use "all possible overt and covert means, including kidnapping" to build a defection program from the Vietminh, targeting Vietminh military and political leaders
- Identify "French Officials of the Colonial Service who have lost their usefulness" and fund their removal from Indochina through jobs with American private firms
- Use all mass media possible to discredit Vietminh and stress their link to China.

The document summarized above, which includes assigning specific tasks to the State Department, to the CIA, and to other agencies (as well as using former Office of Strategic Services [OSS] operatives and private enterprise) exemplifies the reckless nature of the PSB. Although PSB did not set out with the intention of recklessness, their trajectory was a by-product of the haste in which PSB was formed and the rapidly growing urgency of Cold War psychological warfare. Gordon Gray explained to Truman that PSB had been formed in 1951 "to win and hold the confidence of our friends abroad and weaken the will of our enemies" after "some high officials became convinced that we needed the same kind of unified leadership as in a military struggle" to effectively wage a war of words with the Soviets, who had long practiced propaganda "under the cloak of an unnatural peace." However, the PSB "quickly made up their minds that the Board's mandate covered a great deal more than word warfare . . . not to explain—or explain away—events but to shape events." Standing in the way of shaping events were instructions that PSB should "stay out of operational matters" lest it become what it was in fact becoming: "a Board of Improvised Tactics." Nevertheless, tactics were unavoidable because "the task for psychological strategy was to help create situations of strength, not to wait for their creation."[14] Eventually, the PSB was dissolved early in the Eisenhower administration. In its place rose two new entities—the OCB, which in fact kept many of the original PSB tasks and directives in terms of attempting to coordinate psychological warfare across various government agencies—and the creation of a new government unit, the USIA.[15]

Despite its overwhelming emphasis on offensive weaponry in psychological warfare, PSB and its successor agency OCB were becoming aware of the need for weapons such as measurement and assessment of target audience attitudes and message effectiveness—the typical answers public opinion research claims to provide with sufficient accuracy for future planning and deployment of offensive weapons in psychological warfare. One PSB staffer theorized on the inexplicable success the Soviets had in exploiting the idea of "Cultural Imperialism" as a way of blunting American missionary and educational activities in Asia, particularly China. John MacDonald believed the Soviets effectively used the concept of cultural imperialism for bewildered Asians who could not understand the impulse behind the charitable activities of American missionaries and educators, speculated that such charitable activities might actually cause a backlash of xenophobia and nationalism, and concluded that funding expert studies to produce greater understanding of the attitudes of target populations would be "well worthwhile."[16]

The complexities of psychological warfare faced by the Truman administration showed no signs of abating for the newly elected Dwight Eisenhower. In addition to increased activities in established media forms such as newspapers, journals, and radio broadcasting, new forms such as television were now becoming sufficiently established in Europe to present new challenges. Although the British government eventually agreed with the American position that television in Cold War Europe was not so much an issue of national identity as it was an issue of East-West security, at the same time British foreign service officers pushed other nations, such as Canada, to become markets for British as well as American television exports. Of particular interest was arranging for international television broadcast coverage of the coronation of Queen Elizabeth. Even the British cabinet recognized that television was "already revolutionizing publicity and propaganda methods . . . the emergence of television as a permanent feature of modern life cannot be ignored. To omit it from the armoury of our information services will have serious consequences."[17]

The role and impact of television in the International Information Activities (IIA) division of the State Department just prior to the transformation of IIA and other agency units into the USIA was muddled. The IIA Television Development Officer Richard Hubbell, seizing the opportunity of a Senate Foreign Relations Committee hearing on overseas information activities in the grand tradition of many a career civil servant, first warned about new Communist TV developments in East Germany. He then lambasted his own agency for its lack of vision regarding international television, which he believed was largely based on "lip service" rather than concrete plans and action steps. Warning that the Kremlin would first spread Soviet TV through Eastern Europe "for political control purposes" and then move on to target Western European television, Hubbell painted a vivid picture of the power of international television for the senators, telling them "television is to our Information program as Atomic Energy is to our Armed Forces."[18]

The formation of the USIA in 1953 responded to the growing complexities of propaganda, organized overt and public propaganda content production in a single agency of the American government, and just as importantly, relieved agencies such as the State Department from the frontline of offensive psychological warfare. The formation of the USIA also settled once and for all what had become a de facto PSB operating tactic: prior to USIA, the State Department usually engaged in most of the overt and public propaganda, and the CIA usually took on covert or so-called "black" propaganda projects, although heretofore these lines of separation were not always clear. This new separation washed the hands of both the State Department and the new USIA of the ostensibly private propaganda projects (but often bankrolled and programmed through "beards" or CIA cover organizations) such as Radio Liberty, Radio Free Europe, and the Congress of Cultural Freedom.[19] The State Department thus transferred its propaganda and information dissemination activities to the USIA. The USIA grew quickly, immediately taking on propaganda and information dissemination on multiple fronts, including broadcasting, films, lectures, libraries, printed materials, and exhibits. An early global USIA project was the 1956 People's Capitalism exhibit.[20]

People's Capitalism became one of the first major USIA global exhibits, yet the exhibit underscored the emphasis on "telling" target audiences rather than "gauging" or measuring global public opinion. To be fair, the original charge of USIA as first formulated emphasized telling rather than measuring, or creating global public opinion rather than also measuring and analyzing global public opinion. To be even fairer, USIA did, early on and of its own accord, begin to develop measurement and analysis capabilities, particularly in the area of audience measurement toward determining the effectiveness of its own efforts. Yet through most of the first term of the Eisenhower presidency, the USIA was primarily a content producer rather than both a content producer and an analyst of global public opinion. However, the NSC eventually set a course for greater involvement by the USIA in global public opinion polling.

At the 235th meeting of the NSC, held February 3, 1955, Arthur Flemming of the Office of Defense Mobilization raised the question of effectiveness regarding VOA broadcasts in particular and, by implication, of USIA overall activities. Noting that American psychological warfare lacked any substantial basis for passing judgment on the effectiveness of programs broadcast by U.S. agencies, Flemming commented "what were really needed were Hooper Ratings."[21] USIA Assistant Director Abbott Washburn protested that anything like a Hooper rating (a well-known commercial audience measurement service prior to Nielsen ratings) was "next to impossible" and that USIA instead depended on subjective judgment.[22] Taking the middle ground, Eisenhower called for patience, but the NSC had nevertheless signaled a strong interest in audience measurement and evaluating the effectiveness of USIA programming.

Taking its cue from the NSC, the USIA increased its efforts at audience measurement and effectiveness. In part, this meant soliciting advice from familiar colleagues from American universities, such as Wilbur Schramm of the University of Illinois (and later Stanford University) and Ithiel de Sola Pool of MIT.[23] The USIA significantly increased its own internal staff devoted to audience measurement and public opinion polling. Although measurement of the effectiveness of USIA programs and projects continued as a major focus, these measurement and polling activities expanded beyond the scope of self-measurement. This USIA expansion into global public opinion polling would grow considerably during the second term of the Eisenhower presidency, particularly after the Soviet launch of Sputnik.

Sputnik, American Science, and World Public Opinion

Paul Dickson argues that the October 4, 1957, Sputnik launch by the USSR did not begin a popular interest in science and technology. Sputnik catalyzed a rising popular interest that, in American culture, stretched back as least as far as the 1939 World's Fair in New York City.[24] Rocketry experiments in the United States, Russia/USSR, and Europe dated back to the dawn of the twentieth century; the Second World War had seen the rise of German rocket capability in the service of a totalitarian war state; and a wide range of postwar popular press items, scientific studies, and research programs kept rocketry and satellites as an item of popular scientific interest. The International Geophysical Year (an 18–month year from mid-1956 to the end of 1958) had forecast satellite launches as a possible international scientific research activity. Nevertheless, Sputnik was portrayed, particularly in the popular press and media of the United States, as a shock.

The first regular NSC meeting after the Sputnik launch was held on October 10.[25] In a briefing from CIA Director Allen Dulles, the NSC heard the details of the launch, that the CIA did not consider this a surprise, and additional background about Soviet launch capabilities. Dulles then turned to the world reaction noting, "Khrushchev had moved all his propaganda guns into place" and placed Sputnik in a "trilogy of propaganda moves" along with the announcement of a successful intercontinental ballistic missile (ICBM) test and a recent testing of a large-scale hydrogen bomb at Novaya Zemla. Dulles believed the target audience was the Middle East, in particular, and the underdeveloped nations, in general. He saw Sputnik as "following closely on the original Soviet boast relating their scientific accomplishments to the effectiveness of the Communist social system" and concluded that the USSR "was making a major propaganda effort which was exerting a very wide and deep impact."

Deputy Secretary of Defense Donald Quarles then briefed the NSC on American satellite efforts and the upcoming Vanguard satellite project. Quarles confined his remarks to American satellites and reconnaissance implications, scientific achievements, and ballistic missile development. Curious that Vanguard was planned to achieve a lower orbit than Sputnik, Eisenhower first asked if a lower orbit might mean more interference, and then asked if a lower orbit might have a negative impact on American prestige.[26] Quarles responded by arguing Vanguard's more advanced equipment, and therefore greater potential for data gathering, offset these concerns. NSF Director Alan Waterman believed American openness combined with superior scientific design were two important assets in the rivalry with the Soviets. Eisenhower predicted that everyone would soon be involved in rounds of congressional hearings and press interviews and recommended everyone should stay on point that the American plan for satellites was a good plan.

USIA Director Arthur Larson, admitting his own hesitancy on what he was about to say, nevertheless argued while panic over Sputnik was inappropriate, he wondered whether plans were now adequate with regard to global public opinion and the next great breakthrough. If the United States lost repeatedly to the Russians as it had lost with the earth satellite, the accumulated damage to the global image of America would be tremendous.[27] He recommended planning for some of the next breakthroughs first, suggesting a manned satellite or getting to the moon as examples. National Academy of Sciences (NAS) Director Detlev Bronk expanded on Larson's point by arguing the United States could choose to give greater emphasis to a wide range of spectacular achievements in the scientific field, not just space flight, although he noted the difficulty in building press interest in some of these achievements. Closing the NSC discussion on a somber note, Chairman of the Joint Chiefs of Staff Nathan Twining simply cautioned against everyone becoming "hysterical" over Sputnik.

Two months later, meeting just after an unexpected delay in the countdown to launch of Vanguard, Allen Dulles railed to the rest of the NSC against the practice of prelaunch publicity, insisting that the backlash from launch delay had made the United States the "laughing-stock of the whole Free World" and was now a topic of Soviet exploitation.[28] Eisenhower requested, and the NSC approved, the formation of a study group to assess whether public announcement of attempted satellite launches could or should be postponed until after a launch was successful and a satellite in orbit. Space policy and global public opinion continued as a routine agenda item at NSC meetings. By the summer of 1958, the NSC was finishing the formulation of strategic American space policy. NSC 5814 U.S. Policy on Outer Space[29] was in its final drafting, and the question of "exploitation" of outer space capabilities presented NSC with a problem. In a July 3 NSC meeting, Alan Waterman believed it would take great determination to reach parity with the USSR.[30] The NSC chose to pair "exploitation" with the goal of making the United States a "recognized leader" in outer space activities.

With the 1959 creation of the National Aeronautics and Space Administration (NASA), NSC was still considering global public opinion and the image of American science and technology as a component of outer space policy. In a July 30, 1959, NSC meeting, Eisenhower wondered about proposed NSC language and policy in the psychological values of outer space policy, saying such values extended beyond the creation of NASA (and added that NASA was based wholly on psychological values). Abbott Washburn remarked that certain outer space projects carried more "world opinion freight" than others did, offering a soft moon landing as something that captured people's imagination. Eisenhower, perhaps tongue-in-cheek, then asked the difference in psychological impact between a soft moon landing and a trip to Venus.[31]

Washburn, however, from his vantage point at the USIA, by this time knew something of global public opinion regarding outer space activities. Even before Sputnik, but certainly accelerated by it, the USIA began extensive public opinion polling on questions of science, technology, and outer space. These polls were conducted in both Europe and in the underdeveloped world and done extensively. In 1955, the USIA had undertaken self-studies and consulted with outside researchers in planning its own program of public opinion surveys. Recognizing that the USIA needed to listen as well as to speak to the world, one USIA 1955 self-study argued that the superpower conflict in the realm of psychological warfare was "a battle for men's minds" that, as in armed conflict, "cannot be won without the closest attention to fire-control, i.e., systematic measures for localizing targets and for ascertaining whether or not shots are hitting the mark." Global public opinion polling was, therefore, a sort of telemetry for political and psychological warfare because even though official opinion and press opinion helped to set a framework for battle, "only with the third dimension filled in—public opinion—is there really full-bodied guidance for propaganda operations."[32]

The USIA had responded promptly in the wake of the NSC debate in February 1955. Now the USIA was learning and implementing the value of audience measurement, public opinion ratings, and data regarding the effectiveness of American psychological warfare built upon social science methodologies aiming to transcend individual subjective judgments. Global public opinion polling was now a crucial component of national security. Despite this recognition by the NSC and new effort by the USIA, Washington insiders and outsiders still wondered about commitment and professionalism in psychological warfare. Arthur Larson, now departed from Washington and on the faculty at the Duke Law School, appeared on WRCA-TV's *The Open Mind* in October 1958 as part of a discussion of "America's Image Abroad." Larson bluntly told New York City viewers

> We've suddenly come into a position of world prominence, of leadership, that we haven't become accustomed to, and we haven't been professional agitators, we're not conducting a professional world revolution, we're not professional colonialists . . . it's time we took it seriously and did the kind of full-scale job on it that our position in the world demands . . . the key to many of these countries is not the mud hut population or the person back in the bush . . . the key is becoming the band of educated and influential young people, the students, the professors, the young professional people, the young military people, and the lively oncoming groups that have ambitions for their country.[33]

Ithiel de Sola Pool of MIT, Waldemar Nielsen of the Ford Foundation, and C. D. Jackson of *Time-Life* may or may not have seen this telecast, but no matter, they could not have agreed more. All three had a common idea and central theme for recasting the global image of America away from the mud huts and toward the young professionals: science. Dwight Eisenhower was about to give them an opportunity to test their ideas about American science and the global image through a new presidential committee.

The Sprague Committee and the Global Image of America

In July 1959, longtime Eisenhower political advisor and Henry Luce protégé C. D. Jackson wrote to Eisenhower expressing his frustrations over the lack of understanding in the State Department in particular, but generally throughout the Eisenhower administration, on waging political warfare.[34] In December 1959, Eisenhower responded and formed a presidential committee, chaired by former counsel to the Secretary of Defense Mansfield Sprague, to take on questions regarding information activities in the global arena. In addition to Sprague and Jackson (both of whom had experience in OCB and also on NSC), members included USIA Director George Allen, Livingston Merchant of the State Department, Gordon Gray, and Karl Harr, who had served in a variety of Defense Department positions and also on OCB. To serve as executive director, and to direct the research associated with the project, the Ford Foundation allowed a leave of absence to one of its veteran international officers, Waldemar Nielsen.[35]

The Sprague Committee took on the study of both established communication technologies, such as print and radio, as well as the continued emergence of new technologies such as television. Commercial television producer (and former VOA veteran) Louis Cowan wrote Nielsen that Communist exploitation of television was not merely a possibility in Europe, but was already happening. Like many, Cowan hoped for a rising interest in educational and instructional television as a genuine alternative to pinning most hopes for European television growth on a commercial market system.[36]

Of ultimate interest beyond global infrastructures of media technologies, however, was a concern about context, or message: the global image of the United States, particularly in science and technology. Within six months, this question had become the major focal point of the Sprague Committee. The issue came to a head in a remarkable committee session held on June 20, 1960.[37] Waldemar Nielsen asked NSF Director Alan Waterman an oblique question about science funding and national security, querying whether U.S. interests were best served by emphasizing the "basic job" we do in science, or whether it was also useful to give consideration to the "impact factor" in scientific activities. Believing most people suspicious of propaganda, Waterman described what he called "the visual versus the real image in physics" and urged the United States to project its real image. He then differentiated between the opinions of the scientific elite, on the one hand, and the masses, on the other, concluding that the opinion of global scientific elites should be the major priority. Turning to the concept of scientific freedom of inquiry, Waterman warned that further attempts to steer basic research into projects for psychological impact would be a mistake.

As Waterman continued his argument, Jackson asked about situations in which there may be few if any of the scientific elite to influence—for example, Africa. Admitting this was a different case, Waterman suggested the target audience in such situations for improving the image of American science and technology in public opinion was national leaders, and not the masses themselves. Noting that the United States had no choice about playing the Soviet game to some extent, Karl Harr asked how to weigh the factors of scientific importance with other elements of the national interest, contending the United States had so far failed to get its symbol of power communicated to the rest of the world. Jackson again parried, this time more forcefully, telling Waterman that the recent Pioneer satellite may send back data of scientific importance, but it did not do much toward impressing the future leaders of the Belgian Congo.

As the meeting progressed, the committee discussed the pros and cons of publicizing a wide range of possible projects for American science and technology, including orbiting a device that would light up the night sky, nuclear-powered aircraft, using rockets to deliver mail to the American research station at the South Pole in Antarctica, a beam of energy that would disintegrate objects, and anti-gravity devices. It was agreed that all would have maximum potential impact on mass public opinion, but, at the same time, none of the projects could expect to attract significant interest from scientists conducting basic research. The discussion then focused on avoiding mere "stunts" and instead finding "feasible" science projects—feasible for building interest in the scientific elite as well as feasible for exploitation through global public relations. Sprague and Jackson then asked Waterman a series of very pointed questions regarding how the NSF took into account or otherwise measured the potential impact on global public opinion when NSF makes research funding and similar decisions. Dodging the punches, Waterman finally responded that NSF "should play the science fiction aspect with restraint." Harr found no "mechanism" in the American government to consider the factor of global public opinion in science and technology funding and research, complaining decisions were in the hands of scientists who did not consider the impact factor of a given project. Even in this elite group, Harr saw little consensus, believing scientists often shot down the judgment of other scientists on the question of public impact and that scientist's individual views were parochial and colored to a considerable extent.

Gordon Gray then joined the dialogue. An experienced statesman and PSB, NSC, and OCB veteran, Gray confirmed that with respect to two projects of equal scientific value it is clearly the policy of the United States to "give the nod" to the scientific project that has the greater potential for impact on global public opinion. One did have to caution against funding projects that had minimal value beyond public impact, but on projects of equal merit, the impact factor was a key to funding approval. Nielsen then asked Waterman and David Beckler[38] who in the science agencies was responsible for considering the impact factor, and if more people in those agencies could be oriented toward giving the impact factor deeper consideration. Beckler replied that no one in those agencies had that specific charge as part of their duties; rather, when recognition of the impact factor emerged in those agencies, it depended largely on the initiative and creativity of the people involved. Lamenting the lack of impact factor individuals at NSF, the Atomic Energy Commission (AEC), and elsewhere, Nielsen noted there were few if any such people in other government agencies, which would make it even more difficult for the science agencies to "come around" to the value of this skill.

Having heard enough and with the committee now in session for several hours, Jackson cut to the chase, saying the United States could no longer afford to "goof" around and that the United States needed to "draw up its pants and securely anchor them up." Calling the day's testimony a case history of opportunities missed, Jackson said the committee needed to directly influence the president on the importance of waging political and psychological warfare, for there was no hope of nurturing this understanding from the State Department, the CIA, or the USIA. The "P-factor," according to Jackson, cannot get into decisions "by silent osmosis" but needed to be "injected" by spoken commands. Flashing his credentials as a Washington mandarin, Jackson concluded by saying he was fully familiar with the epic struggles that take place in Washington and that decisions "have to be taken even though the blood runs in the corridors." Spilling blood was not to be feared but was part of "the struggle in Washington" for warriors to crank psychological warfare into action, even if "it has to be done over the broken bodies of many people."[39]

The final report of the Sprague Committee included a lengthy section titled "The Impact of Achievements in Science and Technology Upon the Image Abroad of the United States."[40] Its seventeen appendices discussed the impact factor of a host of projects, including manned space flight, manned lunar and/or planetary exploration, nuclear pulse reaction propulsion, controlled thermonuclear reactions for mineral excavation and large-scale construction projects, the Mohole project for deep boring into the earth, cancer research, a commercially feasible air car, rocket transport, drugs to repair radiation damage to humans, charged particle beams (a death ray, a laser, or both), desalination of water, widespread use of audiovisual communications powered by solar energy, instructional television for mass education, and global science education.

In its introduction, subtitled "Shadow and Substance," the committee argued the overall image of a given nation is a "conglomeration of multiple imprints . . . an impressionistic Picasso rather than a sketch by Da Vinci."[41]

Buttressed with USIA public opinion data noting that science and technology are explicitly recognized both as symbols of power and keys to progress, the report recommended the "slow progress of education" as an important component in boosting global perceptions of American science and technology.[42] American science also carried strong connotations of bedrock American values such as freedom, democracy, mobility, and a pluralistic society. Recommendations included that the president stress the importance of "international political-psychological factors" in funding science research and advise science administrators at federal agencies as to the potential for positive psychological impact in their actions and decisions. Suggesting the NSC also weigh in on the psychological impact of science funding, the committee called for "guidance on exploitation of U.S. feats in science and technology . . . and for consideration of ways to improve the image abroad of the United States' scientific and technological capabilities."[43]

Psychological warfare and public opinion polling were seen as issues of national security in the highest echelons of American government during the Cold War. In particular, the attention of the NSC to a lack of audience measurement regarding USIA propaganda activities, plus the importance of assessing the effectiveness of USIA activities on shaping global public opinion, led the USIA to expand its resources in these areas. Analyzing global public opinion on American and Soviet science and technology in 1960, the USIA found assessment of foreign views of American and Soviet science were "fragmentary" and more often than not foreign attitudes were "unformulated and unstable." This meant that "scientific and technological developments lend themselves to highly sensationalized treatment" with a public that "is so responsive to exaggerations, that the tempering effect of expert judgments in these matters is probably more than offset." This all led to global public opinion about science and technology serving as "indices of power." Admitting the exact definition of this kind of power was elusive, it was nevertheless potent, and space exploration, in particular, "seems to have produced the beginnings of a change in man's sense of his cosmos." Achievements in science and technology now carried a "double payload" as "status symbols in the East-West conflict, direct indices of power; and they are promises of directly meaningful, applicable, usable instruments of progress." Concluding that the key to exploiting this new power of science was in cultivating world public opinion to sympathize with and support American efforts in science and technology, the USIA believed that in the future, "those deeds are most successful which most fully convert the foreign spectator into a participant."[44] This demanded, among other things, finding ways to help global audiences see and experience American science in action.

Even though the question of the American image in global science and technology was emergent prior to the 1957 Sputnik launch, Sputnik and the space race added to the urgency of this issue. In addition to government agencies, advice was sought and experts enrolled from universities, foundations, and commercial media—particularly public relations firms and advertising agencies (or what might be called Madison Avenue) on how to consider the question of the American image, as well as how to address perceived shortcomings in the American image abroad. Science and technology, writ large, became a crucial canvas for analyzing the weaknesses in the American global image, as well as for developing strategies and practices for improving the American global image while exploiting weaknesses in the global image of Soviet science and technology. This national security imperative was considered of sufficient importance to introduce psychological impact factors into science planning and science funding at agencies such as the NSF. Furthermore, a working principle recognizing the Cold War psychological impact of science and technology projects penetrated deeply into many facets of American science. American science was not just a Cold War weapon for building components in the physical armory of war; it also became a Cold War weapon for building components in the psychological armory of war.

Questions of loyalty and patriotism of American scientists, burning throughout the 1950s, were still evident into the 1960s. In 1961, the NSF rescinded a graduate fellowship awarded to Edward Yellin, a student at the University of Illinois.[45] Yellin had been cited by the House Un-American Activities Committee for contempt of Congress in 1958 for failing to explain why he had, circa 1950, dropped out of college and gone to work as a laborer for U.S. Steel. With accusations that Yellin was a part of a Soviet plot to put college-educated leftists into American labor movements, his contempt charge led to a conviction in a U.S. district court in 1960 and was upheld on appeal in 1961. Despite signing a loyalty oath as part of his NSF award, the NSF affirmed it "does not knowingly give or continue a grant in support of research for one who is an avowed Communist or anyone established as a Communist by a judicial proceeding"[46] and revoked his funding on the advice of the White House, despite protests from the American Association of University Professors. The Yellin case exemplifies the chilling links between Cold War science policy, propaganda, and patriotism.

Finally, there is another Cold War constraint on our understanding of science and technology, in this case an intellectual constraint. In retrospect, the linking of American science and technology to images of freedom and democracy became a powerful ideology instilled in global consciousness, no more so than within Americans themselves. That is the way propaganda always works—the domestic audience is also an important target audience.[47] Propaganda theory aside, the rough but effective formula "Cold War (Military) (Science & Technology) + Global (Impact Factor) (Public Opinion) $\cong$ Political and Social Freedom" lingers today. Bringing wholesale changes that transform American science policy beyond its Cold War paradigm remains an extraordinarily difficult task, as a quick glance at the amount of government funds devoted to military research and development suggests. Further, as James Der Derian demonstrates in his recent book, this military-based scientific research and development is fully intertwined with private-sector activities in a wide range of areas, not the least of which are media and entertainment.[48] Contemporary society remains shackled with the tensions between the opinions of the scientific elite versus the polled public on a wide range of science and technology research, from missile defense to cloning pets. Feasibility, the impact factor, and the American global image remain as powerful forces influencing—sometimes for better, sometimes for worse—the directions of science. We remain socially shaped by the dialogue built as a discursive weapon for the Cold War.

The power of the basic "Science = Freedom" equation was recognized by a few individuals who had a hand in shaping American Cold War science, technology, and the American global image. Individuals such as Waldemar Nielsen from the Ford Foundation and C. D. Jackson from *Time-Life* had promulgated similar messages in their careers beyond the corridors of Washington. From MIT, Ithiel de Sola Pool argued, "scientific information is one of the few things very much wanted by other countries" and therefore is a "vehicle for establishing contact" and "an ideology favorable to the development of democratic stability in underdeveloped countries." Noting that "universities in those countries often face a choice between working toward modernization through political ideology (which often means Communism or other forms of radicalism) or through science," Pool believed when "the second alternative is recognized as having constructive promise . . . the prospects for evolution in ways desired by us are greatly increased."[49]

In keeping with the findings of the USIA to turn foreign spectators into participants, globalizing American science as a component of Cold War psychological warfare proved to be a new front in the war of words. Indeed, the war would no longer be waged only on the word front, but would expand to multiple fronts and become a war of words, sights, sounds, and experiences mediated through an array of avenues, such as television and other new communications technologies, electronic networks, USIA exhibits, and personal encounters. This new multifront war would ultimately involve a wholesale discursive transformation of the words of the Cold War as well as a trans-

formation away from thinking about global media such as television solely
as a signifier of East-West security. Psychological warfare would begin to
transform, through mediating technologies, into early manifestations of what
is now called information diplomacy. With the help of distinguished Cold
War intellectuals recruited by the Ford Foundation and similar American
philanthropic organizations, television, new communication technologies,
and science would become global signifiers of a new idea, open to participation by citizens the world over: world citizenship shared through global
electronic communications to foster interest in American science, with a
discursive shift toward what is now called globalization.

4. "A Group of Angry Young Intellectuals"

I myself, of course, have a particular taste for the fellow with
innovativeness, interest in the new idea, the unorthodox person
or institution, the border zones, controversy and all . . . [but] . . .
Being the broker of foundation money in transactions with men of
science and thought and education is not a thing to which a really
good man ought to devote his life, and it is not good enough to
have third-rate men devoting their lives to it.
—Waldemar Nielsen, Oral History, 1972

As a senior Ford Foundation officer working on international issues in the
1950s, Waldemar Nielsen proved to be as good as his word, devoting less than
a decade of his own long career specifically to the Ford Foundation. Nielsen
joined the Ford Foundation after helping to implement the Marshall Plan and
came to the foundation with the recommendation of Hans Speier, another
Marshall Plan veteran who had since moved on to become one of the leading
researchers at RAND. With a BA and MA from the University of Missouri,
Nielsen had been named a Rhodes Scholar in 1939, but the Second World
War prevented him from completing study at Oxford. He did graduate work
in law and political science at Wisconsin in 1940, joined the Department of
Agriculture to direct program surveys that same year, moved to the Navy
in 1943 to assist in the tactical deployment of RADAR technology, spent
1946–47 conducting public opinion surveys for the State Department, served
as a senior official in the Department of Commerce from 1947–51, and finally
served as the director of the European Information Division of the Office of
the U.S. Special Representative in Europe (the Marshall Plan) prior to joining
the Ford Foundation in the fall of 1953. From October 1957 until November
1961, he was the foundation's associate director for the International Affairs
Program. He then left the foundation to serve as president of the African-
American Institute.[1] He went on to eventually become, in the latter decades
of the twentieth century, the preeminent consultant and critic regarding
American philanthropy and was honored with both a seminar series and a
professorial chair in his name at Georgetown University.[2]

Although this chapter is partially intended to introduce media studies scholars[3] to Nielsen, the Ford Foundation, and the interactions between American philanthropy and Cold War global media culture, the choice of Nielsen as a seminal figure for understanding these issues is less a biographical exercise and instead more akin to the practice of orienteering. Beyond a brief biography, Nielsen is employed herein as a sort of compass, helping to set bearings for navigating through the incredibly dense and oft-bewildering thickets of American philanthropy, government funding, and Cold War media culture. Therefore, above and beyond providing a useful if contained sketch of Nielsen's contributions to Cold War media culture while he was a senior-level Ford Foundation officer, this chapter also maps a larger and more diverse terrain beyond the career path of one, albeit important, foundation official. Next, this chapter takes a close look at that larger terrain of American philanthropy and media culture at the dawn of the Cold War.

The Ford Foundation and Cold War Communications Research

Using Nielsen as a compass points back at the Marshall Plan and the Allied occupation of postwar Germany. Christopher Simpson concluded that the confluence of American individuals working in various aspects of psychological warfare and information programs during and soon after the Second World War generated a "sociometric effect" that significantly influenced, among other Cold War institutions, the staffing of American foundations dealing with international issues in the early Cold War period.[4] The Ford Foundation experienced a major financial transformation precisely at this time, with the death of Henry Ford in April 1947. Stock transfers into the Ford Foundation resulting from Ford's death gave the foundation nearly $500 million in assets by the end of 1950, making the Ford Foundation the largest philanthropic organization in the world.[5] Coincident with this phenomenal rise in assets was the Ford Foundation's growing interest in global issues. Paul Hoffman was named as the foundation president in September 1950. Hoffman, a former president of the Studebaker Corporation, had served as coordinator of the Marshall Plan. Other Marshall Plan veterans who soon joined the foundation at upper levels of management included Milton Katz, Richard Bissell, Shepard Stone, and Nielsen. Bissell, Stone, and Nielsen had specific experience in various aspects of European psychological warfare, public opinion, and information program management.[6]

The emergence of the Ford Foundation in the early 1950s as a shaper of Cold War information policy, psychological warfare, and media culture is visible in the congeries of issues and individuals involved in the foundation, the RAND Corporation, and the Center for International Studies (CENIS) at MIT. The foundation funded RAND with an interest-free loan later converted to a grant, and Hans Speier, a public opinion specialist who headed up political science research at RAND, had a close relationship with many influential Ford officers.[7] MIT had conducted a top-secret study for the U.S. State Department called Project Troy. Commissioned as a way of investigating countermeasures to the Soviet jamming of Western propaganda radio broadcasts into Eastern Europe, the final Project Troy report was a four-volume assessment on the possibilities of collapsing the government and society of the USSR through an all-out campaign of information overload.[8]

In August 1952, the Board of Trustees of the Ford Foundation approved an $875,000 grant to CENIS for research on international communications.[9] That the foundation intended, at least in part, to build on the impetus of Project Troy is evident in the July 15, 1952, internal report to the board of trustees, which opened the argument for the CENIS-MIT grant by arguing that the foundation aimed to provide some of the Project Troy researchers with "continuing permanent means for bringing the academic resources of the Cambridge community to bear on . . . the position of the United States in world affairs." The board was told that this was the intent of creating CENIS, and CENIS was "in all substantive respects a joint MIT—Harvard operation." Initial CENIS research topics would include the effective dissemination of communication in foreign nations; accurately identifying "the target" of important individuals to reach within a given nation; promoting economic development in those nations as a key to their economic stability; and predicting domestic opinion on American foreign policy as well as shaping that domestic opinion into a stable consensus. The MIT and Harvard faculty members listed as involved in CENIS activities included Walt W. Rostow, Clyde Kluckhohn, Jerome Wiesner, Alex Bavelas, Clifford Geertz, Max Millikan, Richard Pipes, Frederick Barghoorn, Lloyd Berkner, McGeorge Bundy, Barrington Moore, and Philip Mosely.[10]

The Ford grant to CENIS had a relatively long period of gestation, and the initial queries to the Ford Foundation about establishing a research center for international communications did not come from MIT, Harvard, or the Cambridge community. In May 1951, Hans Speier and Donald Marquis (a Project Troy team member then on the faculty at Michigan) wrote Rowan Gaither in favor of the concept. Seeing the need for a research center dealing with international communications that was located outside of government agencies, Speier and Marquis argued in favor of a university home, suggesting Harvard, Columbia, Cornell, Princeton, Chicago, and Michigan as likely

candidates. They also believed that their proposed International Communications Institute and Project Troy could be mutually supportive. Project
Troy could take "principal responsibility for advising policy and operations
in government information services, with operative research of immediate
and direct relevance," and the institute "could be free to conduct studies of
a more general nature."[11]

In essence, both the International Communications Institute that became
CENIS and Project Troy were initially conceptualized by Speier and Marquis
(and echoed by the Ford Foundation) as two sides of the same coin, centered
on problems of international communication. Project Troy aimed at operational and policy problems, or applied research, and the International Communications Institute was first conceptualized around theoretical problems,
or basic research. However, the ways in which CENIS and Project Troy were
intertwined at birth created problems with the inseparability of basic and applied international communications research in the Cold War era. They are
conjoined twins. Therefore, the field of international communications, and
by extension media studies, entered the Cold War—and its first significant
period of growth—with its intellectual compass not so much determined by
the various and disparate researchers and scholars of the field, but rather in a
clandestine crucible forging the intellectual geopolitics of East-West security.
High-level government and philanthropic leaders worked in concert to aim
the vision of the field of international communications and media studies
through the single lens of Cold War psychological warfare. Rarely has any
other academic field or discipline been subject to such a moment of coordinated and covert influence—emanating from the highest and most secret corridors of power—in the shaping of its intellectual history and formation.

The decision by Speier[12] to stay at RAND rather than run the International
Communications Institute that eventually became CENIS did raise questions about who at MIT would do international communications research.
Although he was a member of Project Troy, it is not clear whether Donald
Marquis was offered a directorship at CENIS or if he even would have taken
such an appointment.[13] Though the name of the eventual director was not
listed in materials given to the Ford Foundation Board of Trustees at the July
15, 1952, meeting approving the MIT grant,[14] the major role in shaping international communications research at CENIS was quickly assumed by a relatively
young faculty member named Ithiel de Sola Pool.[15] Pool was apparently an
unknown commodity among senior foundation officials. Waldemar Nielsen
had a discreet background check done in December 1952, as the foundation
did not have a curriculum vitae of Pool in its files. The background check
opened by mentioning that he was the son of David de Sola Pool,[16] the rabbi

of the Sephardic Synagogue in New York City, and stating that Ithiel was believed to be about 35 years old. The background check also noted that Ithiel

> was at Chicago in the old days, at which time he was the leader of the campus
> Trotsky-ites. He studied at the time under Lasswell and Leites. From Chicago
> he went to Hobart College where he organized the social sciences curriculum
> and headed the department until shortly after the war. Then he went to Stanford
> (about three or four years ago) to work on the Revolution of Our Times project,
> on which Harold Lasswell was the major consultant . . . His dissertation (from
> Chicago) was an analysis of Hayek's work on the relationship between economic
> security and political liberty. He has been working part time for RAND during
> the past three years. . . . In connection with this work, he went through a loyalty
> review and was cleared. During the war he changed his political opinion away
> from Trotsky, and as a matter of fact, I think, he is no longer a Socialist.[17]

On the basis of this background check, Nielsen and Ford apparently concluded Pool was, in the vernacular of the day, reliable; no further background
checks on Pool are found in the Ford Foundation materials about the early
days of CENIS. One of Pool's first CENIS projects, a study of political communications in India, did cause some consternation from foundation officials
when Pool conducted fieldwork in 1954. John Howard, in the foundation's
New Delhi offices, called the presence of Pool in India a "powder keg . . .
most naïve to the . . . distrust India experiences toward America . . . [his
study is] oriented toward pulling India's research competence off India's focal
problems."[18] However, there seems to have been no long-term fallout from
this dustup, as Pool remained at MIT and CENIS for the duration of his long
and distinguished career. Additional Ford Foundation funding for CENIS
was granted in 1956, and in 1958, the foundation granted funds to a similar
international communications program at Stanford under the directorship of
Wilbur Schramm.[19] At both universities, the thematic focus of international
communication studies centered on a set of psychological and behavioral
research models designed to explore and predict public opinion, audience
attitudes, and content effectiveness.[20]

With the largest foundation in the world firmly committed to a concept of
international communications that emphasized psychological and behavioral
research models aimed at ascertaining audience predictability and at best
marginally interested in research on organizational, technical, and/or creative
aspects of media technologies, most Cold War funding for international
communications research at American universities tended to go to social
science–based initiatives. Particularly in the early 1950s, coincident with the
hardened attitudes of American policymakers toward Stalinism, the main

thrust of American philanthropic and government support for international communications research viewed the world beyond the shores with hawkish eyes and saw social science research as more likely to produce immediate and applicable results than humanities-based research. These attitudes would change over time, as will be discussed a bit later. For this particular period of the Cold War, however, it is fair to say that, with some exceptions, humanities-based research funding was not at the same scale and scope as social science–based funding.

The major exceptions for the humanities were the many projects aimed at courting the non-Communist left, manifest in the practitioners of arts, letters, and humanities, in Western Europe. Recent works by both Volker Berghahn and Frances Stonor Saunders have, each on their own way, gone into great detail on the Ford Foundation, the CIA, and additional funding for the Congress for Cultural Freedom. Setting aside a few instances, however, these initiatives did not, for the most part, entail the funding of American humanists in Cold War research, art, or performance. Whatever support for American humanists that did emerge during this period usually came from the USIA.

The USIA was formed early in the Eisenhower administration in 1953. The USIA began primarily as an agency that was not so much designed with a clear mission from the start, but rather as an agency designed to alleviate problems elsewhere in the federal government. Various questions, problems, and difficulties within the State Department, CIA, PSB, military, and other agencies on the scale, scope, and conduct of psychological warfare were one spur to the formation of the USIA.[21] A series of investigations on U.S. overseas information activities by the U.S. Senate Foreign Relations Committee, conducted in the context of the growing specter of McCarthyism, was yet another spur. Nielsen had been one of many individuals to testify at these hearings. Nielsen emphasized the differences between overt, indirect, and covert overseas information activities. Overt activities emanated directly from a government; indirect operations meant "activities in which the source of the material or funds is concealed but which would not, if the source were revealed, involve serious damage to the prestige of the American government"; covert activities "would involve serious damage" if the true source of material or funding became known. Adding that he thought the indirect approach was vital, Nielsen believed the American influence "must work with and through indigenous groups with objectives parallel to ours." Arguing for "a substantial reduction of overt activities and a substantial increase in indirect activities in the interest of efficiency and effectiveness of our propaganda operations," Nielsen also advocated the creation of "some new consolidated agency" such as the USIA to undertake indirect activities.[22]

Nielsen's emphasis on indirect approaches is indicative of both the Ford Foundation worldview and of Nielsen's own predilections. The foundation was, as previously mentioned, at this time occasionally engaged in indirect-to-covert support of CIA-initiated efforts such as the Congress for Cultural Freedom. Beyond such delicate cases, the emergent foundation philosophy was more and more in keeping with practices that generally fell in line with the indirect approach to promoting American values in the global arena. As a middle ground between covert and overt, the indirect approach was also in keeping with later actions by Nielsen, such as his recommending that American Cold War science and technology funding be conducted in such a manner to find science projects that were "feasible" for media exploitation of foreign public opinion survey polling results.

So the USIA gestated, and emerged, very much in a maelstrom of hawkish views on Cold War psychological warfare and, by extension, on international communications research. Although the USIA quickly engaged in a wide range of social science–based communication research, it also was one of the few funding agencies at this time that did on occasion commission or internally produce research in the humanities, such as literary and library studies. In one of the few cases of USIA funding of cinema studies in the 1950s, the USIA adapted the indirect approach in 1955 when they funded two members of the University Film Producer's Association—Don Williams of Syracuse University and Herb Farmer of the University of Southern California—to attend the Second International Congress of Cinema and Television School Directors held at Cannes.[23]

In post-Cannes debriefings held in Washington with the U.S. government's Interdepartmental Subcommittee on Official Film Festivals,[24] Williams gave a series of oral reports. In so doing, he emphasized

> the dangers to the Free World of the newer Soviet films, which are of the highest technical and artistic quality and which are produced on apparently unlimited budget. The Soviet Institute of Cinematography is turning out, at a rate unequalled anywhere in the Free World, highly competent technicians, trained not only in cinematography, but in world history, fine arts, and world politics . . . the newer Soviet films, with their softer, less obvious propaganda lines, constitute a threat out of all proportion to their quantity . . . the Institute was far ahead . . . guided by a far deeper appreciation of the potentialities of motion pictures, and demonstrated a determination to spare no expense to make the fullest possible use of motion pictures in quality, kinds, and quantity, to serve the ends of the USSR.

While attending the International Cinema Congress, Williams also had a number of direct encounters with Vladimir Golovnia, the director of the

Moscow State Institute of Cinematography, whom Williams found generally fluent in English and usually without the need of his translators in conversations. After a few days, "Golovnia thawed" and Williams found he could indirectly engage his Soviet counterpart by asking hypothetical questions about pedagogy and curriculum in Soviet film education. On the possibility of exchange visits, Golovnia told Williams, American professors, and students "you would be very welcome, but I doubt your Government would give you a passport" with what Williams described as a "sly grin."

Present not as official USIA representatives but rather as cinema professors from American universities, Williams and Farmer are emblematic of the indirect approach advocated by Nielsen. Apparently on his own initiative, Williams also developed an indirect approach to building an East-West dialogue about film education, posing real and imaginary pedagogical questions to his Soviet counterpart. Williams reported that the institute had eight hundred students, fully funded in both tuition and production materials, enrolled in its six-year program at any given moment, at least two hundred more than the entire total (by his estimate) of full-time American cinema students on all campuses combined. At the institute, "very few indeed flunked their technical work in cinematography, but some failed in their cultural subjects" and failure to demonstrate one was "a good and eager Communist" meant that individual would not graduate and go on to make motion pictures in the USSR. In his briefing, Williams went on to further describe the institute, mainly emphasizing the significant funding the Soviets gave for motion picture training. He concluded that the USSR is "tooling up" for "a massive and highly efficient program of high-quality motion pictures of all kinds, without regard for expense" after having learned that "mallet-headed propaganda" is not well received by Western audiences. Noting that the quality rather than the quantity of Soviet films was the key, Williams argued that "every Soviet film is made for a specific purpose, with a definite target audience in mind" and "the technical, artistic and content quality of these films make them a very potent threat."

Although it would be an interesting exercise to speculate on the political affinities of Williams and Farmer, and by extension of American film education in 1955, I see this rhetoric of Williams primarily as a strategy to try to lay the groundwork for significant increases in federal funding for American film education, and not necessarily as emblematic of a personal hawklike Cold War political philosophy. Williams and Farmer also typify the indirect approach of the USIA in choosing two American film professors to represent American interests (rather than sending official government representatives in a direct approach). The indirect approach also implied protection from attribution and became a common technique for both government and philanthropic Cold War institutions. For example, in discussing the publication of "Target: The World," a USIA-led study of Communist propaganda in 1955, the State Department's Bureau of Intelligence and Research justified publicly attributing the authorship of this report to Evron Kirkpatrick, executive director of the American Political Science Association, because revealing "the fact that 'Target: The World' was produced by a United States intelligence unit would seriously jeopardize the effectiveness of this publication overseas and defeat the primary purpose for which it was written."[25] So even in the underfunded world of Cold War media humanities, creativity, and performance, events such as these suggest that the indirect approach and other similar strategies for international communications research were employed in both the social sciences and the humanities—or in other words, across the entire scale and scope of American liberal arts education.

In the latter half of the 1950s, the USIA focused and refined its own mission. In some instances, particularly as a global public opinion pollster, this refinement of mission came to the USIA from other government agencies, such as the NSC.[26] In terms of political ideology, by the end of the decade, a shift was emergent that suggested a new trajectory away from the strident hawkish rhetoric of the Stalin era and its immediate aftermath and toward a more liberal and inclusive vision stressing more of the similarities, and less of the differences, between the goals and aspirations of everyday Soviet and American citizens. This new ideological trajectory is apparent in the 1959 USIA Moscow Exhibition (best known as the site of the Nixon-Khrushchev kitchen debate).[27] Finally, in terms of media humanities, particularly the performing arts, the USIA became a leading government advocate of the indirect approach to Cold War psychological warfare, sponsoring a wide range of international performances by American artists.[28]

Nielsen's tenure as research director of the Sprague Committee coincided with the tail end of his career at the Ford Foundation. As he was leaving the foundation, Nielsen and Louis Cowan conceived a new idea for promulgating the global image of America and doing so across the sweep of American arts, sciences, and letters. On March 24, 1961, Nielsen wrote McGeorge Bundy (now departed from CENIS and MIT and serving as national security advisor to President John Kennedy) a memo titled "A Plan for the Creation of An Annual President's Honor List," conceived by Nielsen and Cowan.[29] Noting that the United States had not built "a tradition for broader recognition of human achievement," they argued for finding "a reasonable scheme which will provide for intelligent selection and which will protect the system from the kind of conniving and periodic disrepute into which some foreign honors have occasionally fallen."

Projecting awards in categories such as fine arts, humanities scholarship, physical sciences and social sciences, professions, education, and "a miscellaneous category for such things as heroism, community service, race relations, etc.," Nielsen and Cowan called for flexible categories designed "to select outstanding but unorthodox cases from time to time." Calling for a "major White House banquet each year" to present the honors, Nielsen and Cowan also believed this was an ideal event for television to be "witnessed by millions of Americans—and now that intercontinental telecasting is feasible, by millions in other countries as well." They also argued that these awards might prove, in the international arena of public opinion, an effective counterweight to the Lenin Prize, although they rejected matching the $40,000 cash award to any non-Soviet who received the Lenin Prize because "if we give less than that we may look cheesy; if we give more, we will appear crass." In a nod to dignity, Nielsen and Cowan also believed the award ceremonies should carry an air of

> solemnity—the halls of Congress or the White House itself or possibly some open air setting such as the steps of the Lincoln Memorial . . . thought should be given to the academic procession as a model . . . covered by the television and news cameras for transmission not only to the U.S. but throughout the world. . . . The important thing is that the ceremony not be degraded by entertainment. If Leonard Bernstein gets an award, he should not be asked in front of the television cameras to sit down to the piano. . . . It would be important to have the winners make appropriate public use of their award—by using the initials after their name in private correspondence, for example—but rather severe moral obligation should be imposed not to make purely commercialized use of the honor.

I do not know whether or not awardees ever appended their written missives with the award's initials after their signature. However, this idea did coalesce into the Presidential Freedom Awards. Few Americans likely know that these awards had their genesis as part of Cold War psychological warfare and that a Ford Foundation officer and a quiz show television producer were among the creators. Even though by the end of 1961, Nielsen was about to embark on a different career trajectory, Louis Cowan would continue to be centrally involved in the shaping of Ford Foundation thinking about global communications, particularly television. Although earlier in this paragraph I referred to Cowan as a quiz show producer, to focus on that aspect of his career in this study is disorienting. Cowan had a brief tenure as a high-ranking executive at Columbia Broadcasting System (CBS) and, in the 1960s, entered the university world, first through Brandeis, and later became dean of the journalism school at Columbia. Most importantly, Cowan became one of the leading voices in the world of philanthropy, mainly through the Ford Foundation, in shaping a discourse that becomes less concerned with seeing the world of global media strictly through a lens of East-West security and instead views the dialogue about global media through a new lens. Coincident with this discursive transformation in the world of American philanthropy, the USIA of the Kennedy administration also begins to examine its own terminology, under the direction of USIA Director Edward R. Murrow.[30]

Discursive Transformations from East-West Security to Global Concepts

The crafters of this new vision struggled in the 1960s with a term or concept to describe, in a word or two, this new vision, this new way of thinking. Terms used at the time include *world citizenship, world community, general population, mankind as a whole,* and so forth. Although this new vision emerges without a specific name, from the retrospective position of the early twenty-first century, this new vision can be recognized as a way of viewing the world through the lens of globalization. Even though Nielsen had left the Ford Foundation by the end of 1961, the foundation's interest in international communications did not wane with his departure. Coincident with the growing interest in domestic educational television—one of the principal areas of foundation funding in the 1950s and 1960s—attention on international television issues came to the fore in the 1960s. In the wake of Nielsen's departure, Joseph Slater became one of the foundation's key officers dealing with questions of international communication. Yet another Ford Foundation officer with a background in World War II and postwar European information programs.[31] Slater was approached by Louis Cowan in 1962 with an idea for a multinational "Mass Media Authority" aimed at both policy and programming questions for global television.[32] Arguing that "the cultural outpourings of the mass media have become vast in the space of our generation," Cowan nevertheless found that "the content carried by the mass media instruments remains relatively parochial," and in television, the focus was national.[33]

Cowan envisioned responding to this parochialism with an "International Mass Media Authority" in an "American-Western-European-Japanese framework" that could work toward globalizing television program content. As a nonprofit, tax-exempt organization, the institution would serve as a sort of clearinghouse of growing global television facilities and be a "catalyst to guide, improve, and increase the multi-national production flow and exchange."

Such an institution would also need a "Planning Cabinet" that was "selected from the scholarly disciplines" to "formulate philosophies, policies, targets, and priorities" in studying the "socio-psychological problems involved in cultural exchange."[34]

Cowan concluded with a "free-association list of names" for consideration as possible associates to the project, including Ed Murrow, Edward Barrett, Pat Weaver, Theodore White, Robert Saudek, Waldemar Nielsen, Jack Gould, Fred Friendly, Sig Mickelson, Eric Sevareid, Fairfax Cone, Jules Herbevaux, Jean D'Arcy, Henri Cassirer,[35] Leonard Miall, Roland Gass, David Butler, Nicolas Van Vliet, Paul Flamand, Robert McKenzie, and Roland Barthes. Even though a global mass media authority did not come to pass, the idea for a Ford Foundation–sponsored initiative on global television eventually took root in the formation of the International Radio and Television Institute (IRTI), which was conceptualized at a meeting held at Lake Como, Italy, February 23–27, 1966.[36] Hosted at the Bellagio complex of the Rockefeller Foundation, the 1966 Ford Bellagio conference was a mix of Cold War media professionals and intellectuals:

Jean D'Arcy	director, Radio and Visual Services Division, UNESCO
Luigi Barzini	journalist; member of Chamber of Deputies, Italy
Michael Gordey	chief foreign correspondent, *France-Soir*
Klaus Harrprecht	director, S. Fischer-Verlag Pubishers
Robert McKenzie	BBC-TV commentator; professor of Sociology, London School of Economics
Nico J. Van Vliet	TV journalist
David Webster	BBC-TV documentary producer
Peter von Zahn	documentary producer
Paul Hodgson	journalist; BBC-TV research consultant
Louis Cowan	director of Special Programs, Columbia University
Howard Dressner	Ford Foundation
Jack Gould	*New York Times* TV critic
Melvin Lasky	co-editor, *Encounter*
Harold Lasswell	professor of Political Science and Law, Yale
Sig Mickelson	vice president, Time-Life Broadcast, Inc.
Newton Minow	lawyer, former chairman, FCC
Arthur Morse	former executive producer, *CBS Reports*
Joseph Slater	Ford Foundation
Stephen White	Carnegie Commission
Moselle Kimbler	Ford Foundation[37]

A curious group indeed, ranging from the remnants of the Congress for Cultural Freedom (Lasky) to the new frontier of Kennedy (Minow) to pashas of the ivory tower (Lasswell). Basil Thornton, a former BBC man now at National Educational Television (NET), thought the list of invitees aroused a "feeling of puzzlement." Thornton believed they were, on the one hand, "bright people," but they also lacked deep knowledge of current activities in international television. Thornton concluded that the Ford Foundation had different priorities in selecting this group, stating, "an effort was made to collect a group of angry young intellectuals, mixed with a few seers."[38] The seers, according to Thornton, included Lasswell. As for the others, Melvin Lasky certainly did his part at Bellagio to live up to the mantle of an angry young intellectual. A hard-boiled veteran of ideological conflict who had battled against Communism for years by surreptitiously using CIA money to mobilize European intellectuals, Lasky was skeptical of internationalizing television programming, fearing such an action would "make for homogenized television in an already conformist society." In a moment of nihilism and paranoia, Lasky insisted it is "better to be bored than to be rooted in front of a television set. The thought of eighty-two channels available at the flick of a switch is frightening."[39]

Despite Lasky's fears of an eighty-two–channel media universe, the Bellagio conferees developed "three threads of discussion" reiterated throughout the conference and proposed as the first tasks for a new international organization. These three threads included the need to articulate a concept of "Freedom of Television"; more research and knowledge about television as an instrument of communications; and "instrumentalities which would expedite the flow of television across national borders" through program exchange, coproductions, and copresentations.[40] Freedom of television was threatened, among other factors, by the commonality of government control over television broadcasting in many countries of the world and because television journalists had yet to fully adopt standards and practices commonly held in the radio and print journalism professional communities. As an instrument of communication, television was little understood beyond recognizing it was "an instrument of unparalleled power" that most used "blindly." Many profound questions might make it "necessary to create academic sub-disciplines" for proper research. Finally, television flow across international borders was partly stymied by issues similar to those in the area of freedom of television and partly stymied due to the complexities of coproduction among professionals with different national, linguistic, aesthetic, and cultural backgrounds. Although at the time of the meeting, most TV program exchange took place through film or tape shuttled among national networks, satellite TV distribution among national networks had already arrived, and conferees projected a future "when satellites would make possible direct transmission from space into any home equipped to receive it." This meant that the time for action was imminent to resolve practices of international TV program exchange "in some rational fashion before they become too intense to permit a reasonable solution."[41]

Satellite TV transmission had already arrived, fulfilling an American quest for live transatlantic television in 1962 with the launch of Telstar.[42] Telstar, along with other communication satellites of the 1960s, allowed national TV networks to hook up for intercontinental and cross-oceanic TV program exchanges and newsfeeds. Direct satellite-to-home transmission in the mid-1960s, however, was still in the realm of theory rather than practice; the origins of direct satellite-to-home transmission are caught up in, among other events, the transition of American cable television program distribution to satellites in the early 1970s. In fact, a 1966 attempt by the United Arab Republic (Egypt) to introduce restrictive clauses regarding direct-to-home satellite TV transmissions in the drafting of the 1967 Treaty on Peaceful Uses of Outer Space was rejected by both the United States and the USSR as a "diversionary" tactic floated long before the "technical aspects of the problem" needed to "draw up rules and regulations" were understood.[43]

While American and Soviet negotiators to the 1967 Treaty on Peaceful Uses of Outer Space whittled away at third world objections to treaty provisions, the Ford Foundation continued to build momentum for a private international consortium along the lines of IRTI to advance the globalization of television. Shepard Stone informed Ford Foundation President McGeorge Bundy—who had now completed an unusual loop from CENIS and MIT to the Kennedy NSC and now to the Ford Foundation presidency[44]—that IRTI was needed for many reasons. Television was becoming increasingly important in international affairs, but "there is no effective international dialogue among broadcasters," which mitigated against the uses of broadcasting in "nation building" and made difficult "an attempt to preserve a visual history of our times." Any steps to encourage the internationalization of television would also benefit American broadcasters to a large degree.[45]

Finally, Harold Lasswell—present at the postwar creation of international communications as a topic of scholarship and of national policy, and an exemplar of the durability of the small and privileged network of Cold War philanthropic-funded media and communication specialists—articulated the politico-discursive shift from security to globalization by forecasting the future of global television as something akin to astronomers deploying a planetarium:

The idea of a social planetarium extends to the past, present, and future of man the conception that was first effectively applied by astronomers to the field of public information. . . . The emerging technology of television is an instrument capable of providing all men everywhere with a common map of human history and the contingent future. TV libraries and presentations can put at the disposal of every viewer a means of locating his nation, or any other group with which he feels at one, in the total flow of events. The viewer can have access to the best knowledge available; and where interpretations are in conflict, the film presents him with lucid versions of the alternatives. This applies to contending visions of yesterday, as well as of today and tomorrow. The social planetarium can restore the fundamental unity of view that prevails in most primitive societies without returning to the dogmatism that kept man primitive.[46]

Lasswell's televisual planetarium is the theoretical culmination of twenty years of philanthropic and government funding of Cold War research and practice regarding international communications and global media culture. Among those present at the creation of the clandestine crucible of hawkish Cold War social science research on international communications in the late 1940s, as with select others, his durability within an exclusive network of experts gave Lasswell the opportunity to master the discursive transformation from security to globalization without risking his membership in that network. Lasswell signifies an all-too-common condition in American research circles dealing with Cold War international communications and global media culture: the topics of the day, as well as the political spin of those topics, do in fact change over time, but the articulators and spinners of those topics retain their membership within an enduring network of experts, consistently underpinned by government and private research funding.[47]

Therefore, what began in the aftermath of the Second World War and the rise of superpower conflict as global media issues seen in the context of East-West security began to transform, starting in the 1960s, into global media issues seen in the context of globalization, but with the same cast of dramatis personae remarkably intact throughout the entire period of the Cold War. This Cold War discursive journey traversing ideologies within the same select and privileged group of media intellectuals was deftly guided throughout the era by the careful, invisible hand of American philanthropy.

Opening plenary session, 1947 ITU Atlantic City conference. State Department, National Archives.

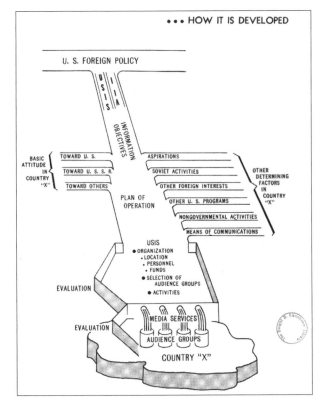

The flow of information: American foreign policy, 1953. C. D. Jackson Records, Eisenhower Library.

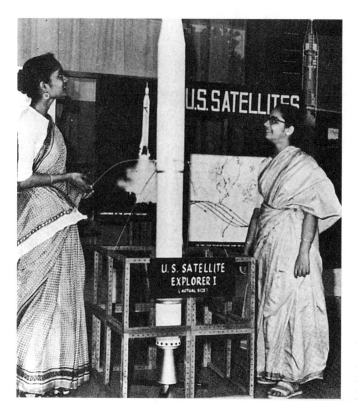

USIA exhibit,
Madras, 1958.
Sprague Committee,
Eisenhower Library.

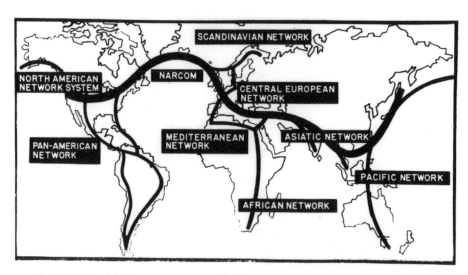

The UNITEL global microwave network plan, 1952. C. D. Jackson Records,
Eisenhower Library.

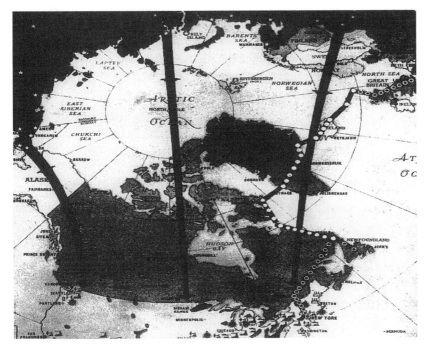

Circumpolar map showing shortest bombing paths from Russia to the U.S. northern boundary and how a transatlantic TV microwave relay network enhances American national security, 1952. Holtusen Papers, Hoover Library.

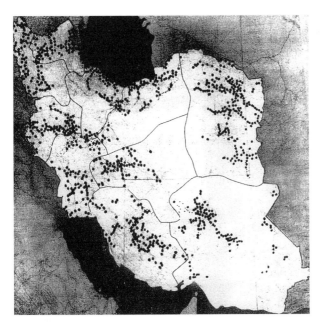

Photo map showing State Department mobile motion picture exhibitions in Iran, 1950–52. Each pin represents at least one mobile unit showing in a village; others indicate as many as ten showings; and 1, 300 villages were visited. Hickenlooper Papers, Hoover Library.

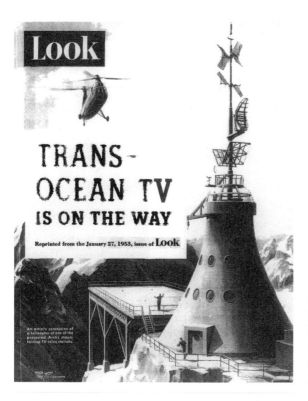

Reprinted from the January 27, 1953, issue of Look

An artist's conception of a helicopter at one of the projected Arctic mountaintop TV relay stations.

Global microwave relay networks will secure the high ground by conquering mountains and leapfrogging oceans, 1953. Holthusen Papers, Hoover Library.

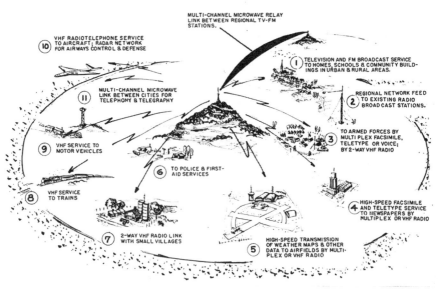

UNITEL—NARCOM "wideband linkage" circa 1952: TV, radio, aviation, rail, trucking, agriculture, education, public services, and business communication via global, national, regional, and local microwave relay networks. C. D. Jackson Records, Eisenhower Library.

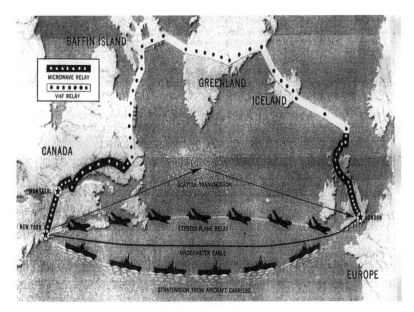

Five possibilities for transatlantic TV networking, 1952: (1) microwave—VHF
combination, (2) scatter-bounce transmissions off the troposphere, (3) express
airplane shuttle relay (the RCA Ultrafax system), (4) underwater coaxial cable,
(5) aircraft carriers and Stratovision. Holthusen Papers, Hoover Library.

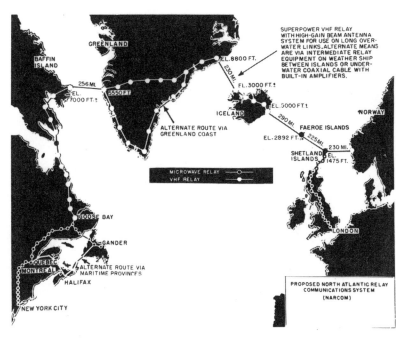

UNITEL and the North Atlantic route, 1952. C. D. Jackson Records,
Eisenhower Library.

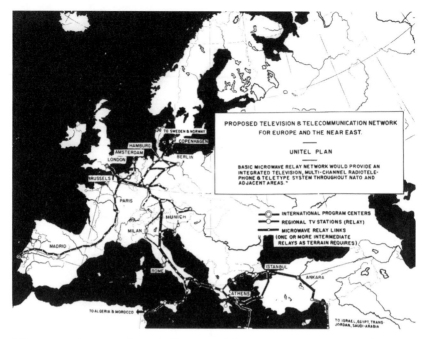

Microwave relay networking for Europe and the Near East, 1951. C. D. Jackson Records, Eisenhower Library.

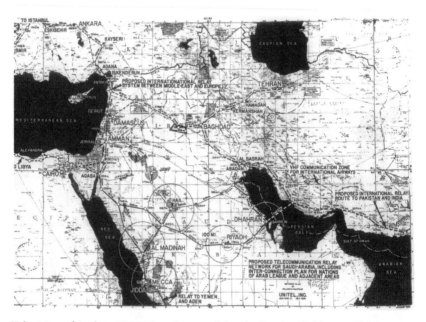

Television of Arabia: UNITEL and networking the Persian Gulf, 1954. Holthusen Papers, Hoover Library.

NTV demonstration on the streets of Tokyo, 1953. Holthusen Papers, Hoover Library.

Mission to Moscow: RAMAC departing New York City, June 1959. USIA, National Archives.

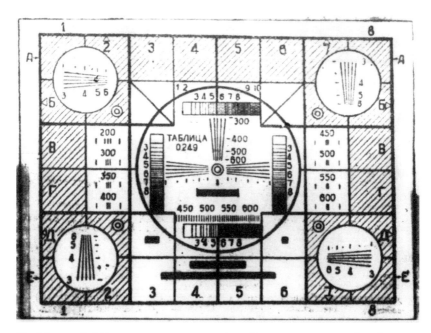

The Moscow TV Center test pattern, 1952. State Department, National Archives.

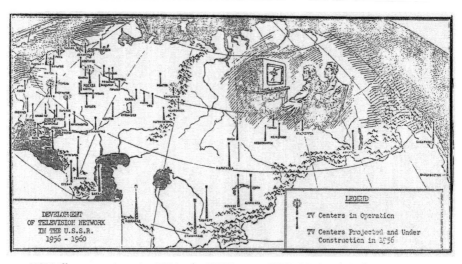

USIA illustrators imagine TV in the USSR, 1956. USIA, National Archives.

PART 2

The Second Strand

5. "We Can Give the World a Vision of America"

The concept of global television networks is considered a recent phenomenon, emergent in the last years of the Cold War. Seen as an outgrowth of the communications satellite, worldwide plunging costs of television set ownership, global cross-investments involving media industries, and the collapse of the superpower conflict, global television networks represent, for most observers, a relatively new idea. Though the maturation of many global TV networks (as well as multiple global electronic information networks) may be relatively recent, the ideas, theories, and visions of global television networks and multiple electronic information networks are not new. Rather, the visions are a direct product of the dawn of the Cold War. Furthermore, the idea of global networks was first spurred in large part by the worldwide postwar interest in television; the fascination within the United States over the growth of coaxial cable and its role in networking American television; the global pursuit of a wide range of new electronic communication technologies; and most of all, by strategies and tactics for military security, for psychological warfare, and for addressing anxieties about the global image of America.

Therefore, the idea of live global electronic information networks converging a number of electronic communication technologies, simultaneously reaching worldwide audiences, and delivering multimedia content laced with political ideology is an idea that is over fifty years old. The evidence for the relative antiquity of this idea—at least shading toward antique for historians of electronic media—is borne out by the elaborate planning, engineering, lobbying, world travel, and rhetoric formulated by the advocates of these global networks over a half century ago. Some of these advocates inhabited the corridors of power in Washington: the State Department, the Defense

Department, the various intelligence agencies, and several influential U.S. senators. Still others were found in the ranks of American business, and yet others still were found overseas, scattered across the globe: Japan, Turkey, the United Kingdom, Latin America, and the new nations of the crumbling colonial world, first tasting their political independence. Although American interests dominated this quest for live global TV networks, the United Kingdom had its own distinct vision, which became operational around the coronation of Elizabeth II. No matter the nation, no matter the institutional fit, and no matter the ideology, one thing was certain in the early 1950s: they were all working on global TV.

As early as 1946, the activities of the UN sparked dialogue about the need for international distribution of television news material. Secretary of State James Byrnes believed opening the UN Security Council and other UN commission meetings to the press was a "revolutionary step" but lamented the lack of UN budget and global infrastructure for rapid and complete dissemination of press, radio, and television coverage.[1] The rise of Cold War tensions, coupled with a perception that the United Nations Educational, Scientific, and Cultural Organization (UNESCO) was becoming politicized in a manner inimical to American interests, meant that American attention to global television quickly turned to other vistas. These new vistas would be positions hardened by superpower conflict, arms races, quests for strategic security, conflicts from Berlin to Korea, and black (clandestine), gray (unattributed), and white (known source) propaganda.

For several reasons, television clearly fell into the realm of white propaganda. The very large investment costs for both producers and users, the small number of television stations operable in a given geographic location due to frequency assignments and engineering practices then in use, and the near impossibility of misdirecting the location of a television transmitter from ELEINT technicians working in adversarial intelligence agencies all meant that television could be neither gray (unattributed) nor black (falsely identified) broadcast propaganda. Even in Berlin, the first hotbed of postwar television superpower conflict, American policymakers quickly realized that television more often than not had to be "white" in its message.[2]

Therefore, in the realm of psychological warfare, television was different in its potentials, and flexibility, from radio, print, and film. These other three media all had enough flexibility in their systems of production, distribution, and reception to allow their applications in all three shades of propaganda. Furthermore, all three were generally applicable in both targeted situations as well as worldwide strategies of psychological warfare. Last—but certainly not least—radio, print, and film were, technologically speaking, all more or less operating on a single universal technological standard. Radio sets picked up transmissions no matter the country or region of signal origin.[3] Film prints crossed borders and were projectable to audiences anywhere. Print propaganda, like radio news, needed an army of language experts and translators, but that army could be assembled. Television had no similar conditions of universal global standards, and the 1948–52 TV freeze by the FCC had the unanticipated consequence of derailing early efforts by American diplomats to impose the American (NTSC) television technology standards on Europe.[4]

Global TV, Cold War Rhetoric, and the Search for Network Technologies

This turned attention toward real-time, or live, global distribution systems whereby the world's continents might be—somehow—electronically linked. Once a signal crossed continents, it could then be converted for rebroadcast (or further distribution) consistent with a given nation's or region's technical systems for television transmission. Even though the circulation of TV programs via kinescope and other filmed material was already underway, these systems of film-based TV program distribution did not offer the possibilities of live, synchronized viewing by mass audiences spanning an entire nation, region, or continent and were subject to the whims of local programmers. The quest pointed to new electronic distribution technologies whereby live television might span continents and thereby play its own vital role in psychological warfare. Hopes were high for a relatively new distribution technology, microwave relay. The trade newsletter *Tele-Tech* in December 1952 hailed microwaves as a "weapon in the global battle of ideas."[5]

The standard distribution technology for broadcast networks, since the early 1920s, was wire. The American radio networks emerged via experimentation with both telegraph and telephone wireline distribution. American Telephone and Telegraph (AT&T) had also, in the mid-1940s, begun disseminating coaxial cable, a large-trunk (greater bandwidth) wire system that could be used for carrying many telephone calls, multiplexing a number of different kinds of electronic communication systems, and most important of all, for networking television. However, other distribution systems for networking had also emerged. For nonsynchronous networking (where simultaneous reception by large, geographically disparate audiences was not crucial), various forms of transcription recordings, passed on or "bicycled" from station to station, were one alternative. These transcriptions could be on disk (for radio) or on film and later in the 1950s on videotape (for television). Cheap, effective, and easy to use, nonsynchronous networking had its drawbacks: no large-scale simultaneity, and no "liveness" crucial for block-buster events or breaking news. Although it was true that shortwave radio reached vast audiences with a small number of transmitters since the late 1920s, the larger bandwidth, spectrum allocation, and transmitter power requirements of a television signal meant that a shortwave type application for global television networking was technically unfeasible. A TV signal had vastly different characteristics of propagation, thus making a shortwave style intercontinental telecast physically impossible.[6]

In the 1930s, however, a wave-based system of synchronous networking emerged. Simultaneous with the emergence of FM radio broadcasting, exper-iments began in using higher frequencies in the electromagnetic spectrum—commonly known as microwaves—to distribute electronic communications in a network system. A microwave relay chain known as the Yankee Network was established in New York State in the 1930s to form a FM radio network. Common carriers such as AT&T experimented with, and later built, micro-wave relay stations for the distribution of long-distance telephony, moving American telephony away from a fully wire-based distribution system into an integrative technical system of wires and microwaves. Microwave network relay also had the requisite bandwidth for multiplexing a number of differ-ent applications of electronic communication, not just radio broadcasting and telephony. Finally, microwave relay also had the requisite bandwidth to distribute a live, synchronous television network.

Microwave relay networks in the 1950s became the first distribution tech-nology undergirding a Cold War vision of global TV. Before turning to the conception, planning, and attempts at building these networks, however, this chapter first finishes setting the ideological context for this 1950s vision of microwave relay global TV networks. Totally cast in the context of the Cold War, envisioned as weapons for psychological warfare, and intended to serve as one of the vehicles for freedom's destiny—rolling back and crush-ing Communism—the idea of microwave global TV networks needed its advocates. Among the most strident stentors for these networks were several influential U.S. senators.

Senators Karl Mundt (R-SD) and Bourke Hickenlooper (R-IA) led the charge for global TV networks in the 1950s. Mundt, an author of 1948 legisla-tion establishing the VOA, was among the first elected American politicians to extol the virtues of a VOA-type approach to television. In 1950, Mundt proposed a "bold plan for using television to turn neutrals into friends and friends into strong and reliable allies for the U.S."[7] He looked to fund the construction of large-screen television projection systems, centrally located, in cities, towns, and villages across the world.[8] Stressing that America needed to augment its "know how" and "hear how" with "see-how," Mundt's "Vision of America" predicted that such a TV system would make a star of "every 4–H youth" in the United States. He assured Congress that the 1948 Smith-Mundt Act already provided all of the necessary legal authorization to fund such a TV project. Speaking for Congress at large, Mundt proclaimed, "we can give the world a vision of America!"[9] Above all other considerations, global TV was needed to wage the war of words through a new medium that reached beyond national leaders and opinion elites. Even though radio, film, and print had begun to make such inroads, Mundt saw TV as the most favorable medium of all to reach beyond such leaders and elites and thereby communicate directly with the masses of the world.

Hickenlooper had a deep interest in the effectiveness of government-run international information activities, and believed in waging full-strength psychological warfare. His long tenure as a member of the Senate Foreign Relations Committee gave him intimate knowledge and influence regarding American foreign policy, and he chaired subcommittees specifically tasked with assessing the effectiveness of government-run international informa-tion activities. In 1953, Hickenlooper was the principal sponsor of Senate Joint Resolution 96, calling to strengthen the foreign relations of the United States through greater attention to international telecommunications. S.J. 96 reported that Hickenlooper's subcommittee had already confirmed "the feasibility of linking the Atlantic nations and much of the non-Communist world in vast television networks is established."[10] Calling for a Commission on International Telecommunications, the tasks of the proposed commission included studying possibilities for the expanded use of television in carrying out government-run international information activities. In a 1953 interview, Hickenlooper explained Senate involvement in a "system of intercontinental telecommunications suitable for the use of television" was mandatory "so that the communications systems of the world may be used for the propagation of democracy, and may not be controlled by an authoritarian state," adding that Soviet jamming of shortwave radio risked "seriously disrupting" international television for the free world.[11] Declaring, "we must adopt our own thinking to this new medium," Senate Foreign Relations Committee Chair Alexander Wiley (R-WI) believed "democracy and freedom can be promoted via global TV" and called S.J. 96 "a magnificent opportunity" for global television.[12]

Both Hickenlooper and Mundt had already established their bona fides as experts on government-run international information activities by the late 1940s, at the dawn of Cold War hostilities. As Republicans, both were more or less immune from the damaging attacks of Senator Joseph McCarthy (R-WI) on individuals involved in American foreign policy and thus could operate with impunity in advocating increased government psychological warfare. Finally, both were, in the vernacular of the day, Cold War hawks. All these factors gave both senators a large degree of influence. Mundt and Hickenlooper had at least one more thing in common: a close working relationship with Henry Holthusen. Holthusen—discussed at greater length later in this chapter—was the link between the Senate and the private investors interested in building microwave-based global TV networks. Beyond Holthusen, other American industrialists of the era had their own vision of global networked TV.

David Sarnoff, as a lad in 1912, claimed to be among the first on American soil to receive a wireless distress signal from the sinking luxury liner *Titanic* and parleyed that claim up the corporate ladder to climb into the chairmanship of RCA. Sarnoff was transformed yet again during the Second World War. He became a general. General Sarnoff (preserving rank and title through his postwar enlistment in the Reserve Corps) now spoke not only the language of technological progress and ever-expanding frontiers of communication, but also the language of national security. Sarnoff's first Cold War technosecurity gambit was Ultrafax. Pitching Ultrafax over different months in 1948 to FCC Chairman Wayne Coy, Secretary of the Defense James Forrestal, and President Truman, Sarnoff painted Ultrafax as the ultimate Cold War international telecommunications system.[13] Sarnoff assured Truman that the RCA Ultrafax system, recently tested, would have a transmission rate when completed of a million words per minute and could provide a wide range of telecommunication services: telegraph, telephone, television, teleprinter, and weather information.

Installed on fleets of transoceanic aircraft—both commercial and military—Ultrafax also had a strategic security component. Sarnoff believed that Ultrafax could include

> an airborne radio relay system [that] could serve as a constant watchman to intercept guided missiles that might be traveling in our direction . . . [and] detect and furnish information about enemy projectiles thousands of miles from our borders. . . . As a result, counter measures could be taken which would locate and destroy the missiles before they could reach the United States . . . from the standpoint of secrecy and national security, such a system would have the further advantage that the enemy need not know of the incidental, although very important, military significance of the aircraft which appeared to be engaged only in transport or commercial aviation. Thus the system could be world-wide in scope.[14]

Sarnoff also argued that RCA Ultrafax was superior to the Westinghouse-proposed Stratovision plan for airborne TV transmitters. Stratovision merely envisioned television transmitters in airplanes circling above major American cities as a technology to increase the signal range of domestic television stations. Ultrafax included television, added a wide range of additional telecommunication services, and was globally projected.

There is much that is both astonishing and chilling about Sarnoff's scheme. In a vision eerily prescient of arguments for strategic missile defense—ranging from antiballistic missiles to "Star Wars" to current policy of the twenty-first century Bush administration—Sarnoff painted Ultrafax as the watchtower of national security to guard against missile attack, a vision predating the establishment of North American radar defense in the Arctic, such as the DEW Line and NORAD. Ultrafax and missile defense are jointly conceived in 1948, almost a decade before Sputnik, derived from extrapolating out a future vision of the postwar development of German V2 (A-4) rocket research by the Cold War superpowers. The V2 had, during the war, achieved a typical maximum range of less than 300 miles and never came close to transcontinental range. The implicit references to the redundancy of the system (placed in many airplanes) combined with the suggestion that the hidden deployment of Ultrafax on commercial air transport helps protect the secrecy of Ultrafax brings up a chilling vision of secreting Ultrafax literally under the rumps of clueless transcontinental travelers. Presumably, the Ultrafax system would be sufficiently redundant to avoid complete destruction by the enemy at the onset of general hostilities. The collateral damage to innocent and unwitting transcontinental air passengers as some, but not all, of the secret Ultrafax planes are shot out of the sky by the enemy is the kind of collateral damage that Sarnoff presumably sees as one of the many unavoidable tragedies of war.

RCA hosted a demonstration of Ultrafax at the Library of Congress on October 21, 1948, transmitting the text of *Gone with the Wind* in two minutes and twenty-one seconds and showing on a large screen the handwritten missive of a new father announcing his daughter's birth. This presentation was televised to Schenectady, Boston, New York, Philadelphia, Baltimore, Washington, and Richmond, Virginia. Although Sarnoff hailed Ultrafax as "a milestone in communications as was the splitting of the atom in the world of energy" and invoked the Berlin crisis by calling for an "airlift" of Ultrafax to bring live American television to Europe, Ultrafax never became a regular television technology. It is likely that the quest and expenses of domestic color television service took priority in RCA engineering developments.[15] Nevertheless, Sarnoff continued to push for global television, arguing before the UN in 1949 that "the freedom of radio is a mere figure of speech without the corollary principle of Freedom to Listen. We can foresee the day when television will enable us to look around the world" but that would be "an empty dream unless the Freedom to Look is given assurance among our human rights." Sarnoff also turned to the popular press for his message, telling *Look* magazine in a 1950 interview that television will "sell democracy abroad." Although democracy in theory "begs for the ear," democracy in action, according to Sarnoff, "challenges the eye." Thus, the "American way of life must be seen as well as heard." Even though radio could talk about the problems democracy faces, Sarnoff assured *Look* readers that television can show the results democracy produces.[16] Following up on his 1949 UN award, *Look* reported that television may soon allow everyone "to see as well as hear around the world; when that happens, we will have a great new tool working for freedom and brotherhood."[17]

Various aspects of the technological environment spurred the dialogue about global television in the early 1950s. Television was seen as a potential tool for mass education—and propaganda—and studies were already underway to determine how to best exploit this potential. The linkage of television to the Cold War included strategic security issues, as exemplified by the vision of Sarnoff for Ultrafax, by the call for action on microwave relay for transatlantic television, and by S.J. 96, all of which saw live global TV and electronic information networks as part of an electrotechnical fortress for North America. This discourse about global TV networks was fomenting at precisely the same time that new innovations in domestic American television were common news items in the trade press as well as the popular press. By 1952, the FCC had finally ended its freeze on the issuance of new construction permits for American television stations. Stations holding construction permits prior to the freeze were now firing up and telecasting programs. New construction permits were now being issued at a rapid pace, and the ultrahigh frequency (UHF) bandwidth was opened for TV broadcast licenses. TV set purchases skyrocketed. Although little remembered today, the incremental, city-by-city growth of the AT&T coaxial cable system, making American network television a reality, was exciting news. Therefore, the discussion of global television in 1950s American society was contextualized and framed from a host of issues: Cold War; new technology; national security; new and multiple electronic information networks; and the rising dominance of the postwar consumer society, a society of nuclear families nationally conjoined by the new technology of network television. It is, in retrospect, unsurprising that these frames and contexts within American society and culture were spilling beyond their borders into discussions and ideas about global television and electronic information networks.

Henry Holthusen, UNITEL, and Global Microwave Networks

The State Department had continued its pursuit of propaganda activities after the Second World War, through its International Information Activities (IIA) branch. Even though postwar radio was now operating through a quasi-independent VOA, print, film, exhibits, and lectures continued as an IIA activity until the formation of the USIA in 1953. The USIA took over all State Department information activities and became the overt branch of American psychological warfare (with covert activities going to the intelligence community as well as certain military operations).[18] Disseminating moving images via film exhibitions as part of offensive psychological warfare was difficult, particularly in rural and underdeveloped regions of the world. For example, during a fourteen-month period from 1950 to 1952 in Iran, the IIA screened films, often on multiple occasions, in over 1,300 Iranian cities, towns, and villages.[19] Although USIA mobile motion picture units continued to operate worldwide throughout the Cold War, global television networks—if built, globally developed, and then successfully programmed— would be much more efficient in quickly disseminating audiovisual materials to world populations.

Henry Holthusen knew these challenges, as he had long advised the State Department on international information activities. Who was Henry Holthusen?[20] Born in 1894 and trained as a lawyer, Holthusen retained a private practice from the 1930s until passing away in 1971. An appointment as U.S. Minister to Czechoslovakia during the Hoover administration failed nomination procedures in the Senate; however, Holthusen returned to American diplomacy in 1947 as a consultant to the Senate Foreign Relations Committee. Tasked with assessing information activities, Holthusen served as a committee consultant through the 1950s at the request of Mundt and Hickenlooper and toured twenty-three European nations, eventually touring the entire globe. In 1950, Holthusen became a leading advocate of television as a component for Cold War psychological warfare. Holthusen drafted several speeches for Hickenlooper and Mundt on this topic.

In his private legal practice, Holthusen forged a relationship with William Halstead, a broadcast engineer who had been involved in constructing the FM microwave relay network (Yankee Network) in New York State. Holthusen connected Halstead with both the State Department and the Senate, and they worked together forging plans for global TV networks based on microwave relay stations. Through a corporation called UNITEL, Holthusen and Halstead sought funding from a number of sources, ranging from U.S.

government Cold War development programs such as the Marshall Plan and Point 4 to private investors worldwide.

The UNITEL plan had a number of components for various regions of the world, such as the North Atlantic Relay Communications System (NARCOM) for its transatlantic link. UNITEL envisioned a vast engineering project of huge microwave relay towers strategically placed on mountaintops, islands, and rimming the oceans of the world. These plans included electronically connecting these stations in a relay chain such that no station was more than 300 miles from its nearest neighboring station—a plan that did in fact allow for bridging the Atlantic Ocean. UNITEL was a massive task, and if it had in fact been built to completion, would have surely been considered one of the largest engineering projects ever undertaken in entire span of world history. Microwave relay stations were required in harsh and demanding terrain, including mountaintops, remote islands, and glaciers. The UNITEL plan for building microwave relay stations in challenging terrain is oddly prescient of the actual deployment of the DEW Line and NORAD radar defense system later in the 1950s.

UNITEL promised global TV network capabilities and always prominently mentioned this capability in its business plans. This TV network capability was invariably painted in the Cold War rhetoric of freedom, democracy, education, science, and culture, proclaiming television had a paramount role in promoting these values to counter Soviet propaganda. Holthusen corresponded globally in the 1950s, extolling a grand vision of global television in the name of the free world. His exchange with Frederick Daniell in Australia was typical; Holthusen told Daniell television could be "a single method for mankind to communicate together by the picture language as a means for mutual understanding to combat the insidiousness of the Cold War." Daniell agreed, adding "television is bound to dominate world affairs in a way that is generally undreamed of . . . I believe we must have a global master plan, and I pledge myself to do my utmost as far as Australia is concerned."[21] UNITEL also envisioned a vast range of services beyond television: telephony, telegraphy, education, transit communications, local fire and safety communications, agricultural applications, and business communications. Labeling this strategy as "wideband linkage," UNITEL was, in this sense, an early vision of—well, of broadband convergence. UNITEL was the crypto-Internet.[22]

Discussions about possible global TV networking technologies at this time were a bit reminiscent of the ITU discussions about TV technical standards: many possibilities conceptualized with few, if any, proven in practice. Global TV networking ideas in the early 1950s included microwave-VHF combinations, scatter-bounce transmissions off the troposphere, Ultrafax, underwater coaxial cable, and Stratovision variants of airplanes with transmitters flying above ocean-going aircraft carriers.[23] Halstead argued that of the five known possible technologies for early 1950s global TV networking, the UNITEL system was superior. Even though bouncing a TV signal off the troposphere was possible, changing atmospheric conditions and the sunspot cycle had already proven problematic in many areas of the spectrum, and a bounce signal would be no different. The laying of a coaxial cable, though possible, would require repeaters, inspections, cable ships, and landing rights—and the bandwidth available on coaxial was less than that available on microwave relay.[24] The UNITEL plan was complex, involving different sizes of relay stations and state-of-the-art broadcast engineering. Though never precise about costs, the transatlantic span alone was estimated to need at least $30 million in funding to become a reality. Maps produced by UNITEL depict their global network microwave relay plans. All of these maps share some common features: linking major cities, using extant transport routes, rimming seacoasts, key island landings for leapfrogging oceans, linking to the capital city of every non-Communist nation, a hub-and-spoke system of major and lesser stations, transcontinental and transoceanic linkage, and as a whole, a geography networking the entire non-Communist world for simultaneous real-time dissemination of electronic information. Furthermore, as individual components, the possibility of a wide range of telecommunication services in local areas and/or a single nation was also present.

The UNITEL global microwave relay TV network was never built. However, UNITEL did have a role in bringing television to the world. Plans for Turkey influenced the development of Turkish television, although not specifically along the lines UNITEL forecast.[25] UNITEL was one of the early voices promulgating educational television. UNITEL was also instrumental in privatizing television for one Asian nation: Japan. Holthusen and Halstead, on visits to Japan, had become acquainted with several potential investors. Of this group, the major Japanese newspapers formed a coalition to back UNITEL and their networking system. The UNITEL Japan network was never built. However, this momentum led to the establishment of Japan's first privately owned TV station, NTV Tokyo, in August 1953.

The emergence of NTV (Nippon Television Network) had its origins in the activities of Senator Mundt; as early as 1950, Mundt identified Japan as a particular threat for Communist influence and suggested that television in Japan was an important weapon in the battle against Communism. Holthusen made Japan one of his first stops while touring the world on behalf of the Senate Foreign Relations Committee. The history of postwar Japanese television is rooted in American psychological warfare during the Cold War.[26]

The United States was not the only nation interested in the geopolitics of 1950s television. The United Kingdom had monitored the growing global reach of American television activity since the late 1940s with a combination of envy and anxiety. The first occupying power to bring television to postwar Germany, by the end of German occupation the United Kingdom had grudgingly acquiesced to the American view of German (and by extension, European) television: the growth of television in Germany and Europe needed strategic consideration and implementation in light of East-West security issues, rather than only as an expression of national identity.

Even though the British Government eventually agreed with the American position that television in Cold War Europe was not so much an issue of national identity as it was an issue of East-West security, at the same time British foreign service officers looked to internationalize British television. Of particular interest was Canada, seen as a prime market for British as well as American television exports. The British cabinet in 1952 recognized that television would become a global medium and that British involvement at global levels was in the national interest. Arguing that the United Kingdom should "lose no further time" in building a global market for British TV exports, the cabinet believed the coronation was a tremendous opportunity to build global demand for British television programs, "but it will not recur and it would be an incalculable pity to lose it." Seeing that the United States already had a commanding presence in global television program exports and that this presence would become even more extreme without action to support the British television industry, the cabinet argued the "coronation is approaching at a time when television is on the verge of great expansion in the United States, and is just finding its feet in Latin America, Japan, and Western Europe." There was a chance that British TV program exports built around interest in the coronation could successfully ride the first major wave of global TV growth.[27]

The BBC also considered a number of technologies for enhancing international distribution of the BBC TV signal, beginning with experiments across the English Channel in 1951 and also investigating a variation of Stratovision, with TV transmitters in British air force planes. NBC was interested in this idea, as well as the feasibility of a high-powered transmitter in the United Kingdom beamed toward North America, but the sunspot cycle and an increasingly crowded VHF spectrum suggested both transatlantic plans presented difficulties, despite the occasional over-the-air reception since 1936 of BBC TV at the RCA engineering station in Riverhead, Long Island.[28]

Arranging for international television broadcast coverage of the 1953 coronation of Queen Elizabeth became a key moment in the internationalization of British TV. Wave-based links were established between London and the European continent to bring live coverage to France, Belgium, the Netherlands, and Germany. Kinescope recordings of the coronation ceremonies were couriered by airplane to Montreal, New York, Milan, and Tokyo. At a more intimate level, TV set owners in the British zone of occupied Germany extended invitations to local British subjects living in the zone to visit German homes and watch the coronation ceremonies, relayed live from London.[29] Thus the coronation of Elizabeth II also became the coronation of international television activities by the United Kingdom.

Both NBC and CBS were intensely interested in televising the coronation. NBC had used the funeral of George VI as a test run for the coronation, analyzing transatlantic air transit times to forecast the shuttling of coronation film footage for televising in the United States. NBC also commissioned a lengthy study of the media coverage of the coronation of George VI in 1937 and found that the archbishop of Canterbury and the duke of Norfolk had exercised censorship over the motion picture footage of the event. At Westminster Abbey during the 1937 ceremony, Queen Mary had been caught in a newsreel close-up "drying her eyes during a period of emotion." The archbishop and duke feared the impact upon the public and censored this footage, arguing very few British subjects had, up to that time, ever seen a display of emotion from their royal family.[30]

At one point, the American networks had reason to believe the coronation of Elizabeth II might never become a live TV event. In October 1952, the royal family spoke out against the idea of live TV coverage of the coronation "based on fears some incident might upset the planned perfection of the semi-religious rite. If the Queen should drop her crown or scepter, or stumble for instance . . ." or to otherwise guard against what the duke of Norfolk called some "untoward" occurrence (although he hypothesized the archbishop dropping the crown). This meant American audiences might end up seeing nothing more than "bits and pieces" of the ceremony.[31] Live coronation TV was saved, however, by no less an eminence than Winston Churchill, who spoke of the benefits modern technology would bring to the public. Churchill gave a British flavor to the democratic values of letting the masses see and hear. "There is, I feel, a broad general opinion that fuller advantage should be taken of the modern mechanical arrangement now available through television to enable the many millions of people outside the Abbey to see what is seen by the congregation of notables in the Abbey. It is our hope that it will prove possible in practice to carry into effect the principle that the world should see and hear what the congregation in the Abbey see and hear."[32]

Churchill's opinion carried the day, much to the relief of both the American and British television industries. Although massive plans for speedy airplane delivery by both CBS and NBC went awry and led to the very first American TV coverage of the coronation coming from a CBC feed in Montreal, the delayed coronation footage was a huge hit with American TV audiences, reaching over 18 million homes and capturing the attention of 81 percent of the total available TV audience.[33] In its postcoronation publicity materials, CBS claimed the individual TV network winner of "the great plane race" was unimportant, as the most important winner was "television itself." Comparing the transatlantic TV coverage by plane-relayed kinescopes to past news distribution milestones such as the homing pigeons of Richard Harding Davis, CBS called the coronation telecast and its global coverage "an extension of the democratic process through cathode rays." Television proved powerful in advancing world understanding and for CBS did so with intimacy: "The restlessness of a child prince developed more goodwill in a few seconds of broadcast than frock-coated diplomacy could achieve in a century," thus proving television "equal to the challenge of a thousand-year-old spectacle."[34]

Within a year, the growing ability of the BBC and other European telecasters to achieve live program exchanges across Western Europe led to Eurovision, a program exchange organization. Eurovision was formally launched in the summer of 1954 by Pope Pius XII after a six-week experimental period during which the programming included French horse racing and Queen Elizabeth reviewing the Royal Navy.[35] Eurovision would continue to grow throughout the 1950s and, as will be discussed in chapter 7, reached the USSR in April 1961. Although both East and West Europe, and also Canada and the United States, became internally networked for live television distribution in the 1950s, live networked TV program distribution either across the Iron Curtain, or across the Atlantic, remained beyond the reach of everyone throughout the decade.

From the vantage point of the early twenty-first century, the reasons why UNITEL failed to become a global TV network system are obvious. The tremendous amount of capital investment that UNITEL required was never sufficiently generated, either by government funding or by private investment. Even if such investment had been forthcoming, one still wonders if UNITEL could have been built. The construction of the DEW Line and the NORAD system in the Arctic regions of North America took almost the entire decade of the 1950s to near completion. UNITEL had similar scale and faced similar logistical obstacles of terrain. Furthermore, UNITEL planned to conquer not only the Arctic, but also the entire globe. It is difficult to imagine building the worldwide UNITEL system, even with full funding, in less than ten to fifteen years. As the testimony of David Sarnoff demonstrates, UNITEL was not the only voice in Washington with a plan for global television.

Conceptually if nothing else, UNITEL and Ultrafax were marvels of their age, despite never having been put into full operation. Both Ultrafax and UNITEL presaged strategic defenses that became key components of American strategic and missile defense. Although the terminology is different, UNITEL and its concept of wideband linkage for live synchronous networking of a wide range of new electronic communication technologies also demonstrates a prescient view of today's Internet, broadband convergence, and multiple networks. Although the ambitious visions of technology were in many ways futuristic, UNITEL and Ultrafax were also time-bound creatures of the Cold War, with rationalizing rhetorics steeped in the language of psychological warfare; their advocates were among the leading cold warriors found anywhere in the United States. UNITEL, Ultrafax, and similar globally cast technosecurity information systems of the early 1950s represent a crypto-convergence: an early failed vision of present-day broadband convergence of information technology, as well as an idea totally encrypted in the security rhetoric of the Cold War.

UNITEL and similar systems were ultimately never built to completion because of the emergence of the communications satellite. The rise of the communications satellite is analyzed in chapters 7 and 8 of this study. Before turning to the heavens above, however, this story now takes a brief but important detour to Moscow during the 1950s to better understand the Soviet experience of television, consumer society, and the rhetorical transformation of Cold War communications technology.

6. "A Record of Some Kind in the History of International Communication"

A civilization's culture, at any stage of its existence, is its total achievement, individually and collectively, in the fields of intellectual and aesthetic effort usually referred to generically as the seven lively arts. . . . Culture itself is intangible and cannot be measured by precise units or pre-determined standards. However, its manifestations such as works of art, pieces of literature, declamations of drama and compositions of music, may be reduced to tangible form . . . these manifestations . . . are capable of *impressing* the consumers—even if the normal reaction is so simple as "like" or "dislike." However, in a vast majority of instances, an impression carries with it an idea; consequently cultural manifestations may well be considered vehicles for specifically designed impressions—in short, *propaganda* . . . [including] sponsorship of exhibits, festivals, etc. . . . . emphasizing the contrast in ideas between the free and totalitarian worlds.

—Col. Charles McCarthy, report to Psychological
    Strategy Board, 1952

"Ambassador" RAMAC communicated with more Soviet citizens than any other American representative at the massive USIA 1959 Moscow Exhibition, yet RAMAC is all but forgotten today. Best remembered as the site of the famous Richard Nixon–Nikita Khrushchev "kitchen debate," the USIA 1959 Moscow Exhibition was the first major American exhibition mounted in the Soviet capital since the Bolshevik Revolution. As such, it became a key moment in the superpower competition over competing visions of science, technology, and consumer culture, a competition that provided one of the grand narratives for the Cold War. This particular exhibition not only experienced the kitchen debate. Other exhibits included the controversial American ranch-style home dubbed the "splitnik"; mock-ups of U.S. satellites; modern art (which turned Nikita Khrushchev into an impromptu art critic defending realism); closed-circuit color television; and RAMAC.

RAMAC was a machine diplomat. A creation of International Business Machines (IBM), the IBM 305, popularly known as RAMAC, was a state-of-the-art computer programmed to answer over three thousand different questions about American life, values, and ideals. Soviet citizens attending the exhibition grounds made RAMAC a moderately popular attraction, with queues often taking more than two hours from the point of entry to the answering of the question. Those receiving counsel from RAMAC would wait in line, choose a prewritten question and receive keyboard assistance in entering that question, and then within ninety seconds of entering their question, receive their answer as both a personal printout and a mass-audience video display from RAMAC. Among the most popular questions included "What is the price of American cigarettes?" and "What is jazz music?" Even though RAMAC had appeared previously at the 1958 Brussels World's Fair, the 1959 Moscow Exhibition was RAMAC's first encounter with an all-Communist audience.

The RAMAC experience at Moscow was a crucial moment for the interplay between electronic communication technology, American-Soviet dialogue, and the Cold War. In this regard, RAMAC, the 1959 exhibition, and the emergence of American electronic communication technologies in direct contact with Soviet and other foreign populations marks an early milestone in the origins of what is now often called "information diplomacy." Contemporary examples in the early twenty-first century of information diplomacy include the uses of electronic media such as the Internet for public diplomacy; electronic dissemination of government reports on foreign policy; online transcripts of meetings, interviews, and speeches; and routine appearances by world leaders in the nonstop global TV news cycle. Although information diplomacy in the twenty-first century is far more prevalent and much more sophisticated than what went on in the past, RAMAC and the 1959 USIA exhibition stand as precursors of the present-day world of information diplomacy, albeit with communication technologies that are now relics.

RAMAC also stands as a precursor to contemporary database and Internet search engines. Not only did RAMAC answer questions for Soviet attendees at the 1959 exhibition, RAMAC also collected data about which questions were asked, and with what frequency each question was asked. Again, by twenty-first century standards, these examples to contemporary search engines are modest, quaint, and outdated. RAMAC needed constant assistance from its dozen IBM handlers, and various USIA personnel worked with the Soviet audience to help individuals select a RAMAC question, enter the question into RAMAC, and then receive a printout of the answer. As UNITEL was a crypto-Internet, RAMAC was a crypto-search engine—a beast that apparently once semi-existed in the past, whose modest skeletal remains scattered across a handful of archives and news clippings represent all a contemporary researcher has left to work with by way of analysis.

However, even these archeological shards of RAMAC, particularly in context with other aspects of the 1959 USIA Moscow Exhibition, suffice for glimpsing several attributes found across the contemporary world of search engines. These attributes include questions of audience surveillance, comparisons of data gleaned about searches with other machine-based information sources, unanticipated results regarding the frequency (or lack thereof) for individual queries on particular topics, technical glitches and slower-than-desired output, public relations ballyhoo reporting to the press about popular queries placed to RAMAC, and use of data gleaned about searching RAMAC for follow-up tactics and strategies regarding future Cold War diplomacy. So even though RAMAC is light-years away from the contemporary world of search engines, an investigation of RAMAC reveals core attributes still at the center of understanding search engines in the twenty-first century. Some of those core attributes are who wants to know what from this computer, why do they want to know that, what is revealed about the person making the query, how can the query be compared with other queries as well as other uses of mediated communication, and how can this help to better understand the audience of computer users and their search engine habits so that the owners and operators of the search engines may more effectively exercise knowledge and power over the users of the search engines.

Much more went on at the Moscow exhibit, including the display of new American cars. Another hit was color television, then relatively unknown in the USSR. Closed-circuit color television broadcasts (within the fairgrounds) took place each day, with a range of programming. One popular TV contest, with audience participation, was in voting for who at the fair that day had the biggest Russian-style beard. Another interesting moment took place when television eavesdropped on a debate between an African American[1] exhibition guide and a Soviet official on race relations in the United States. Although the 1959 USIA Moscow Exhibition is but one very small slice of the Cold War, an investigation into this exhibit reveals interesting aspects of American diplomacy, of suppositions and ideologies of pedagogy, and of the nascent information age, albeit in protodevelopment. The 1959 exhibit arrived in Moscow after a decade of growth in Moscow TV, and the exhibit responded in several ways to emergent images of Soviet consumer life as seen on Soviet TV. In particular, the Moscow exhibition became a major testing ground for an expanded global dialogue between American propagandists and Soviet citizens about consumer life, a dialogue supplemented by direct human-machine interaction at an unprecedented scale and scope.[2]

Technology on Display: USIA Exhibits and the 1959 Exhibition

The 1959 Moscow Exhibition was not the first USIA exhibition mounted in the Cold War era. By the mid-1950s, the USIA viewed exhibitions as a countermeasure to trade fairs, which often included extensive displays from the USSR and its Eastern European satellite nations.[3] In 1956, the USIA mounted a Space Unlimited exhibition in Berlin, focusing on the future of space travel and its implications. Visitors polled by the USIA rated this exhibit one of the highlights of the entire fair, with visitors reporting they were surprised to find space research to be a "peaceful" and "open" activity, thus anchoring space research into a scientific (rather than military) sphere. This exhibit later toured several other cities in West Germany.[4]

More ambitious was the People's Capitalism exhibition that same year.[5] Tested at Union Station in Washington, D.C., and then packaged for a world tour, People's Capitalism was a coventure with the Advertising Council of America. USIA Assistant Director Abbot Washburn opened his pitch for the planned exhibit to USIA Director Henry Loomis with this question: "If you had an Iranian as a captive audience for only 25 minutes, what would you tell him about the American economic system?" Speaking for the Ad Council, Washburn explained that the display exemplified how American capitalism is capitalism in the service of the people. Ad Council President Theodore Repplier anguished in 1955 that the American system was nameless, lamenting "imagine Communism without a name!," and offered up People's Capitalism as a worthy brand. Arguing in favor of the term *people* and noting the word's prominent appearance in the Constitution and the Gettysburg Address, Repplier said, "it is high time we liberated this noun from the Russians" and offered up People's Capitalism to display a free and decent life for all humanity. Some within the USIA found the concept muddled and lacking in clarity; one officer, in the early phases of planning, observed that "not knowing the degree of blatancy desired in setting forth the message of this exhibit, it is difficult to suggest specific changes . . . the phrase 'People's Capitalism' may be misunderstood and a purely materialistic impression left where an ideological battle is being fought."[6] Despite questions of blatancy and clarity, momentum ensued and the exhibit opened in February 1956 for a test preview at Union Station in Washington, D.C.

With a hard-hitting rhetoric proclaiming that People's Capitalism was a display aimed at a war of ideas, the Washington visitors were told that for Americans, the ideas of the exhibit were not news. However, for the rest of the world, this is news that would otherwise be "drowned out by the never-ceasing bombardment of Communist falsehoods." Filled with data about the 70 million U.S. savings accounts, 115 million life insurance policyholders, and the like, the display also showed how the U.S. worker of the day outproduced preceding generations: for example, contrasting a nail worker of 1776 who made sixteen nails each hour with a modern nail machine manufacturing fifteen thousand nails each hour. People's Capitalism was eventually broken down into a wide range of components separately used by the USIA in various areas around the world. Corporations helping to produce the exhibit in conjunction with the Ad Council included Eastman Kodak, DuPont, *LIFE* magazine, McCann-Erickson, and U.S. Steel.[7] While on its world tour, the exhibit was routinely attacked by the Soviet bloc press, including editorials from Prague, Warsaw, and Moscow. The VOA counterattacked by giving the exhibit wide coverage on its Armenian, Bulgarian, Czechoslovak, Latvian, Rumanian, Russian, Yugoslav, and Chinese services. On the bright side, the USIA noted several professors and intellectuals in Colombia and India either gave favorable press reviews to the exhibit, or had recently published articles in social science journals advocating the global export of American economic practices.[8]

In hindsight, People's Capitalism is somewhat of an anomaly for USIA exhibitions during the Cold War. By the time of the 1959 Moscow Exhibition, the rhetoric had toned down away from direct confrontation in favor of a more spirited competition between the United States and the USSR. Vice President Richard Nixon was to open the USIA Moscow Exhibit, and in his typical attention to detail and power, Nixon specified who was to fly on Air Force Two, and who on the following plane (accepting cabinet members on Air Force Two, rejecting anyone below the assistant secretary of State level and any members of Congress, and rejecting all spouses except his own). Nixon particularly pushed for a personal one-on-one public encounter with Khrushchev, adding that only U.S. Ambassador to USSR Llewellyn Thompson (and interpreters) could appear with him. He also rejected the idea of a gift of Steuben glassware for Khrushchev, stating that Steuben gifts have "already been overdone" and proposed "a first rate Hi-Fi Stereo instrument with a set of records, for example, with all the Tchaikovsky ballets."[9]

Although Nixon fretted the details, this trip to the USSR in conjunction with the Moscow exhibition would be one of the high points of his career; his speeches and television appearances were given great attention within

Soviet society and were received as indicative of a new, direct dialogue with the Soviet people.[10] This new, direct dialogue on the ground in the Soviet Union would include individual speeches by Nixon and other Americans; active one-on-one engagement of fairgoers by USIA exhibition guides; and for the first time, direct human-machine communication between Soviet citizens and an American computer. Richard Nixon stood as the man of the hour at the 1959 Moscow Exhibition, and RAMAC stood as the mediating machine agent proclaiming the American message of technology, liberalism, and the benefits of American consumer society.

RAMAC, the Exhibit, and Information Diplomacy in Moscow

While Nixon planned his itinerary and gifts, RAMAC arrived in Moscow on June 21, 1959, along with its twelve IBM handlers. An IBM press release stated, "when the first of an estimated 4,000,000 visitors begin inspecting exhibits . . . they will find RAMAC conveniently situated to answer all questions about the United States."[11] By the end of August and with the exhibition in full swing, IBM released a list of the most-asked questions to that date (all below asked and answered a minimum of one hundred times):

1. What is meant by the American Dream?
2. What is the present direction in the development of American Jazz?
3. What is American rock and roll music?
4. How much do U.S. cigarettes cost?
5. How old is Louis Armstrong?
6. What is the wardrobe of the average American woman?
7. What is the most popular U.S. jazz orchestra?
8. What is the average income of the American family?
9. What are the reasons for the rise in abstract painting and sculpture?
10. The mineature [*sic*] radio receiver in the U.S.
11. How many Negroes have been lynched in the U.S. since 1950?
12. What is the minimum wage in the U.S.?
13. What is the salary of the American scientist compared with other professions?
14. What is the Liberty Bell, which is a symbol of independence to Americans?
15. What is the division of budget planning between husband and wife in the U.S.?
16. Who is currently the most popular jazz artist in the U.S.?
17. What is the relationship between costs and earnings in the U.S.?

18. What are the origins of American jazz?

19. How long does the American factory worker have to work to earn the price of a new car?

20. Has U.S. medicine found any drugs successful in the treatment of cancer?

21. What type of dance is most popular in the U.S.?

22. How many professional mathematicians are there in the U.S., and what are some of their recent contributions?

23. What is the number of unmarried men and women in the U.S.?

24. How much does travel between the U.S. and the U.S.S.R. cost?

25. What have been some recent overall developments in physics in the U.S.?

26. How much aid did the U.S. give the U.S.S.R. during and after the 2nd World War?

27. How does the young engineer usually get started on his career?

28. Why don't all American families have automobiles?

29. How many stellites [sic] has the U.S. fired successfully?

30. How much do new automobiles cost in the U.S.?[12]

Here are a few answers, verbatim, from RAMAC:

1. What is meant by the American Dream? The American Dream is the fundamental belief by Americans that America has meant and must always mean that all men shall be free to seek for themselves and their children a better life. Americans interpret this in terms of a demand for freedom, of worship, freedom in the expression of belief, universal suffrage and universal education.

2. What is the present direction in the development of American jazz? Today's American jazz musicians are better educated in music than the jazz musicians of a generation ago. Consequently American jazz today musically is more sophisticated, the composers and arrangers employing more extended musical forms and more complex devices in their original work. However, a breaking away from the icily cool intellectualizations of the "progressives" of the late '40s and early '50s is apparent in the performances of men such as Gerry Mulligan and indicates a tendency to return to the older tradition of the freely improvised solo jazz is accepted as a serious art form and study of it is included in the curricula of American colleges and universities.

4. How much do American cigarettes cost? In the U.S. the price of a package of 20 cigarettes varies from 20 to 30 cents. The average semi-skilled worker in the U.S. earns enough money in one hour to buy about 8 packages. Almost all cigarettes sold in the U.S. are of American manufacture.

6. What is the wardrobe of the average American woman? The wardrobe of the average American woman in the middle income group includes one winter weight long coat (fur trimmed or untrimmed), one spring weight

coat—sometimes with a zip-out lining, a raincoat, five house type dresses, four afternoon "dressy" dresses, three skirts, three suits, six blouses, three sweaters, four slips, two petticoats, five nightgowns, eight panties, five brassieres, two corsets or girdles, two robes, six pairs of nylon stockings, two pairs of sport type socks, three pairs of dress gloves, one bathing suit, three pairs of play shorts, one pair of slacks and one play suit as well as accessories.

11. How many Negroes have been lynched in the U.S. since 1950? Since 1950 a total of 7 deaths—6 Negroes and 1 white person—have been classified as lynchings by Tuskegee Institute, the Negro college which has compiled records on lynchings in the U.S.A. Lynching in the U.S. is the execution of a person for an alleged crime without a fair and public trial before a qualified judge and jury of his peers. Originally lynching was a form of hasty neighborhood action designed to maintain order in the absence of adequate police and courts. All responsible Americans condemn lynching. The perpetrators of these crimes are prosecuted under state laws.

RAMAC was an attraction, but not the most popular exhibit; RAMAC ranked tenth overall in popularity of all exhibits at the Moscow exhibition. Nor was RAMAC the only machine calculating visitor opinions. Voting machines were also used to tally rankings of various individual exhibits.[13] Soviet visitors were more interested in the display of American automobiles, abstract art (in this case, interested in that it generated controversy), the Family of Man pavilion, color television, a circular widescreen film exhibition known as Circarama, and the American ranch-style home dubbed the "splitnik."

In part, the RAMAC experience was negated by operational difficulties.[14] RAMAC operated at a slower speed than expected, which meant patrons typically stood in line for sixty to ninety minutes awaiting their encounter. In addition, the physical space of RAMAC was poorly designed for crowd flow. RAMAC, to quote from a USIA report, "occupied a section along the wall of the aluminum dome . . . located in a balustraded enclosure which resembled half of a hexagon." The TV monitors producing RAMAC answers were situated in such a way that the sight lines of the queued crowd did not easily view the monitors, and the monitors also broke down repeatedly. RAMAC took input from two individuals at once. Individuals received printouts of their answers, which became valued souvenirs. RAMAC answered questions in eight categories: the American People and Land; American Education; How Americans Live; Americans at Work; American Culture; American Science and Technology; the American Economy; and Americans and the World. RAMAC was not programmed solely to dispense information, but also to "register precisely the interest of visitors in every aspect of information" contained in RAMAC. "It was completely impartial; it recorded interest without prejudice, and it forgot no detail of this interest." Of its 3,477 questions, 10% were asked more than 20 times, and 60% fewer than 5 times.

Turning from popular RAMAC questions, what were among the least asked? Soviet visitors apparently cared little about the American view on such topics as the consumption of dairy products, retirement and private pension systems, American magazines, manufacturing packaging techniques, nongovernmental organizations, urban-rural changes, synthetic fibers, or general mining practices. In scanning the full list of popular and unpopular RAMAC question topics, one can see the roots of People's Capitalism, particularly the connections to American industry. In fact, many of the mundane RAMAC questions—and many RAMAC questions are indeed mundane—are little more than public relations bromides for American industries. In addition, these RAMAC questions and answers are in keeping with a business rhetoric codeveloped by industry, sponsors, and media outlets as an anti-New Deal strategy to promote American life as constantly delivering "more, new, and better," or what William L. Bird calls the rhetoric of "Better Living."[15] As a USIA planning document put it, the exhibition was designed to show "our technology is for us only a means to an end, not an end in itself" and that a better life for the individual was the goal. Arguing that this led to better security and health and increases in standards of living, the USIA counseled that what other nations mistakenly labeled as American "materialism" should more correctly be seen as "only a means to a greater humanism."[16]

RAMAC also has roots to a major USIA project of the Cold War era: global public opinion polling. The USIA expanded public opinion polling far beyond the industrialized world, and the scale and scope—as well as location—of regular public opinion polling by the USIA during the Cold War was truly remarkable. Moving far beyond Europe (although very active there as well), the USIA regularly polled Asian, African, and Latin American citizens on a range of Cold War themes, particularly questions related to leadership in science and technology. Though heightened by the 1957 Sputnik launch, the investment in gauging global public opinion on hundreds of variants of a basic question—Who leads the world in the development of science and technology, the United States or USSR?—was immense. By 1963, the USIA had fully embarked on regular world public opinion polling. Results at that time tended to indicate "a generally good disposition toward the U.S., but a disturbing belief in many places that the U.S. trails the Soviet Union in military power . . . and is badly behind in the space race . . . the USSR is believed to be ahead of the United States in space development everywhere except Saigon, although the margins are small in West Germany, Mexico City, and Bangkok."[17] One would wonder about any other result out of Saigon at that time.

RAMAC certainly was designed in part to respond to Soviet science and technology, particularly in electronics, but also in behavioral sciences. The Sprague Committee had found that "although the U.S. enjoys a clear lead in the number and quality of its computers, much evidence suggests that the Soviet's strong mathematical background permits them to use their fewer computers more effectively, and Soviet mathematicians are also engaged in very long-range speculation of unique character with respect to the development of radically new computer devices . . . [and also show] emphasis on research toward a unified theory of human behavior embracing the biological, psychological, and social facets of man. This broad interdisciplinary approach is directed toward understanding, control, and predictability of human behavior."[18]

In addition, the USIA Moscow Exhibition followed a decision by the NSC that seeking global leadership in outer space development and exploration was in the strategic interests of the United States.[19] The NSC observed that "the United States should continue actively to pursue programs to develop and exploit outer space and . . . ensure that the United States is a recognized leader in the field. . . . Due consideration should be given to the psychological values of solid technical and scientific advancement." Because of the highly classified nature of this NSC directive, it is unlikely most USIA officers were intimately familiar with its contents. However, the directive indicates the high priority of the space race for American policymakers, particularly after Sputnik in 1957.

RAMAC, of course, does double duty on this question, not only serving as a surreptitious poll-meister testing the Moscow exhibition visitors, but also simultaneously signifying American advances in computer science and information processing. As such, RAMAC stood as a counterforce against the hotly debated Soviet cybernetics campaign.[20] In the 1950s, cybernetics and computer software sparked a heated dialogue within the Soviet Union on whether computer programming was reconcilable with the scientific and philosophical principles of Marxism-Leninism. As Loren Graham notes, the history of computers in the Soviet Union can be described as an early attempt to sustain Soviet exceptionalism, but eventually (during the 1960s) exceptionalism had eroded to the point where the Soviet Union had little choice but to adopt Western trends in computer programming, thus hastening the decay of Marxist-Leninist scientific method as a philosophical approach for controlling its systems of information.[21] Control over information flow in the USSR began its great erosion in the late 1950s and continued until its dissolution in 1991; and RAMAC, along with the entire 1959 Moscow Exhibition, contributed to this decay (which must have pleased the researchers of Project Troy).

RAMAC thus also represented an oblique Western incursion into Marxist-Leninist scientific method. Coming on the heels of a collapsing belief in Lysenkoism,[22] RAMAC may well have, in a modest way, also pushed Soviet computer scientists to reassess their own Marxist-Leninist methodologies. So even though the Soviets could still, in 1959, legitimately claim world leadership in such areas as space technologies, developments such as RAMAC discreetly demonstrated that such examples of Soviet technological and scientific leadership were few in number and likely to decline in the years ahead. President Dwight Eisenhower was so confident of American leadership in science and technology "across the board" that he actually argued against competition in the space race, noting that this would simply legitimate one of the very few cases in which Soviets could claim a temporary superiority. Although basically ignored by all his policymakers (and politically countered by aspiring 1960 presidential candidates Lyndon Johnson and John Kennedy), in retrospect Eisenhower's assessment appears very accurate.[23]

In a postexhibition report that surveyed all questions put to USIA workers by Soviet fairgoers, the RAMAC questions were folded in with questions asked at other exhibits in an attempt to get a general view of Soviet curiosity regarding America.[24] Over 70% of all questions fell into the following categories (the USIA identified the first six as "friendly" and the remaining three as "antagonistic"): living conditions, American awareness of the USSR, technology (especially consumer technology), education, music (especially jazz), freedoms and ideals, unemployment, the "Negro problem," and bases around the USSR (U.S. military installations). Because Soviet visitors showed a keen interest in technology, the report suggested continued emphasis on promoting consumer technology in future exhibits. RAMAC questions on science and technology accounted for 25% of all RAMAC questions asked, with most of these in applied technology rather than basic research. Some of this may have stemmed from housing RAMAC in an area filled with other scientific and technical displays, possibly skewing the RAMAC audience by drawing people who already had an interest in science and technology. The impersonal nature of a RAMAC encounter also may have played a role, with the USIA believing "on such sensitive subjects as unemployment, racial discrimination and overseas bases, the public obviously was not satisfied with a mechanical answer . . . this reliance on the spoken word for the "real truth" was very evident in the kind of face-to-face questioning encountered by Exhibit personnel."[25]

RAMAC appears, discursively speaking, to have mastered the technological rhetoric of a benign American liberal, but not the intimacy of a personal confidant.[26] Nevertheless, this benign liberalism had real value, particularly in the dissemination of American scientific research. Soon after the Moscow exhibition, Ithiel de Sola Pool postulated "scientific information is one of the few things very much wanted by other countries," which meant "science becomes a vehicle for establishing contact." Particularly in the case of a closed society like the USSR, American science could put "a few significant chinks in this wall of secrecy" and, therefore, anything "that can be done to increase Soviet desire for contact with American science is to the good."[27] In this sense, getting American science directly from the RAMAC itself was definitely "to the good" for increasing contact and breaking down a closed society, through a very benign, muted, and subtle application of information overload first secretly advocated several years earlier by Pool and others at MIT in the Project Troy report.

Though RAMAC is a central topic of this chapter, other interesting exhibits and events relevant to information diplomacy and human-machine dialogue also occurred at the 1959 USIA Moscow Exhibition. This chapter now reviews of some of these developments, centering on hi-fi music, television, race, and consumer culture. The popularity of RAMAC questions concerning jazz, in particular, and American popular music, in general, is evident throughout the USIA reports about the exhibition. High-fidelity music systems from Ampex, Klipsch, Marantz, Pickering, Rek-O-Kut, Fisher, Scott, Zenith, Westinghouse, General Electric, RCA Victor, Wollensack, and Shure were on display and used throughout the exhibition to play music for audiences. Jazz requests were so numerous that classical and semi-classical recordings were dropped from the program schedule in favor of additional recordings by Louis Armstrong, Dave Brubeck, Gerry Mulligan, Oscar Peterson, and many other performers. One USIA officer working in the hi-fi area noted the many references to VOA broadcaster and jazz-spinner Willis Conover, and added another "frequent and odd" question was to ask the age of the Andrews Sisters.[28]

The color television studio was one of the most popular sites on the exhibition grounds. Color television was not yet in regular production in the USSR, although television growth in the USSR had proceeded at a relatively robust pace in the 1950s, in part built upon research and manufacture in the Soviet zone of Germany and in part built on prewar research and postwar expansion in Moscow and Leningrad. Although Soviet television grew rapidly, complaints of poor reception and low-quality sets were common throughout the Soviet bloc, and plans for regular color television service, despite impending Soviet announcements through much of the decade, were forecast to be at least two years away.[29]

Audience participation at the exhibition television studio was an ongoing activity as evidenced by the following reports from USIA exhibition workers:

> The color TV studio recently began putting on a game of musical chairs each evening (which is televised and played back to the audience). The winner is given a prize—usually a toy—since the participants are limited to children and youths. The studio is mobbed at the time the game is usually played. . . . The color TV studio has a library of Disney type animated cartoons . . . these attract tremendous crowds of young and old whose rapt attention and amusement undoubtedly demonstrate a widespread thirst here for pure fantasy in entertainment . . . a film describing the inner workings of the US stock market [is called by a Soviet professor of economics] a waste of time because most of the terms in it as well as the processes portrayed are so alien to a Soviet audience that little is understood.[30]

> For the first weeks of the exposition, the color television studio ran a periodic telecast of a contest for the best and most luxurious growth of beard among the male members of the Soviet audience. The hirsute champion was selected by the audience itself through the use of an applause meter. He received a prize consisting of the "give-away" items RCA and Ampex were able to scrape up in the glass pavilion. Also pinned on each proud winner's chest was a flamboyant cockade of ribbons left behind at the studio during the first days of the Exhibition by some representatives of the West Texas Cattle Breeder's Association. (The Association uses these cockades back home to decorate the bovine winners of its cattle shows). . . . These shaggy competitions were immensely popular with the TV studio's audience and had all comers rolling in the aisles with mirth. However, someone from the Party or bureaucracy must have happened by at the wrong time and submitted his report. The TV studio management was eventually approached by "a representative of the Ministry of Culture" who discretely [sic] suggested that the contests lacked taste. . . . They were reluctantly dropped by the studio.[31]

> I was standing on the second floor of the glass pavilion when I noticed a large crowd beginning to form around one of the monitor sets of the color television exhibit. Edging closer, I saw that what had interested them was the transmission of a live interview which was taking place outside the building between one of the Negro guides and a Soviet citizen. The latter was being extremely aggressive and was not too bright, whereas the guide was remaining calm and supplying the interrogator with intelligent, well thought-out answers. In general, the Soviet was commenting on the race problem in the United States in a manner which may have had a certain limited validity twenty years or more ago. The guide countered these outdated generalities with up-to-date facts backed by meaningful statistical comparisons on the improvement of the

Negro's position in the United States. Interestingly . . . the Soviets composing the crowd around me seemed to be universally in sympathy with the guide and critical of their countryman's questions and accusations. Time and time again the Soviet's remarks evoked from the crowd cries of "What a silly question," "Ours is so stupid," "Doesn't he know anything?" etc. In response to the guide's replies, however, from the crowd came murmurs of "Why, certainly they have made progress," "Of course things have changed," "the guide is clever," etc.[32]

Also, although not from the television exhibit, one more observation about race relations in the United States: "[An observer] . . . was present at the Helena Rubenstein pavilion when the following happened: a young Negro girl was being given a facial. A Russian woman seeing this began to shout hysterically that this was all propaganda, it wasn't true, that everyone knew that in the US no white would serve a Negro. The other Soviet citizens told her to keep quiet and when she persisted they removed her bodily from the scene."[33]

These various accounts demonstrate one major function of the entire Moscow exhibition was to provide opportunities for observation and surveillance of ordinary Soviet citizens interacting with simulations of American consumer society, as well as ordinary Soviets interacting with the Soviet bureaucracy. These USIA manuscript collections chronicling the 1959 exhibition are filled with dozens and dozens of pages of accounts (all typed single-spaced) similar to these, on all aspects of the entire exhibition. The USIA guides and American diplomats in Moscow routinely queried their Soviet contacts from all walks of life regarding the exhibition and reported back to Washington on their findings. This also included follow-up reports from U.S. Foreign Service officers throughout the USSR on Soviet-wide circulation of exhibition souvenirs, including RAMAC printouts. The 1959 exhibition produced a massive behavioral science research laboratory for two different investigative teams: both the United States and USSR conducted extensive observations of fairgoers. Frankly, attendees at the 1959 exhibition were among the most closely watched group of people, or sample population, in the history of the Cold War. An entire fairground was elaborately constructed, entrance to the fairground controlled by a ticket system, and attendees carefully monitored by an armada of both American and Soviet observers, recording the responses of subjects with incredible detail and, on a few occasions, stimulating or provoking a subject response in hopes of observing a particular behavioral expression. In this sense, the exhibit was the ultimate Cold War social science experimental research project aimed at a target group, and it was unusual in that one target group provided an opportunity for close observation and analysis by both superpowers. It is tempting to say the fairgoers were like rats in a maze, but that does not do justice to either the rats or the fairgoers—

the rats negotiate a simple scientific physical geography to get food, and the fairgoers negotiated a complex scientific social geography to get ideology.

Soviet government reaction to the Moscow exhibition also took place in the wake of the Moscow exhibition. In addition to staging its own exhibition in New York City concurrent with the USIA Moscow exhibition, the Soviet news agency TASS occasionally swiped at American home building, race relations, and American unemployment. The Soviets also announced, during the run of the USIA exhibit, that they would soon hold an international film festival in Moscow, unveiling "Circorama," a Soviet version of the USIA exhibition's popular Circarama projection process, and that a new, permanent pavilion devoted to economic development would soon open in Moscow with exhibits showing Soviet progress in radio electronics, communication technologies, science, and electrification.[34] *Komsomol Pravda* expressed "disgust" when the exhibition fashion show played an Elvis Presley record and demonstrated American-teenage dancing.[35] However, the major move came in the waning days of the fair, when the Soviets literally hit the moon on September 15 with Luna 2 and released Luna 3 photographs of the dark side of the moon on October 4, the second anniversary of Sputnik.[36] Leslie Brady, the cultural affairs counselor at the Moscow embassy, commented on the lack of exhibition coverage in the Moscow press, ruing it "could not have held the headlines in competition with Khrushchev's UN speech and sputniks shooting off hither and yon . . . (but) the public remembers, whether the press does or not."[37]

Representations of race are another fascinating facet of the Moscow exhibition activities. RAMAC offered several race-related questions (including the example on lynching), African Americans were among the USIA staff, and the projection of American race relations was clearly an important, if muted, concern of the Moscow exhibition. The USIA aimed to project a liberal and inclusive vision of race and society in the United States.[38] American race relations had long been a propaganda staple of the USSR and countering that propaganda is one reason for this attitude. Despite its anti-Communism, the USIA was in many ways a comparatively liberal-minded institution within the American government at this time, and the attempts to portray race relations in the United States as inclusive, improving, and aimed toward the betterment of all society are not incompatible with majority sentiments of USIA personnel.[39]

Deep within this majority sentiment, however, one can also read the continuing presence of an ongoing question concerning race that occupied the American diplomatic and security community throughout the Cold War. This question was not about race in the United States; rather, it was a question of policy toward non-Russian minorities in the USSR. Briefly stated, a small but vocal minority within the American diplomatic and security community had always called for actions that would incite the non-Russian minorities of the Soviet Union to rise up against Russian attitudes of moral and cultural superiority and thus bring down the Soviet Union. From the earliest days of the Cold War, this policy was always rejected at higher levels and by the majority for the following reason: even if this could be accomplished, to do so would simultaneously create a set of conditions that American policy could not control. No credible way could be found (more accurately, no strategic policy could be developed) to contain these non-Russian minorities, after their success at toppling the USSR, within the influence of American policymakers. So, in fact, the representation of American race relations by the USIA at the 1959 Moscow Exhibition is very much in keeping with American strategic and diplomatic policy at that time regarding non-Russian minorities in the Soviet Union. This American attitude would not appreciably change until after the 1979 Soviet invasion of Afghanistan.

Finally, while writing a USIA preliminary report on the Moscow exhibition, Ralph White commented on the many fairgoers who demonstrated a visual fascination with machines at work building the products of American consumer society. White noticed that "people watch any machine that is in motion, like the plastic-cup machine or the fiberglass machine, the electric train, the cut-away Chevrolet with its slowly rotating engine or even the slowly-rotating stainless-steel design in three dimensions." This was not the trained eye of a Soviet engineer, but "more like a little boy's fascinated wonderment at mechanical parts busy in motion, with a glimmer of understanding as to how it works but with much feeling of something magical that is far beyond his power of comprehension."[40] White endorsed exploiting the visual nature of technology in future exhibitions. His examples included additional technical details, several movie projectors in simultaneous operation, scientific demonstrations "with a semi-magical quality . . . like the more dramatic demonstrations that occur in a good university course in physics," and a colossal display "massive enough to appeal to the Soviet taste for sheer size" in recognition that the Soviet public has made it clear "they *want* to be amazed."

An analysis of these observations surprisingly leans toward somewhat reclaiming and justifying the words and actions of Richard Nixon. In his kitchen debate (and in a sentence that came back to haunt him in the 1960 presidential campaign), Nixon observed there were some areas where the USSR perhaps led the United States, for example, in rocketry and launch thrust abilities, and there were other areas, perhaps color television, where the United States led the USSR. John Kennedy jumped all over this in the 1960 presidential debates with his view that leadership in rocketry was more important. Yet Nixon, perhaps by virtue of his first-hand experiences at the Moscow exhibition, had a point. The incredible popularity of, frankly, banal American-style television program concepts (musical chairs, applause meter, game show–like contests, etc.) is telling and points to perceived values present in American consumer society and relatively absent in Soviet consumer society. Ralph White recognized that color TV was also a glimpse into the coming future of Soviet life with TV "on a mass scale (Moscow's shacks, like comparable shacks in the United States, are very often crowned by television antennas)," and Soviet color TV, though "inferior" to color TV in the United States, was on the way. When Soviets watched American closed-circuit color television at the Moscow exhibition, White thought, "in looking at our color TV, as in looking at our cars, they could thrill at the thought that they were getting a glimpse of their own bright future."[41] Nixon also appeared on Soviet television during the exhibition, not only on the closed-circuit television system at the exhibition grounds. This televised speech was noted by many fairgoers in written and spoken comments, and Nixon drew praise for speaking in a plain and direct manner to the Soviet peoples, rather than aiming his remarks solely at Soviet leadership. Nixon's TV speech appeared on Moscow's third channel and was not relayed beyond Moscow; viewers found the telecast despite advance notices announcing the telecast would be on the second, rather than third, channel.[42]

1950s Moscow TV and the Rise of a Soviet Consumer Society

By 1959, the USIA estimated over 4 million television sets were in use in the Soviet Union, and that color TV was just beginning test transmissions. About 1 million new TV sets were slated for production, and the opening of a "people's television university" in October was celebrated as a festive occasion.[43] Despite the costs of sets, TV seemed to be reaching, albeit haphazardly, a broad spectrum of Soviet citizens. Television had been growing in Moscow for over a decade, and that early growth was observed by diplomats in the American embassy in the early 1950s and later by the USIA. The initial embassy interest in Moscow television was, like other early interest in Cold War television from the State Department, circumstantial rather than strategic. Monitoring of Moscow TV and reporting back to Washington apparently began in 1950 as an embassy initiative rather than a department policy when an embassy officer—probably either M. Gordon Knox or Norman Stines— brought an American-manufactured 8½-inch Motorola TV set to Moscow and had it converted to local standards.[44] At this time, Moscow had fewer than ten thousand TV sets. Moscow TV Center broadcast four nights a week and also on Sunday afternoons.[45]

In November 1950, Ralph Collins reported from the embassy with one of the first detailed accounts of a Moscow TV evening, a program called *Soviet Art and Literature in the Cause of Peace* followed by a prewar movie titled *Far-Away Bride.* Collins found the first program theme as "one and unchanging, peace Soviet-style, threatened by the American war mongers. It was like a Partisans of Peace meeting" and wondered why with less than ten thousand sets in use and most of those in the hands of the Communist "aristocracy," viewers were "fed such a strong dose of propaganda, which through the medium of television becomes even stronger medicine than the usual gruel dispensed every day and hour over the Soviet radio on the theme of peace."[46] This example of detailed reporting from the embassy to the State Department became typical from 1950 to 1953, before the formation of the USIA. In these detailed reports, a handful of embassy staff not only provided a very thorough collection of accounts describing early Moscow television programming, they also occasionally showed an authorial flair for television criticism and analysis worthy of Jack Gould.

Gordon Knox, discussing the March 31, 1951, Moscow program honoring recent winners of the Stalin Prize, reported the heavy and obvious use of scripts, a film clip of a giant walking excavator with a promise of "many more giant excavators for the great Stalinist construction jobs ahead," a leather worker who economized leather scraps for the Soviet cause, and many testimonies to the "rich Soviet culture of today." Included were brief theatrical scenes from current plays, including a naval drama depicting a corrupt Admiral Nelson at Trafalgar, and as a finale, the recitation of a brief excerpt from the prize-winning Alexis Surkov poem, "Peace for the World": "Stalin, Stalin, Stalin, peace, peace, peace, Stalin, peace, Stalin, peace." The program opened with images of giant posters of Lenin and Stalin and ended, according to Knox, with this visual motif: "And there He was again, Stalin on a poster, His hand upraised, the happy peoples of the world behind Him, adoring Him."[47]

Knox later added that Moscow television in the spring of 1951 spent about half of its program hours on motion pictures, and about one-third of its hours on various forms of drama. Live broadcasts of current events were "virtually non-existent" and there was not much in the way of anything resembling news programs. A few sports programs showed up from time to time, as well as the rare educational program; children's programs were also present on the screen. Virtually all of this was done with talent from other venues around Moscow brought into the studio; the only television performer specific to the TV station was a "pretty girl announcer. She announces each program, reads off lists of performers, marches on and off the television stage during concert programs in the usual Moscow concert hall fashion." He also, in a comparative moment, revealed his familiarity with television in his homeland (although did so with the proper intellectual disdain) and confided there are

a number of programs familiar to American listeners which do *not* appear on Moscow television. There is no roller derby, no soap opera (although on occasion Moscow drama approaches it), no give-aways, no "meet the press," no "enquiring reporter" to roam Gorky Street and plumb public opinion, no Dagmar, no Ed Sullivan with Kremlin gossip. Perhaps this is to the good. How-ever, taken all in all, Moscow television suffers from too much formality, from a dull conference hall approach, from its desire to reproduce other forms of art (concerts, opera, theater, movies) instead of creating forms of its own, from lack of experimentation, from an ostrich-like attitude toward news events. It may be true there are no commercials—but there is plenty of propaganda. As one American spectator remarked on International Woman's Day, U.S. televi-sion is entertainment interrupted by commercials, while Soviet television is propaganda interrupted by entertainment.

Tempering the propaganda charge to a degree, Knox concluded that "one surprising fact" about Soviet television was its relative lack of propaganda compared to other Soviet mass media and popular arts, noting that while on the one hand Moscow TV did "pay its measure of tribute" to propaganda themes, "it isn't required to do so every night." In the end, the main criticism of Moscow TV, as seen by the American embassy, was a lack of "boldness and experimentation" typical of American television, instead providing little more than a "pale reflection" of other forms of Soviet entertainment.[48]

Over the rest of 1951, American embassy officers reported back to Wash-ington on such Moscow TV programs as Bolshoi Theatre specials, football (soccer), the unveiling of a Gorky statue, musical competitions, the "Decade of Ukrainian Literature" spectacular, Railroad Day, Air Force Day, Navy Day, Coal Miner's Day, the Stalingrad power and irrigation project, Tank Day, and a celebration of progress on constructing the Turkmen Canal.[49] Norman Stines found the programs generally improved in production quality during the course of 1951, but leading party members remained absent from the TV cameras more often than not, and though Air Force Day and Navy Day did show some military equipment, Tank Day showed none and received no TV coverage. Railroad Day and Coal Miner's Day, on the other hand, received "voluminous" TV coverage, and Stines closed his Coal Miner's Day report by adding, "it is obvious that there are many more television antennas around Moscow than a year ago." The Turkmen Canal program was, in Stine's eyes, "the best organized of the series and proved to be impressive propaganda."

In a rare instance, Coal Miner's Day on TV included a non-Russian Soviet "Deputy from the Turkmen Supreme Soviet, whose name sounded like KLIV. Kliv was obviously a real Turkmen, speaking Russian in a harsh Central Asian accent" who, though a powerful speaker in the party mold, was unaccustomed to speaking in an empty studio rather than in front of a live audience. Kliv, "befitting a Soviet politician," attacked American warmongering in the Soviet style, but "after he pronounced the name of Stalin midway in his speech, he paused somewhat automatically to deliver a black-eyed stare into space. Possibly he was waiting for applause, but there was no studio audience. Only the rustling of a script could be heard."

Reporting about a Moscow TV music spectacular in September 1951, Stines found Moscow TV productions increasingly ambitious. Professionalism among the staff and announcers had notably improved, and Stines thought the use of the Moscow concert hall announcer for the music fest was a good move, noting this announcer compared favorably with "Milton J. Cross from the golden days of NBC," and that the musical performers themselves were all good, with a few even outstanding. However, after watching through a Russian soprano, a Russian ballet team, a Russian pianist, a Tadzhik dancer, a Kigriz soprano, a Russian violinist, another Russian ballet team, a Kazakh woman instrumentalist, two more ballet dancers from Sverdlosk, a tenor from Sverdlosk, and a ballet team from the Kirov, he had had enough Soviet music and culture and longed for the music of his own land. Despite only seeing half of the program, Stines admitted his patience had worn thin, and he "switched off the television set, turned up the volume on his three-speed record player and put on an LP record of Benny Goodman."[50]

By January 1952, Moscow-area set ownership was estimated to be more than thirty thousand homes and had begun to spread to nearby cities and a few dachas. A rumored 19-inch set was supposedly in production but not yet seen by embassy staff. One staffer had overheard talk of this set between a Soviet military officer and a Russian civilian while on a train journey and gathered that the 19-inch set was intended for community viewing in various "houses of culture" such as museums and other public organizations. A third transmitting station in Kiev was in experimental phases and expected to join those in Moscow and Leningrad in offering regular programming. Leningrad TV was up to four nights a week, and Moscow now telecast six nights a week.[51] By April 1952, Moscow had over sixty thousand TV sets with about 15% of the viewers in the outlying areas of the Moscow oblast.[52]

By the end of 1952, television had begun to be something beyond a small service for party loyalists and had grown in size, scope, and viewership into the daily fabric of Moscow life. Various officers at the Moscow Embassy increasingly heard reports of Muscovites complaining about the inability to find competent TV repairmen and a general lack of spare parts and tubes. Beyond the technological frustrations of set ownership, television and family life in Moscow had also begun to show the signs of tension familiar to TV families everywhere. One embassy officer reported a story of a "Soviet citizen in a bakery queue describing the complications which television set ownership has brought to his family life. Some of them sounded remarkably like the troubles which television has produced for American families." This Soviet family had "no life of its own since it bought a television set. The neighbors, and especially the neighbor's children, come at all hours, invited or uninvited, to watch the programs." These interloping TV viewers protested even the family's bedtime. Additional reports about TV in the lives of other Soviet families confirmed this basic tale, with one wife begging her husband not to repair a broken TV set so they could enjoy some peace and quiet because life without TV was now "simpler since the breakdown." Despite the challenges, "receiver ownership seems increasing steadily. Several persons have reported seeing new antennae going up all over the city" and even the "oldest, most dilapidated small houses on the city's outskirts—by American standards no more than huts—now possess a television antenna propped on the rickety roof."[53]

In February 1953, Moscow TV announced it planned 175 productions for the year, surpassing the 1952 total of 147 productions, and promised each would be broadcast only once except "in rare cases at the request of the television viewers themselves." Propaganda programs, usually under the rubric of "scientific—social—political programs," were planned to increase to over one hundred, up from eighty-nine in 1952, thirty-three in 1951, and six in 1950. However, sports programs were also planned to increase significantly. Finally, the announcement for 1953 TV programming also took a swipe at American TV culture: "Scoundrels, murderers, bandits, thieves, robbers, detectives, and policemen are the principal heroes of the American television programs. American television typifies the complete depravity and collapse of bourgeois culture. The American business leaders have turned television into a commercial enterprise, into a weapon of oppression and baneful corruption of people."[54] The American Embassy forecast that this program schedule would be "very appealing to the average Soviet television set owner." That same year, Pat Murrin of NBC found himself in the USSR, and gave Soviet TV programs generally high marks on technical quality, ballet, and variety shows, although he also reported no live telecasts, and far too many "documentary films of 'Life-Down-In-A-Russian-Coal Mine' kind of thing."[55] By 1954, this TV audience was estimated at over one hundred thousand homes in the Moscow area, and TV was expanding throughout the Soviet world geographically and socially. Relay stations had also begun to carry programs from Kiev, Moscow, and Leningrad beyond transmitter range and to new Soviet audiences in 1955, and Soviet manufacturing expected to build 750,000 new TV sets that year.[56] In 1956, William McFadden reported from the embassy in Moscow that "television antennae appear on the most beaten down hovels around Moscow." Though admitting his contacts were limited, he also noted, "the Russians who have access to TV seem to watch it continuously" and seemed to prefer TV to radio.[57] By the time the 1959 USIA Moscow Exhibit was winding down, TV had entered nearly 5 million Soviet homes.

New Electronic Media and Cold War Consumer Culture

Coming on the heels of a decade of growth in Moscow and Soviet TV and, by extension, the early beginnings of a Soviet-style consumer society based in part on expanding mass media and technology, RAMAC proved a valuable asset for American public diplomacy both during and also after the exhibition. Data collected by RAMAC on questions chosen by Soviets was published in condensed book form and also used for a USIA cartoon feature on the American way of life. The VOA; Vice President Nixon; the Department of Agriculture; Department of Health, Education, and Welfare; and Department of Labor all used RAMAC data.[58] RAMAC answered over thirty-five thousand questions in a six-week period, far beyond the capacity of the approximately eighty USIA exhibition guides, and proved an influential exercise for enhancing the reach of public diplomacy and propaganda through information and communication technologies. Just as important, the data collected by RAMAC was a valuable window on Soviet curiosity.

A follow-up study on the 1959 exhibition conducted by the USIA in early 1960 compared 924 questions asked by visitors to RAMAC, to USIA exhibit guides, and to Americans traveling in the USSR during the exhibit. Taken as a whole, the questions represented "the best opportunity we have had to document the specific interests the Soviet public has in America."[59] Noting the paradox of a lack of Soviet interest in the philosophy of political freedom combined with a keen interest in knowing what the rest of the world thinks about the Soviet Union, the USIA concluded that the average Soviet citizen had a concern for identity, an interest in the newest developments in technology and culture, searched for knowledge pertaining to the living of everyday life, and wanted to be liked. Of these, how to best respond to the question concerning technology remained, in the eyes of the USIA, unresolved. Many attendees at the 1959 exhibit regretted there were not even more machines on display, and the USIA concluded that "the Soviet public's interest in American technology—however strong it may or may not be—is largely of a familiar and very untechnical kind. With the more esoteric forms of science and technology it is no more engrossed than its counterparts elsewhere. What it is primarily concerned with is technology as it affects the *consumer*."[60]

Realizing that virtually all science and technology questions were a result of RAMAC, the report drove home that Soviet popular interest in science was not in "abstract" science but in its applications. Given that RAMAC served as a sort of "source book" for questions concerning technology, RAMAC thus represented a range of "interests that could be satisfied by the more impersonal approach." Guides and travelers, on the other hand, often fielded the kinds of questions "on which the public wanted a direct reassurance of sincerity." In the terminology of Waldemar Nielsen, RAMAC was a technological manifestation of the indirect approach to public diplomacy. Although some questions remained unresolved on how to improve the quality of experiencing the direct American-Soviet dialogue, the quantitative output of that dialogue as represented by the 1959 Moscow Exhibition was staggering. No single event throughout the Cold War had heretofore provided so many communication opportunities. Ralph White believed an estimated count of "communication units" produced between Americans and Soviets during the exhibition was on the order of 30 to 40 million units and "probably represents a record of some kind in the history of international communication."[61]

Leslie Brady, in his final report on the exhibition, believed the real success of the exhibit was the transcending of old messages, strident in tone, and exchanged only through official propaganda outlets, into an interactive dialogue between the exhibition and the Soviet people. This new dialogue, "rather than the constant monologue which is Soviet propaganda," was highlighted by Nixon speeches, accomplished through human contacts with exhibition guides, strengthened by cultural contacts demonstrated in the displays, enhanced by exhibits of technology in action, and augmented by machine-based interactions with RAMAC.[62] Ithiel de Sola Pool ruminated after the exhibition that when the exhibit "portrayed the consumer goods available to the American people," this forced the Soviet hand into action despite the problematic implications of that action.

> The Soviet propagandists felt constrained to reply. Soviet citizens, they said, had the same things too and to underscore the point they opened their own exhibit of Soviet cars, TVs, housing, etc. at the entrance gate of the American exhibit. Thus, to compete in the propaganda field, the regime itself had to become a perhaps unwilling agent of liberalization . . . [most Westerners] may appreciate

that a democratic government can be hamstrung by public opinion, but may doubt that this applies also to the Kremlin. That view underestimates the role of public opinion in a totalitarian society. . . . The iron curtain is a porous one . . . public opinion is important in Russia . . . controls are not adequate to isolate Soviet thought from major concepts circulating the world or from major news events . . . the regime fails in its attempts to keep out interest in jazz, lipstick, TV, or French Impressionism.[63]

Thus, the RAMAC experience, the USIA exhibition, and a decade of monitoring Moscow TV all drove home for American policymakers the need for simultaneous human and machine contact with the Soviet peoples to reach out and, hopefully, sway public opinion in the Soviet world through a dialogue based in part on human interaction, in part on consumer aspirations, and in part on an emergent form of information diplomacy. In this way, the RAMAC experience, the emergence of a Soviet consumer society, and the growth of Moscow TV in the 1950s serve as precursors for the combination of television, new communication technologies such as satellites, emphasis on both daily life and world affairs, and a new dialogue on world citizenship that would soon become hallmarks of the Kennedy and Johnson presidencies.

7. "Something of That Sense of World Citizenship"

On April 14, 1961, as the CIA ratcheted up the Bay of Pigs invasion, cosmonaut Yuri Gagarin arrived at the Moscow airport to celebrate his pioneering outer space orbit of two days earlier. Television cameras beamed the celebration to millions of homes in the USSR and Eastern Europe. However, for the first time, live television transmissions crossed the Iron Curtain and relayed the Gagarin celebration on to the national television networks of Western Europe. The first live all-Europe telecast of the Cold War projected a triumphant Soviet space program.[1] Within a few months, Gagarin would visit London, lunch with Queen Elizabeth, and shake hands with Prime Minister Harold Macmillan. Within a fortnight, TV coverage of the Red Army's annual May Day parade in Moscow's Red Square was also telecast live across the Iron Curtain and throughout Europe. American television audiences saw coverage of the Gagarin celebration and May Day events a day or so later via videotape recordings and film newsreels shuttled by airplane across the Atlantic Ocean. Over a year before the first Telstar live transatlantic television satellite relay from the United States to Europe, live television from the USSR had penetrated the televisual manifestation of the Iron Curtain and reached television audiences across all of Europe, depicting Soviet space heroes and military prowess. Earlier warnings from a 1960 Sprague Committee report that "the linkage of the Soviet television system with Eurovision will create in the future a significant problem that has not existed in the past" had now become a reality.[2] Meanwhile, transatlantic television remained a tape-delayed, film-in-the-can, ocean-crossing experience devoid of live television programming and news coverage for European and American viewers. Live television programming from the United States to Europe and the world at large seemed to have as much trouble getting off the ground as did so many of the early American rockets and satellites of the space race.

Although live television coverage of Soviet space achievements to all of Europe was certainly a propaganda coup for the Soviets, the Soviets themselves were not solely responsible for this engineering feat. Rather, the engineering heroes—or culprits, depending on your point of view—resided at the BBC. The 1961 Soviet telecasts were the high point in a decade of BBC engineering accomplishments toward live all-Europe television, including the challenge of immediate conversion and subsequent network distribution of differing television technical standards. Live conversion had begun in a series of exchanges with France in 1952, and had reached over one thousand such programs yearly among Western European television networks by 1959, usually via Eurovision arrangements. In 1961, BBC, Finnish, and Soviet engineers tackled the difficult task of accomplishing a live hook-up between the TV towers in Helsinki and Tallinn.[3] In exchange for coverage of Gagarin and May Day, Soviet TV engineers cooperated in this project and also telecast a number of British programs across the Soviet TV network.[4] Describing these events to the New York chapter of the Academy of Television Arts and Sciences in October 1961, former BBC President Gerald Beadle told the Americans that in the case of the Gagarin and May Day telecasts

> of course, you saw them several hours late. The 3,000 miles of the Atlantic Ocean has so far proved to be an insuperable barrier to live television. The bridging of this gap is going to be the most important event of all in global television. . . . It will open up possibilities of tremendous value to my country and to yours. . . . We want to be able to see your great events in their entirety while they are in progress . . . there would be great political advantages to sharing such experiences . . . the absence of a live television link between us is a defect in our equipment which should be repaired at the earliest possible moment . . . [global television will] give us all something of that sense of world citizenship, without which the human race is surely doomed.[5]

In the twenty-first century, whether we are all surely doomed without something of that sense of world citizenship is a crucial question for global society, although the question is not always posed as starkly as Gerald Beadle did. In the context of October 1961—after the Bay of Pigs fiasco, the rise of the Berlin Wall that summer, American military buildup in Southeast Asia, an unproductive superpower summit, and the resumption of nuclear weapons testing—global observers such as Beadle had good reason to speak with such a stark rhetoric. Beadle, like some others in the 1960s, also began to speak about global communication—in this case, television—as a possible catalyst for mutual understanding and shared interests through a consensual global public opinion. For others in 1961 who were intensely concerned with global public opinion, such as the USIA, the impact of Soviet space and military achievements broadcast live on television screens across Europe represented a disaster for the global image of America. From the perspective of USIA public opinion polling on global leadership in outer space, it was not a sense of world citizenship but rather the global image of America that was surely doomed.

Looking back at the superpower space race, global prestige, and the summer of 1961, one is hard pressed to find a moment between 1946 and 1969 when overseas public opinion was worse for American interests.[6] In fact, the one time throughout the 1960s when public opinion of the American space program appeared even worse than that in the summer of 1961 was in August 1962, soon after the USSR first sent two humans into outer space in the same space vehicle. The zenith of American prestige to date came in July 1962 with the launch of Telstar. Sputnik had established a trend. The Eisenhower-era Sprague Committee, analyzing global public opinion about American science in the late 1950s, had earlier unearthed this British schoolboy ditty during its research:

> Catch a falling Sputnik,
> Put it in a basket,
> Send it to the USA.
> They'll be glad to have it,
> Very glad to have it,
> And never let it get away.[7]

Witty juvenile doggerel such as this did, alas, represent majority attitudes across the United Kingdom. The first time a majority of Britons would place the United States ahead in the space race was five years away, during the middle phase of the Gemini project circa January 1966. The comfort of historical hindsight tempts trivializing these concerns regarding the global image of America in science, technology, and space achievements during the summer of 1961, but a preponderance of public opinion, global images, and stark rhetoric throughout 1961 bode ill from an American Cold War perspective. Now the Soviets had a live television feed into Western Europe, courtesy of British engineering knowledge. Furthermore, Soviet and Eastern European television had a working relationship for live television program exchanges across Europe with the BBC, the world's most venerable broadcast institution and a paragon of global audience trust and credibility. For Americans interested in globalizing American television, never had the oceans been so vast; one might as well dream of finding a technology to conquer the heavens above rather than try and cross the Atlantic Ocean via microwave relays with a live TV signal.

When all was done that is exactly what happened: American television used satellites and brought liveness to the heavens well before live American television regularly crossed the oceans via microwave links, undersea cables, or fiber optics. However, knowing American television conquered outer space is one thing. How American television turned to the satellite as a technological path, what other electronic communication networking technologies were explored, and what it all meant for the global image of America, for global electronic communication networks, and for promoting something of that sense of world citizenship in the 1960s are questions worth exploring in detail.

Satellites and the Search for Secure Global Electronic Communications

Despite a growing awareness of the potential of communication satellites among more and more individuals starting around 1955, detailed knowledge about satellites was a rather closely held secret prior to the mid-1950s. Indeed, virtually all of the individuals, including prominent U.S. Senators, deeply involved in the failed global microwave TV network project of the 1950s have few satellite-related materials in their manuscript collections prior to the Sputnik launch. This compartmentalized world of knowledge and delayed awareness regarding satellites may have been a factor in allowing the microwave group to go as far as they did along that technological path.

Given this context, the early emergence of a discreet dialogue about communication satellites and American foreign policy confined in such areas as the military, the intelligence community, the executive branch, and the NSC is predictable. Questions about satellites had roots in dialogues stemming from the Second World War about ballistic missiles and about photoreconnaissance. Within days of the formal surrender of Japan in 1945, the OSS finished a report on global intelligence and photoreconnaissance that called for the first global photomapping project by the United States.[8] This report recommended photomapping based on future potential hostilities involving a major land and sea power within the next five years. The OSS envisioned a one-time plan of photomapping followed up by using human intelligence assets on a regular returning basis to targeted areas for updates; routine HUMINT would follow one-time PHOTOINT.

Even though the OSS global photomapping project indicates early strategic thinking about postwar global photo surveillance, its problems included a dependence on HUMINT as a follow-up and a lack of continuous PHOTOINT over time. The RAND Corporation; the air force; and other defense, intelligence, and military agencies, both public and private, first reported on satellites as a possible technology for reconnaissance in 1946. A decade of research led to two major developments: the formal inauguration of a highly classified design and development project between the air force and Lockheed Missiles and Space Company that would eventually result in the Corona photoreconnaissance satellite system, and the very public announcements that satellites for science would be a part of the upcoming IGY.[9]

Public predictions at this time included a prominent role for satellites and television, but omitted the details on how this might be accomplished. One book written for a general audience forecast jet airliners with in-flight television. Television viewers were promised a future of direct-to-home satellite reception from all over the world.[10] Furthermore, satellites would someday mean worldwide audiences receiving a "message transmitted economically, instantaneously and simultaneously." This meant that someday satellites would bring the message of freedom to the entire planet: "How would an enslaved people react if day after day they were to see the goods and services being offered and bought by the world's free people—the automobiles, refrigerators, clothes, food, and furniture? . . . What would be the effect if through television these people visited American factories, Scandinavian homes, German fairs, and French resorts—if they saw the roads and schools and theaters and farmlands—and the Easter parade on New York's Fifth Avenue, and on London's Bond Street? If they saw the free world?"[11] These passages demonstrate an articulation of satellites, space research, and the "science = freedom" formula emergent in American global policy discourse at this phase of the Cold War. Bringing this message to Cold War audiences included such events as the Space Unlimited exhibit mounted by the United States at the September 1956 Berlin Fair.[12] Survey research conducted on attendees found that a majority of exhibit viewers believed that space research was a positive, peaceful activity and that the United States shared scientific knowledge gained through space research with the rest of the world. Exhibit reports do not mention whether any attendees recognized the recycling of German World War II rocket research and development in the American Cold War space program.

Beyond examples such as the 1956 Space Unlimited exhibit, the overarching public information regarding space, satellites, and science during this period was the IGY, which operationalized international scientific research and cooperation for space and satellite research, oceanic research, geodetics, atmospheric and solar research, and polar research. Sputniks 1 and 2 were launched during the IGY, and after some early failures, the United States successfully launched[13] its first satellite, Explorer 1, in January 1958 and launched three more satellites in 1958 as a part of the IGY. The fifth U.S. satellite in 1958, Project SCORE, was not part of IGY but rather a direct address regarding the global image of America.

Project SCORE, launched December 18 as an Advanced Research Projects Agency (ARPA)[14] project in conjunction with the air force, specifically demonstrated the potential of communication satellites to the world. SCORE was an acronym for Signal Communications Orbital Relay Experiment and was the world's first broadcast satellite. SCORE carried modified radio transmitting, recording, and receiving equipment as well as a radio beacon and transmitted a prerecorded message from President Eisenhower: "This is the President of the United States speaking. Through the marvels of scientific advance, my voice is coming to you from a satellite circling in outer space. My message is a simple one. Through this unique means I convey to you and all mankind America's wish for peace on Earth and goodwill toward men everywhere."[15] SCORE did not merely orbit a satellite after a series of discarded rocket stages, but placed an entire Atlas missile into orbit. The total weight placed in orbit (payload) tripled the weight of the recent Sputnik 3 and thus set a new mark in what Paul Dickson has called the "Cold War weight-lifting contest."[16] Although SCORE had been programmed to send its messages in Russian, French, Chinese, and Spanish as well as English, the NSC decided against using languages other than English.[17]

The American formula of linking space-based telecommunications with missile strength reached another zenith at this time. Experiments investigated the possibility of temporarily creating an atmospheric zone—usually somewhere in the troposphere or ionosphere—to serve as a passive reflector for telecommunications signals. The most spectacular, and reckless, of these trials were among several experiments folded into a series of nuclear weapons tests, ranging in altitude from twenty-five to three hundred fifty miles, over the Pacific Ocean.[18] The signal communications component of these weapons tests (code named Teak, Orange, and Argus) tried to temporarily increase the reflectivity of the ionosphere to make possible, for example, beaming RADAR signals into remote regions of the USSR. Presumably, this heightened reflectivity could also be used for transoceanic signal relay. Atmospheric reflectivity could also be augmented by releasing a metallic cloud of small metal fragments (usually copper) into an upper atmospheric layer. This particular application, code-named West Ford,[19] also boosted upper atmospheric reflectivity to improve transoceanic telecommunications.

By twenty-first-century standards these temporary conditions enhancing transoceanic communications may seem fruitless, but full-time round-the-clock wireless transoceanic communications were still not reliable services even in standard shortwave-based transoceanic telephone services through much of the 1950s.[20] So telecommunications engineers and scientists research-ing applications for enhancing global and transoceanic wireless communica-tions in this period would not have necessarily demanded that their research only produce systems with round-the-clock reliability but rather would have looked for a wide range of possible enhancements to the global telecom-munications systems of their own era.[21] West Ford experiments by the air force continued into May 1963, beyond the initial success of Telstar and other communications satellites.[22] These West Ford experiments centered on ques-tions of global defense communications capabilities and not on commercial or non-defense-related government global communications. The Kennedy administration had throughout 1961 and 1962 abolished the Eisenhower-era OCB,[23] reorganized telecommunications management at the executive level,[24] established a task group to develop plans for survivable communications re-quirements in the event of general hostilities,[25] and gone through the Cuban Missile Crisis with serious strategic communication challenges. On October 25, 1962, McGeorge Bundy and Robert McNamara convened a National Com-munications Systems Working Group tasked with improving communica-tions between the United States and Latin America. The group learned that strategic and military communications were its "highest urgency" and that the intelligence agencies[26] had already recommended increasing circuitry between the United States and Panama, exploring "the crash installation of a tropospheric scatter system" in the region.[27] The National Communications Systems Working Group coalesced into the NSC Subcommittee on Commu-nications, which reported in May 1963 (soon after a West Ford test) "marked improvement" in communications with Latin America, where electronic communications problems had previously "loomed so large" in the Cuban Missile Crisis. Now, round-the-clock survivable and restorable electronic communications were in place for hemispheric security, and "slower, but measurable progress has been witnessed in the construction of the European and Trans-Mediterranean tropospheric scatter systems, as well as in com-munications improvements in other areas of the world."[28]

In retrospect, SCORE, Teak, Orange, Argus, and West Ford along with NSC committees, White House telecommunications reorganization, communica-tions survivability, tropospheric scatter systems, and the Cuban Missile Crisis suggest that, despite the increasing success of satellites as a communications resource, the quest to develop a wide range of feasible American technologies of global strategic communication begun in the early 1950s by systems such as Ultrafax, Stratovision, and the UNITEL global microwave network did not come to a quick end after the first successful satellite launches. Looking back at both the strategic tensions of the Cold War and the rapid developments in global communications technologies over the late 1950s and early 1960s, and remembering that satellites were as yet an unproven technology for providing round-the-clock global communications and being cognizant that as of mid-1963 absolutely no treaties existed that directly or indirectly protected orbiting satellites[29]—which meant that communication satellite assets in space could be attacked in times of war—the American strategy of pursuing any and all feasible technologies for strategic global telecommunications becomes more understandable. These pursuits of global telecommunications technologies in the 1950s and 1960s were yet another extraterritorial arena for superpower contestation.

Strategic and defense communication issues were not the only global communication concern of the Kennedy administration. Global television also drew attention, and in the waning months before Telstar, the Kennedy administration pursued with the USSR the possibility of an exchange of television programs between the two nations, with Kennedy and Khrushchev speaking on the TV networks of each other's nation. U.S. Ambassador to Moscow Llewellyn Thompson suggested disarmament as a general topic for a Kennedy telecast, believing that the average Soviet citizen would be reached not only on the basis of peace, but also on the possibility that mutual disarmament could lead to increased spending on consumer goods within the USSR.[30] George Kennan, also asked to comment, found recommendations difficult without first knowing the focus, purpose, and length of the telecast, but thought it was not a "suitable occasion for direct personal solemnizing with Khrushchev" and instead suggested "skillful indirection" against the work of Soviet propagandists. Kennan also indirectly suggested disarmament comments and put an emphasis on the need for mutual inspection of weapons. He closed on a personal note suggesting a new, global theme:

> I have personally long wished to see our government espouse [the] principle that all matters affecting physically [the] lives and interests of [the] world population as a whole, as for example use [of] outer space, development [of] Antarctica, protection [of] purity and resources of oceans, atmospheric purity, [the] preservation of migratory wild life, etc., ought eventually to be [the] subject not . . . just of coordination [of] national efforts but rather of direct administration by international authority with real power to decide and act . . . [if the] President could invoke this particular concept as [a] goal [of] US Policy, something of comparably broad nature . . . [this] would make [the] best possible central

point . . . with [a] view to taking [the] attention of [the] listening public off
sterile and shopworn polemics of [the] Cold War and directing it to a hopeful,
constructive, and arresting objective.[31]

This advice from Kennan demonstrates that the politico-discursive transformation from security to globalization discussed earlier in this study is
apparent beyond the nurturing environments of the Ford Foundation and
other philanthropic enterprises concerned with global television and the
Cold War. Rather than only advocate a static security discourse, Kennan
also argued to open up a new rhetorical and theoretical line for international
relations, offering up a cornucopia of extraterritorial spaces and places for
superpower reconsideration as sites of current tension and future resolution:
environmental issues, Antarctica, and outer space. This new line of thought
echoed Gerald Beadle and his call to promote "something of that sense of
world citizenship." Although for various reasons—mainly the resumption
of nuclear weapons tests[32]—the planned superpower TV exchange never
came to pass, policymakers and intellectuals showed signs of rethinking the
basic values and beliefs of superpower rhetoric, global public opinion, and
Cold War propaganda just as television was becoming a global phenomena
in practice as well as in theory. Postwar growth of consumer culture, international science such as the IGY, Antarctica, natural resources, outer space,
atomic weapons testing, and mutually assured destruction all, in their own
way, represented extraterritorialities that signified world citizenship. Perhaps
global television also belonged, or could be placed, on that list of signifiers.

Any applications of global television in the early 1960s would have to
be mediated, or filtered, through the various national television networks
of the world. For satellite relay, this meant arrangements and agreements
with national networks, whether public or private, to accept and receive
live satellite feeds that they would then retransmit to viewers over their own
domestic terrestrial networks. So in effect, what people such as Beadle and
Kennan probably imagined was global program themes distributed over
national television networks. One American TV success story in this regard
had already been achieved prior to satellite distribution: *A Tour of the White
House With Mrs. John F. Kennedy* was widely circulated by the USIA, and
over a dozen nations broadcast the tour on their own national networks in
1962, including Japan, Australia, the United Kingdom, Switzerland, Sweden,
New Zealand, Finland, and Norway.[33] Capitalizing on the world popularity
of the glamorous first lady, this was, nevertheless, not an example of live
international TV program distribution. Similarly, the orbital flight of astronaut John Glenn on February 20, 1962, was watched live by 40 million TV

homes in the United States, but coverage of the Glenn flight on overseas TV sets in Europe and elsewhere had to be done by tape and film relay across the Atlantic and Pacific oceans.[34]

In the weeks preceding the Telstar launch and tests of July 10 and 11, 1962, the potential implications of global television for American interests were analyzed in detail by Tedson Meyers, then an assistant to FCC Chairman Newton Minow.[35] Meyers warned to "prepare now for the imminent era of global mass communication through international television and radio broadcasting," arguing the moment was propitious for the United States to "begin to exploit the power of international television and radio broadcasting in our own national interest."[36] Recognizing the paradox that global television would in fact be accomplished through distribution to national television networks, Meyers forecast the distinction of global television, unlike radio with the possibility of direct shortwave reception, would be the need for television programs to be placed, by agreement, on to the national network of a given nation: a "central authority will be in a position to decide whether or not a television broadcast will be able to reach individual listeners."[37] Global television would "open a new era of massive and immediate contact among all peoples," where "a single broadcast will touch the minds of millions. Whatever these millions will see or hear can teach or distort, enrich or debase, preserve peace or stir to war." This would raise the power of broadcasting in international affairs, and mean that any nation "with the imagination and money, technical resources and the will, can exploit international broadcasting as an unparalleled instrument in the achievement of its international objectives." Seeing that global television distribution through national networks would also stimulate domestic media growth in many participating nations, Meyers argued that television broadcasting needed to be fostered where it did not yet exist and that program exchange with the United States needed to be expanded where television broadcasting had already found a domestic footing.[38]

Meyers also discussed educational possibilities, television growth in Europe, and the recent round of Soviet and Eastern European TV activities, hinting that the United States had failed to keep pace with recent developments in international television. He found inactivity in Latin America particularly damning and compared American neglect in its own backyard with recent Soviet activity in Europe, pointing to, among other examples, the failure in the 1950s to develop the South American portion of the UNITEL global microwave relay network. Meyers saw the globalization of American television and electronic communications as overly cautious and aimed only at the most lucrative trade routes, chiding, "our efforts have been concentrated along the more traditional routes of international communication, across the North Atlantic. If television linkage had already existed in the Western Hemisphere, its usefulness in helping to launch the Alliance for Progress would have been obvious." Meyers rejected this narrow vision, warning that in "1961, international broadcasts of the Gagarin and Titov receptions, and of the May Day celebration, emanated from Moscow, were carried live to viewers throughout Europe, and marked the beginning of live international television broadcasting from the Soviet Union."[39] Closing with the observation that "mankind's saving grace may be that our technological capacity for mass communication has kept pace with our mastery of the means of mass destruction," Meyers concluded "at this moment in history, keeping pace is not enough" and that the "rewards of mass communication must overtake and extinguish the threat of mass destruction" in the future.[40]

The imminent saving grace of mass communication was about to go celestial, courtesy of AT&T: on July 10 and 11, 1962, Telstar, the first privately funded commercial satellite, launched, reached orbit, and successfully began an array of high-publicity global communications experiments and demonstrations. During a nationwide TV program about Telstar, a telephone call relayed via Telstar from AT&T Chairman Frederick Kappel in Andover, Maine, reached Vice President Lyndon Johnson in Washington, D.C., who reported Kappel's voice was "coming through nicely." The TV program also showed prominent senators commenting on Telstar, as well as Telstar breakthroughs including the first facsimile from a satellite, data transmission via satellite, and news that a TV signal showing the image of the American flag had been received at an earth station in France. In Andover, FCC Chairman Newton Minow forecast Telstar and communication satellites would improve the flow of global communication and would serve as an antidote to global conflict.[41] Television coverage of a Kennedy presidential press conference was relayed live across the Atlantic. Despite an orbit that only allowed for very limited periods of transatlantic relay, Telstar proved incredibly popular as a global marvel of American science, spawning a multitude of newspaper articles, outpourings of mail, and a hit song by the British rock group the Tornadoes, later covered on an American label by the Ventures.

From Italy, Joseph Colella, a University of Rochester medical student studying in Florence, wrote the president on July 26 that a recent America-Europe Telstar relay was "received with great enthusiasm here, as people hurried home from work or gathered in neighborhood cafes so as not to miss any of the long-awaited program." Colella told Kennedy that viewers "were often heard to exclaim or sigh at views of the Statue of Liberty, the World's Fair, and Niagara Falls," and flattered the president that his own "image was received with many smiles and a good deal of conversation as parents explained who you were to their youngsters." Remembering in the days after the Telstar relay "America was on the lips of everyone with whom I spoke," Colella believed Telstar promoted a greater degree of global intimacy and closed with confirming that Telstar had "done a great deal to stimulate thoughts and ideas about America, making the world more receptive to exchanges of opinion on a personal basis."[42]

Vice President Lyndon Johnson, as head of the Space Council, also received numerous congratulatory messages from Americans excited about Telstar. Albert Price of Philadelphia proclaimed worldwide television was now a reality. The Van Broock family of Scranton, Pennsylvania, sent an elaborate greeting card with the handwritten missive that Telstar will broadcast live television all over the universe. C. G. Wykoff of New York City, writing on July 12, reported he saw the vice president on television the night before and thought "being Vice President has agreed with you very much indeed. You looked wonderful." He added Telstar was a stunning "piece of public relations" that Khrushchev could not, for once, claim the Russians had invented. The private ownership of Telstar was not lost on some correspondents. Writing in black crayon from Hollywood, Florida, A. Arthur Gardner, a self-proclaimed "lobbyist for the people," asked Johnson to make sure that AT&T did not extend its current world monopoly to a monopoly of the entire universe. M. M. "Pop" Myers, the district governor of the Downtown Lions Club of Dallas, assured the vice president that the Lions of Dallas were behind him all the way, exclaiming, "the 200 members of the Downtown Lions Club of Dallas at noon today voted to wire you to influence the Senate, as only you can, to allow Telstar to remain under private enterprise with government supervision." Elizabeth Rogers of Hyde Park, Mississippi, summed it all up with this succinct message: "You, the space people, and the Telephone Company are certainly to be congratulated for making this possible."[43] Finally, British public opinion of the American space program in the wake of Telstar during July 1962 reached the highest approval ratings ever given by British samples—still slightly behind the USSR, but nearly even—and an approval rating that would be equaled only by Ranger moon probes in 1964 and finally surpassed by various Gemini space missions in 1965.[44]

What only a select number of high-ranking American military, intelligence, and executive branch officials knew (along with a few observant scientists) was that the saving grace of mass communications represented by Telstar was nearly done in by the increasing mastery of the means for mass destruction. On July 9, 1962, Project Starfish Prime, part of a series of American high-altitude nuclear tests known as Operation Fishbowl, had successfully detonated a 1.45 megaton explosion about 400 kilometers above Johnson

Island in the Pacific Ocean. Starfish Prime introduced significant radiation into the upper atmospheric layers that eventually reached the Van Allen belts (and temporarily increased the radioactive levels of the Van Allen belts), while also creating an electromagnetic pulse (EMP) that disrupted power across the Pacific from Hawaii to New Zealand. This was the first of several Fishbowl high-altitude nuclear explosions that conclusively proved, by the end of 1962, that high-altitude nuclear explosions were a very effective antisatellite weapon: the explosions, EMP, and radiation seriously damaged satellite circuitry and reduced the operating life of satellites.[45] Telstar's relay circuitry, damaged by Starfish Prime, first failed in August 1962, and though engineers staved off total failure for several months, Starfish Prime had on its virgin orbit exposed Telstar to more radiation than had been expected for the entire life of the satellite. Telstar—what Tedson Meyers would have undoubtedly considered a saving grace of global communication, what Gerald Beadle may well have labeled a technology to promote something of that sense of world citizenship—was also a casualty of the weapons of mass destruction, its shelf life shortened by excessive radiation in its orbital regions of the upper atmosphere.[46] So the greatest American device yet developed for global communication fell victim to the greatest American device yet developed for global destruction.

A second model of the Telstar series of satellites (several Telstars had been manufactured by AT&T) was subsequently launched and live transatlantic television continued beyond the shortened shelf life of the original Telstar, but the threat of high-altitude nuclear testing to satellite technologies was becoming better known in the international scientific community. Allouette, the first Canadian satellite—and a satellite designed to specifically measure the topside ionogram, or measures of the highest level of the ionosphere (important for distinguishing between things such as aurora borealis flares and incoming missiles in NORAD radar readings, for example)—launched in September 1962 after undergoing extensive engineering tests for reliability.[47] At least seven of the twenty-one known LEO (low-earth orbit) satellites in orbit during Starfish Prime suffered damage from the blast and radioactivity.[48] High-altitude nuclear testing presented long-term problems for satellite growth, particularly at this moment in satellite development. Even though it was possible to build or "harden" satellites with sufficient shielding to give greater protection against radioactive contamination, this was still an era when questions of maximum orbital payload, or weight, of satellites was a significant challenge, and shielding added considerable weight to the orbital payload. Photo surveillance satellites of this era, such as Corona, returned canisters of exposed film to Earth, rather than relay electronic images to Earth, and film was also susceptible to radiation damage.[49] So both superpowers, now deploying their first round of elaborate space reconnaissance systems, had good reasons for concern over high-altitude nuclear testing and subsequent radioactive fallout lingering in the upper regions of the atmosphere, troposphere, and ionosphere risking their emergent technical intelligence systems.

Additional high-altitude nonatomic experiments, particularly West Ford, also received new scrutiny late in 1962 and early in 1963. In May 1963, the USSR filed a written protest with the UN titled "Dangerous United States Activities in Outer Space."[50] Claiming West Ford was a danger undertaken without consulting the international scientific community (and throwing in for good measure charges that the United States failed to properly register orbiting objects under the guidelines of General Assembly Resolution 1721), the Soviets also denounced American high-altitude nuclear tests. Secretary of State Dean Rusk pointed out that the Soviets had been less than forthcoming on their own high-altitude nuclear tests and presented a list of Soviet-orbited objects that also had not been registered with the UN. Regarding West Ford, Rusk acknowledged that the first West Ford launch in October 1961 of 75 pounds of copper dipoles suspended in naphthalene had not properly formed an orbital ring but "rather remained in five or six small clumps." The May 1963 West Ford deployment did successfully form a copper dipole–naphthalene orbital ring that increased in size over time and was expected to last a maximum of three years. Finally, the second West Ford launch had been prepared in consultation with an international team of science advisers. However, these kinds of heated exchanges between the superpowers over high-altitude nuclear testing, cutting-edge global telecommunications experiments, and outer space policy were about to take their first concrete step toward toning down the bellicose rhetoric.

The radiation risk to satellites ended for the Cold War period[51] in October 1963 with the Limited Test Ban Treaty. A genuine milestone in disarmament, the treaty also protected satellites, indeed implicitly depended on satellites for mutual verification of treaty enforcement. The seesawing technological tensions between the warlike technologies of mass destruction and the peaceful technologies of world citizenship are again evident in the background of this treaty, with the peaceful technologies of world citizenship gaining the advantage in this case. The treaty also implied (but does not specifically state) that outer space was a zone of disarmament and a zone deterritorialized, by prohibiting "radioactive debris to be present outside the territorial limits of the State."[52] This hint at deterritorialization, or desovereignization, of outer space was yet another potential signifier of world citizenship and represented a resolution of extraterritorial tensions.

In the era of space satellites before the 1963 treaty, the coincident timing of the Telstar launch and the Starfish Prime test raises a number of questions. For one, the scheduling of these atomic weapons tests was not a complete secret. Cecil Coale, who ran magnetometer tests on Canton Island for the U.S. military as part of the Fishbowl test series, recalls that

> the Hawaiian news media touted this high altitude nuclear test series as the "rainbow bombs" because of the spectacular auroral displays that had been visible from Hawaii. On the night of July 9, 1962 when Starfish Prime was scheduled, the hotels in Hawaii offered roof top bomb watching parties. It seemed that everyone in the Pacific hemisphere was watching the sky . . . a brilliant white flash erased the darkness like a photoflash. Then the entire sky turned light green for about a second. In several more seconds, a deep red aurora, several moon diameters in size, formed where the blast had been. A white plasma jet came slowly out of the top of the red aurora [over Johnston Island] and painted a white stripe across the sky from north to south in about one minute. A deep red aurora appeared over Samoa at the south end of the white plasma jet. This visual display lasted for perhaps ten minutes before slowly fading. There was no sound at all.[53]

To say that most AT&T engineers, global telecommunications specialists, additional members of the scientific community, and other interested observers were shocked by the coincident deployment of Telstar and Starfish Prime would be an accurate statement, because only a select few individuals knew that Telstar, despite all of the publicity before, during, and after launch, was in fact both a communications satellite and also a scientific research satellite. Although virtually everyone now remembers Telstar as a communications satellite, Telstar was also designed for one specific scientific application beyond its formidable communications capabilities: the measurement of radiation levels in the upper atmosphere. AT&T engineer James Early recalls being tasked to "design and test radiation-resistant high-efficiency solar cells" as part of Telstar development, including a potentially lethal test involving exposure of the radiation-resistant solar cells to strontium 90 at a level of 1 million curies that, if unshielded, would deliver a fatal dose to a human up to 100 feet away in 10 to 15 seconds exposure time.[54] Existence of the Van Allen belts and other space radiation fields around the planet was already known, and Early assumed the radiation testing and manufacture for radiation resistance was part of planning for long-duration orbit in the face of these known natural space phenomena.[55] AT&T engineer A. C. Dickieson, Telstar project manager, believed that problems in the Telstar command channel (used by AT&T to send command functions to Telstar) were directly attributable to increased radiation levels in the Van Allen belts from Starfish

Prime. The only person he knew of from AT&T who had prior knowledge of the Starfish Prime test was Walter Brown, who managed the Telstar-based space radiation tests.[56]

The National Space Science Data Center (NSSDC), a subagency of NASA, describes Telstar as "primarily a communications satellite" with an electronics package for "an experiment designed to measure the energetic proton and electron distribution in the Van Allen belts."[57] The NSSDC lists Walter Brown of AT&T as the principal investigator and identifies the subdiscipline as "Space Physics: Magnetospheric Studies," suggesting Telstar may have been designed to provide a parallel outer space measurement along with the land-based magnetometric work of Cecil Coale and others on Canton Island and additional South Pacific islands. Curiously, the replacement Telstar 2 satellite, launched in May 1963, was nearly identical to the first Telstar, except Telstar 2 had radiation-resistant command system transistors and had a higher apogee in order to spend less orbit time in the Van Allen belts.[58] The Telstar series were not geosynchronous satellites (geosynchronous describes an orbit approximately 36,000 kilometers above the equator, which provides fixed, round-the-clock satellite coverage over a given landmass) but rather relay satellites that had a low perigee over the Atlantic and a high apogee over the Pacific, usable for transatlantic signal exchange for about 25 to 40 minutes of each orbital pass at (and near) perigee over the Atlantic. The data below summarizes the temporality of the Telstar launch and the Starfish Prime detonation:

Starfish Prime Moment of Detonation

Local time (Honolulu observation, same time zone as Johnston Island): 23:00
   (11:00 P.M.) July 8, 1962
Zulu time (GMT): 09:00:00 July 9, 1962

Telstar Moment of Launch

Local time (Cape Canaveral, Fla.): 3:35 A.M. July 10, 1962
Zulu time (GMT): 08:35:00 July 10, 1962

Telstar Duration of Orbit and Trajectory

Duration of one Telstar orbit, in minutes: 157.8 minutes
Direction of Telstar launch into orbit: east
Longitudinal separation between Cape Canaveral and Johnston Island when
   traveling east to west: ~ 270 degrees or almost exactly 75% of a Telstar orbit
Cape Canaveral = 80.54°W, Johnston Island = 169.52°W
Minutes after Starfish Prime until Telstar reaches its first orbital pass directly
   above the longitude of Johnston Island ≈ *93 minutes* (157.8 × .75 = 118.35 −
   25 ≈ 93)[59]

In addition to the radiation from Starfish Prime, Telstar and other satellites in orbit faced radiation from a number of other U.S. atomic bomb tests,
most of them airdrops. From June 9, 1962, to August 9, 1962, or from the
month before through the month after Telstar's launch, the United States
conducted thirteen additional atomic tests in the South Pacific for a total
yield (including the Starfish Prime test) of approximately 19.3 megatons.[60]
During the entire so-called broken moratorium aboveground atomic testing
period from September 1, 1961, to December 25, 1962, the USSR conducted
148 atmospheric tests, the United States 35 atmospheric tests, and France 4
atmospheric tests for a total of 187 aboveground tests. Most of these were
from towers or airdrops, but both the United States and USSR also conducted
high-altitude tests. Within the same period as the broken moratorium, the
superpowers conducted a total of 125 known satellite and manned space
missions (including failures).[61]

Atmospheric Nuclear Tests

USSR 148
United States 35
France 4
Total = 187

Satellites and Manned Missions

USSR 26
United States 87
United Kingdom 1
Canada 1
Total known missions (including failures) = 125
At least 43 of the above 125 space missions directly related to U.S.
  PHOTOINT, SIGINT, and similar defense-security uses.

All of this aboveground atomic weapons testing, particularly high-altitude
testing, increased levels of radioactivity in outer space. Of all various belts
of outer space radioactivity in near-earth proximity, the greatest problem
was posed by the South Atlantic Anomaly. Positioned approximately 200
miles above an area roughly bounded by −90° to +40° longitude and −50°
to 0° latitude,[62] the South Atlantic Anomaly is an irregular feature in the
relationship between the magnetic terrestrial field of the earth and the Van
Allen belts. Basically, the South Atlantic Anomaly is an area where the Van
Allen and similar radiation belts come much closer to the earth's surface
than anywhere else on the planet and cause significant increases of radiation
exposure to spacecraft when orbiting within the South Atlantic Anomaly.

Like the entirety of the Van Allen belts, the intensity of radiation in the South Atlantic Anomaly measurably increased as a result of Starfish Prime and other aboveground atomic tests and slowly decreased its radiation levels from the Starfish Prime and other blasts only over a period of several years.

The South Atlantic Anomaly may seem relatively benign, as it does no known harm to Earth's inhabitants, its proximity over the earth partially coincides with an ocean, and it is possible to route manned space missions in ways to minimize the risk of exposure. However, the skies above that sparsely populated area of the South Atlantic Ocean are in fact a prime "highway" of sorts for certain satellites, particularly those in polar, and in sun-synchronous, orbits. All three of the U.S. Mercury manned missions that took place during the broken moratorium period (Glenn, Carpenter, Schirra) had orbital paths passing through, or traversing, the South Atlantic Anomaly. The South Atlantic Anomaly remains a space hazard to this day, as shuttle missions and similar manned missions take the phenomena into account, and communication satellites are often programmed to shut down a number of functions as they pass through the South Atlantic Anomaly. The skies of the South Atlantic Anomaly were accessed by many satellite orbits prior to 1963. Sputnik 1 orbited through the South Atlantic Anomaly in October 1957. A sampling of Sputniks 1, 4, and 6, plus the John Glenn Mercury mission orbital flight paths, suggests that it was routine, if not required due to limited capabilities in the early era of satellites and manned missions, to at some point in the orbital flight plan traverse the South Atlantic Anomaly.[63]

In addition to manned missions, science missions, and communications applications, the South Atlantic Anomaly is also a significant factor in surveillance satellites, particularly those in polar, and in sun-synchronous, orbits (as many are). In the early 1960s, polar orbits and sun-synchronous orbits were the crucial orbits used for photoreconnaissance satellites by the superpowers. Polar orbits were used by the superpowers for satellite PHOTOINT mapping of each other, particularly U.S. PHOTOINT of the USSR. This was routinely accomplished through north-south, or polar, orbits yielding long photographic datasets of the USSR landmass on north-south axes. To analyze infrastructural changes with PHOTOINT, more accurately measure the scale of objects under surveillance, and generally produce more comparable photographic datasets, PHOTOINT satellites often have both polar orbits and sun-synchronous orbits. The latter orbits are timed to place the satellite above the target at the same relative solar or "daylight" time each day, thus producing consistent shadow lengths of photographed objects (which are a key to measurement of land and surface sea-based objects via PHOTOINT). Sun-synchronous orbits are also polar-influenced and often traverse the South Atlantic Anomaly.

Yet another factor for superpower satellite PHOTOINT, particularly U.S. PHOTOINT of the USSR, was the geospatial relationship between the South Atlantic Anomaly and the USSR landmass. To conduct satellite PHOTOINT over the USSR via polar and sun-synchronous orbits, the United States had to use flight plans that routinely traversed the South Atlantic Anomaly. Among the surveillance targets in the USSR in orbits coinciding with the South Atlantic Anomaly were the USSR-Finland border, Murmansk, Leningrad, the Ukraine, Magnitogorsk, Sverdlosk, virtually the entire northern half of Siberia, the Kamchatka peninsula, and the Bering Straits. In other words, nearly half of the landmass of the USSR coincided with polar and sun-synchronous U.S. PHOTOINT satellite orbits traversing the South Atlantic Anomaly. Therefore, in the early era of satellites and manned missions, it was basically inconceivable to orbit objects without traversing the South Atlantic Anomaly. Increasing radiation levels in the South Atlantic Anomaly as a by-product of aboveground and high-altitude atomic testing posed serious risks to space travel, communications satellites, and most of all satellite surveillance of the USSR by the United States. Because surveillance imperatives had now become both global and continuous for the indeterminate strategic future of the United States, and surveillance satellites were a vital component of the growing arsenal of global surveillance, the South Atlantic Anomaly and the Van Allen belts needed to be protected from excessive levels of radioactivity. Thus, both superpowers had mutual strategic defense interests in the Limited Test Ban Treaty of 1963: the treaty was vital for preventing excessive space radiation to ensure the future growth of space-based surveillance.

Aboveground and high-altitude atomic testing prior to the Limited Test Ban Treaty of 1963 did more than create EMPs, entertain Hawaiian tourists, visually overwhelm atomic veterans, stoke the fires of disarmament protestors, and disrupt Telstar and communication satellites: testing also increased radiation levels in the Van Allen belts and especially in the South Atlantic Anomaly. The Telstar–Starfish Prime experience hints that atomic weapons testing risked the long-term security and espionage applications of satellite technology just as both superpowers were beginning to fully deploy PHOTOINT and SIGINT satellite reconnaissance systems at global scales. At particular risk were certain satellite orbit patterns, such as polar orbits and sun-synchronous orbits, orbits and flight paths absolutely crucial for strategic security. Testing also risked future access to the geosynchronous orbit—the prime orbit for communications and the only orbit where a satellite remains fixed above its relative point on earth, allowing for round-the-clock transmission and reception without satellite switching—by threatening to so overly irradiate the Van Allen belts as to make it impossible for a functional satellite to successfully pass through that area undamaged on its way to achieve access to the geosynchronous orbit. Given the brief history of satellite orbits and space science up to the Starfish Prime test and subsequent radiation increases of July 1962, denial of access to the area of outer space encompassed by the Van Allen belts and the South Atlantic Anomaly was most likely unthinkable to the superpowers, for there was little, if any, experience in satellite orbits that did *not* involve access to the area of the South Atlantic Anomaly. Thus, it is likely that space reconnaissance circa 1962 without orbital access to the South Atlantic Anomaly for polar and sun-synchronous orbits was scientifically and strategically inconceivable by both superpowers.

The Limited Test Ban Treaty of 1963 can be rightfully hailed as a victory for disarmament, for the environment, for the peace movement, even for trans-oceanic television viewers, and for global society. Aboveground and high-altitude atomic testing created health hazards, stoked the arms race, added to world tension, disrupted global electronic communications, and damaged the planet. If anyone lost anything from the prohibition of aboveground and high-altitude atomic testing, it was the hoteliers and tourism entrepreneurs of Hawaii, and they had plenty of other spectacles and attractions to turn to in making up lost revenues from filling hotels with tourists eager to watch atomic tests.

In the end, the biggest winner from the prohibition of aboveground, atmospheric, and high-altitude atomic testing codified by the 1963 treaty was probably not the environment, the disarmament movement, the people of the South Pacific, global TV audiences, the global image of America, or global society. The biggest beneficiaries were the individuals and institutions at the center of the American nexus of global security. Without the 1963 treaty and the protection it offered to strange space phenomena such as Van Allen belts and the South Atlantic Anomaly, the American global electronic surveillance network we have lived with for over forty years, now the most extensive information network surrounding and permeating planet Earth, may have never emerged and grown to the levels of scale, scope, and complexity we now take for granted.

One final factor needs to be mentioned in all of this, and that is the factor of chance, because the confluence of Starfish Prime and Telstar is a chapter in the history of error. For the series of atomic weapons tests including Starfish Prime, the designation "prime" indicates the second attempt at that test. Starfish was originally scheduled for June 20, 1962, but launch pad and takeoff malfunctions scuttled the original test, thus inadvertently putting Starfish Prime on the same countdown as Telstar. Although Fred Kappel had no problem chatting with Lyndon Johnson via a Telstar telephone call after the Telstar launch, it appears that the telephone company and the military somehow had a missed connection just before that launch. Despite the mutual interests and intertwined agendas of the federal government's biggest user of telecommunications and the biggest American telecommunications corporation, what the Department of Defense and AT&T shared between July 9, 1962, and July 10, 1962, was chance, coincidence, error, unanticipated outcomes, and unintended consequences. Their 1962 chance encounter, manifest in the confluence of Starfish Prime and Telstar, presaged the famous pop culture utterance from the 1967 movie *Cool Hand Luke:* "What we've got here is failure to communicate."

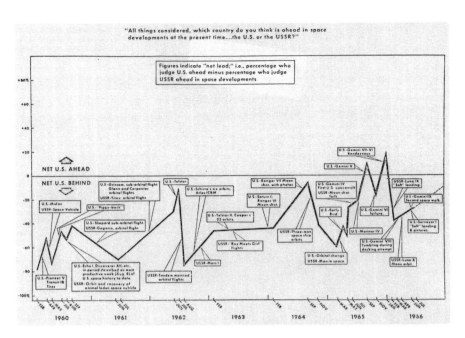

"All things considered, which country do you think is ahead in space developments at the present time....the U.S. or the USSR?"

British public opinion regarding the superpower space race, 1960–66.
USIA, National Archives.

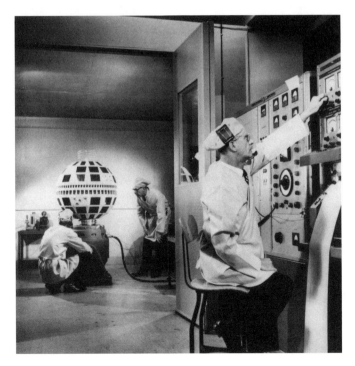

Making Telstar,
AT&T Labs, 1962.
Minow Papers,
WHS. Image
#WHi-43346.
Used with
permission.

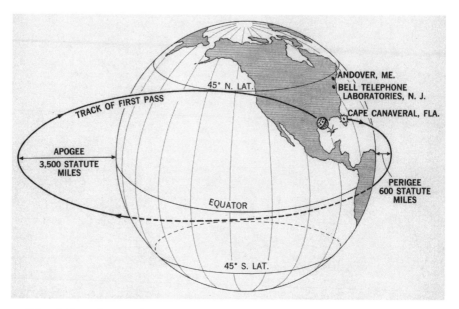

Telstar's first orbit, 10 July 1962. Minow Papers, WHS. Image #WHi-43347.
Used with permission.

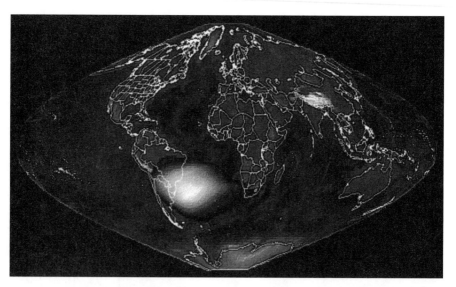

The South Atlantic Anomaly. European Space Agency. Used with permission.

RCA tests Ultrafax, 1948. NBC Records, WHS. Image #WHi-43342. Used with permission.

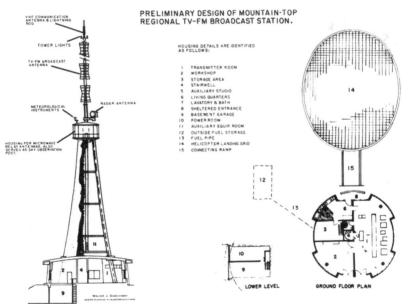

PRELIMINARY DESIGN OF MOUNTAIN-TOP REGIONAL TV-FM BROADCAST STATION.

VHF COMMUNICATION ANTENNA & LIGHTNING ROD

TOWER LIGHTS

TV-FM BROADCAST ANTENNA

RADAR ANTENNA

METEOROLOGICAL INSTRUMENTS

HOUSING FOR MICROWAVE RELAY ANTENNAE, ALSO SERVES AS SKY OBSERVATION POST.

WALTER J. OUBCHINSKI
MASTER PLANNING IN TELECOMMUNICATIONS

HOUSING DETAILS ARE IDENTIFIED AS FOLLOWS:

1   TRANSMITTER ROOM
2   WORKSHOP
3   STORAGE AREA
4   STAIRWELL
5   AUXILIARY STUDIO
6   LIVING QUARTERS
7   LAVATORY & BATH
8   SHELTERED ENTRANCE
9   BASEMENT GARAGE
10 POWER ROOM
11 AUXILIARY EQUIP ROOM
12 OUTSIDE FUEL STORAGE
13 FUEL PIPE
14 HELICOPTER LANDING GRID
15 CONNECTING RAMP

LOWER LEVEL

GROUND FLOOR PLAN

Schematic for NARCOM Regional Broadcast Station, 1952. C. D. Jackson Records, Eisenhower Library.

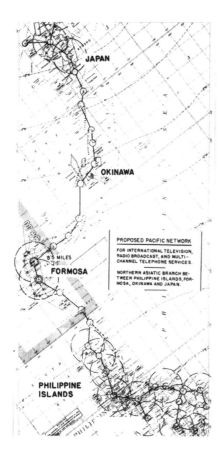

Networking the Pacific Rim, 1952. C. D. Jackson Records, Eisenhower Library.

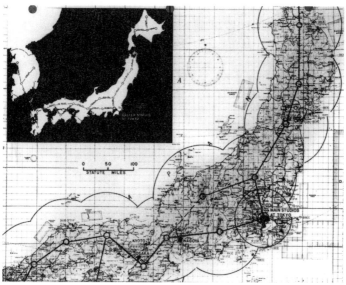

UNITEL and NTV plans for Japan, 1952. C. D. Jackson Records, Eisenhower Library.

Ford Foundation Bellagio conferees, 1966. *Back left to right:* Van Vliet, Hodgson, Lasky, Mickelson, Gould, Cowan, Haarprecht, Morse, D'Arcy, Dressner, White, Von Zahn. *Front:* Webster, Lasswell, Barzini, Slater, Gordey, Kimbler, Minow, MacKenzie. Mickelson Papers, WHS. Image #WHi-43336. Used with permission.

Arthur Morse, Mel Lasky, and Jack Gould enjoying a casual moment at the Ford Foundation Bellagio global TV conference, 1966. Mickelson Papers, WHS. Image #WHi-43329. Used with permission.

The Telstar earth station, Andover, 1962. A giant 340-ton antenna is inside the radome. Housing at left holds maser and other gear enable antenna to send signals to satellite and receive faint signals sent back to Earth. Minow Papers, WHS. Image #WHi-43344. Used with permission.

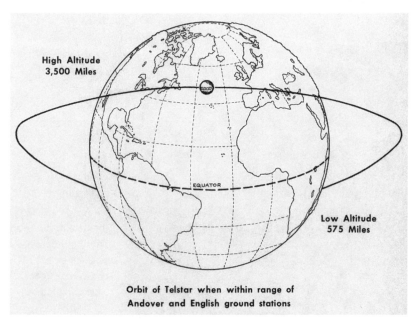

Another view of the Telstar orbit, July 1962. Minow Papers, WHS. Image #WHi-43347. Used with permission.

8. "A New Idea Capable of Uniting the Thoughts of People All Over the Earth"

Although Telstar proved the value of international television program distribution by satellite, a series of questions remained about effective implementation and expansion of satellite-distributed global television contextualized with the global image of America. Frankly, the Kennedy administration faced a fundamental domestic problem regarding the overseas expansion of telecommunications: the traditional American position of politically supporting the leadership of private enterprise in the global expansion of American commercial electronic communications would probably lead to private enterprise concentrating its efforts on expansion of the most lucrative commercial trade routes in global telecommunications—most prominently, the transatlantic trade route—while building out at best minimal service connections to much of the rest of the world. To take this traditional domestic political stance risked fully globalizing television into vast areas of the world now among the most ideologically contested areas of the Cold War: Africa, Asia, and Latin America. A global image of America might then be reduced to a Western European image of America. In July 1961, the National Aeronautics and Space Council (NASC) argued for a fundamental difference in a satellite system designed for lucrative international trade, as opposed to a global system of satellite communications. A global system "is one with the potential and the objective to provide efficient communication service throughout the whole world as soon as technically feasible, including service where individual portions of the coverage are not profitable or even have no expectation of future profit." The NASC labeled a global system as "a national objective" and recommended such a system be "operable as soon as possible within the limits of the technology."[1]

The corporate policy in 1961 for satellite expansion by AT&T, creator of Telstar, gave pause regarding the difference between lucrative trade routes and fully global systems. During the development of Telstar, AT&T forecast an eventual AT&T satellite network of twenty-five to forty satellites configured in different nongeosynchronous orbits, linked via the switching capacities of the AT&T telephone network, and capable of circulating television network exchanges among interested national networks.[2] Such a satellite constellation would not use geosynchronous orbits and would not necessarily provide full global reach, but would maximize AT&T transatlantic telephony revenues. This debate over geosynchronous global satellites versus nongeosynchronous satellites sparked what might be called competing positions over the political economy of satellite orbits, a rather esoteric yet extremely important debate about future satellite planning, production, and use in the area of global telecommunications. The AT&T network of nongeosynchronous satellites needed the complex interconnection of those satellites with AT&T switching and networking facilities on the planet itself; AT&T was arguably the only American commercial telecommunications network on the planet then capable of this level of complexity in signal distribution. In short, for all intents and purposes, AT&T planned a communications satellite monopoly for itself. Despite the technical ability to relay live international TV program exchanges among paying parties, the AT&T-proposed satellite system was aimed primarily at high-traffic commercial telecommunication and telephony routes. Fred Kappel of AT&T argued in June 1961 that the AT&T satellite system served proven global telecommunications demands, adding "time, analysis, and experience" were needed before AT&T or any other entity in the telecommunications business knew "whether there is a field of use for broadcasting satellites." Raising the specter of censorship, Kappel warned "a nation that does not wish its citizens to listen to broadcasts from satellites will forbid them to do so."[3]

Like many others at this time both within and outside of the American government, Kappel had obliquely hinted at the future prize: direct-to-home satellite television, from America to global viewers, bypassing what Tedson Meyers called the "central authority," or the national networks of other nations. If a satellite system could be globally deployed, and if direct-to-home satellite television reception promulgated, then television would become akin to shortwave radio reception, namely a direct address to the viewers of the world, unmediated by the national TV networks of their own nations: the ultimate conduit for reaching worldwide viewers with a global image of America. President Kennedy set this tone in the closing sentences of his 1961 "Report to Congress on United States Aeronautic and Space Activities" by hailing communication satellites as a "new technology to bring the farthest corner of the globe within reach by voice and visual communication" as a goal in the national interest.[4] Congressional and public opinion questioning the extension of AT&T's corporate reach into space communications had surfaced even before the flood of letters prompted by the Telstar launch. Frederick Dutton advised Kennedy in November 1961 that some members of Congress as well as the press criticized AT&T's "strangle hold" over communication satellites, and Congress threatened investigative hearings in its next session.[5]

As the Cuban Missile Crisis stewed, a policy paper on global satellite communications circulated within the Kennedy administration.[6] Dated October 4, 1962, and designed to guide future talks with the United Kingdom, Canada, and other nations, this memorandum explored the geopolitical extraterritorialities of satellite networks and stressed that getting "a communications satellite system operating as soon as possible" would enhance American prestige and produce economic benefits. Such a system could "achieve political gains resulting from increased international communication, including communication with Communist countries" and "augment the economic development of less developed countries and our political relations with them by means of a global system which links low traffic areas as well as the main industrial countries." The system would give the United States leadership in planning at the ITU for the allocation of spectrum to be used in space communications. The memorandum cast the "central question" concerning global communication satellite growth between a single American-led system and competing international systems, with the latter alternative likely to include the Communist bloc, Europe, and multiple American systems. Coming down squarely in favor of a single system, competition risked excessive duplication of equipment, squandered scarce frequencies in the electromagnetic spectrum, and especially negated any possible geopolitical gains through global television. Echoing arguments put forward by American delegates during television technical standards debates at ITU regional European conferences a decade or so earlier, multiple systems of satellite networks "would reduce the possibility for the worldwide exchange of programs." Multiple systems also reduced the possibility "to link the Soviet Bloc into a global communications network" and risked competition with European nations promoting their own national interests by seeking to electronically reify colonial relationships with Asia, Africa, and Latin America. This meant instead of the United States fully exercising global access via a single satellite system, "the less developed countries will be adopted as members of more or less exclusive communications clubs."[7]

The need for decisions was again, as had so often been the case since the occupation of Germany, driven by external and extraterritorial factors.

The United Kingdom and Canada had already begun early talks about a Commonwealth satellite system. An ITU conference on space communications scheduled for October 1963 would determine frequency allocations for space communication systems, and if a "genuine international arrangement" could be crafted, this could "foreclose the establishment of competing systems" and encourage other nations to "accept a self-denying ordinance" at ITU frequency allocations. Although there were risks in striking a balance between an "arrangement which is international enough to assure foreign participation in a single enterprise and yet which safeguards the U.S. position sufficiently to assure rapid progress" an American-led consortium was a goal worth the work.

Prior to the 1963 ITU space communications conference, both the United Kingdom and France discussed the feasibility of a cooperative European initiative in global satellite systems. A British diplomat confidentially advised the State Department that "there was some feeling in Europe that [the] French were trying to dominate [the] European space communications scene" and that while the British Foreign Office did favor a single global system, the United Kingdom needed to remain open to other alternatives if the American-led single global system proved too restrictive and prevented "participation in all phases."[8] A European conference on satellite communications held in Paris in May 1963 recommended satellite communication on an international basis that allowed for full European participation in system design, ownership, management, and future expansion of technical equipment including satellites and launch systems. The United States believed that the factors favoring a single global system were "persuasive." While agreeing that any founding participants in a single global satellite system should be nations with the means to make meaningful technical and economic contributions, the United States argued these same nations also needed to "acknowledge the goal to be global coverage" with service to be "provided at some point in all major geographical areas of the world." Financial assistance to developing nations would also be important for their "meaningful participation in the global system."[9]

When the European Allied occupiers of postwar Germany and other Western European nations in the late 1940s pursued a policy for the allocation of European TV frequencies that suited their own national interests and did not consider the needs of Germany, the American government objected and firmly cast European television in the framework of a security issue, labeling European television as what Lucius Clay called "a facet of east-west problems." In the early 1960s, the United States now spoke to its European allies (and North Atlantic Treaty Organization partners) not only with the rhetoric of security but more often with the new rhetoric of world citizenship, advising them that the paramount principle in communication satellite growth was a single global system in which all nations could eventually enjoy the benefits of meaningful participation. Yet the goal was the same despite the changing rhetoric: security for European television growth in the late 1940s and world citizenship through global satellite communications in the early 1960s were different discursive models toward a strategic goal of American influence in global electronic communications. As an example of single systems, the United States could point to its own domestic satellite policy and the emergence of the COMSAT as a model of a cooperative plan for a single system.

Incorporated in 1962 through an act of Congress, COMSAT was a coinvestment project between the American government and the major American telecommunications entities. Satisfying the goal of a single system and neatly obviating the possibility of AT&T extending its monopoly into space, the new corporation was not necessarily assured of early profits, despite its status as a single entity in a newly emergent field of commercial space communications. In fact, a major area of financial risk for COMSAT was international telecommunications traffic. Despite interest in the new corporation from established transatlantic telecommunication service entities such as AT&T, nothing on the face of things would prevent AT&T from theoretically expanding its undersea cable telephony system in direct competition with satellites on transatlantic and other lucrative trade routes. David Sarnoff believed in 1963 that COMSAT had a "rocky road" to travel because profits were still some years off and advised the Kennedy administration that AT&T could "keep it down" by building out its own transcontinental undersea cable facilities. Arguing the federal government should proactively "separate off from AT&T and all other companies the facilities and licenses for international communications," the federal government could then marshal those resources through "the Satellite Corporation into one chosen instrument to handle all international commercial communications between the United States and the rest of the world." Sarnoff believed this would "eliminate the AT&T domination, encourage the technological development of satellites" and offer consumers a choice of systems "rather than have the choice markets always subject to AT&T's decision as to whether or not to build cables" while also giving the United States "one company to negotiate with other countries which have communication monopolies."[10]

Sarnoff was, among other things, thinking about the genesis of his own corporation, RCA, in 1919. The State Department's Office of International Economic and Social Affairs and several members from the Board of Directors of COMSAT forged an agreement on November 21, 1963, to work toward "the negotiation and establishment of an intergovernmental agree-

ment to set up an intergovernmental agency on satellite communications"
that would be modeled on a range of other intergovernmental organizations
and agreements from postal services to the World Bank.[11] A plenary conference on European satellite communications held in Rome in December 1963
formed a regional organization as a counterpart to the COMSAT serving as
the European partner for a United States–led single global system of communication satellites.[12] In August 1964, the INTELSAT was formed with an
interim partnership between the United States, Canada, Japan, Australia,
and several nations of Western Europe.[13]

While a single American-led global communication satellite system was
in gestation, other observers not directly involved in its formation wondered
about the implications of such a system for global television. Jean D'Arcy, a UN
official long involved in UN public information activities and former director
of Eurovision (as well as a future participant in the Ford Foundation Bellagio
conference on global television in 1966) reported the USSR and other nations
harbored a "fear about direct broadcasting from communication satellites to
the home receiver."[14] Although a recent ITU conference had chosen not to in-
vestigate direct satellite broadcasting, the French delegation had arrived with
instructions to oppose direct satellite broadcasting if the subject arose. Furthermore, D'Arcy claimed the newly independent nations of the world were
"properly fearful of the ability of the space powers to communicate directly to
their citizens." He confided that an Indonesian representative at a recent ITU
meeting found it "intolerable if President Kennedy used a communication
satellite to speak directly to large numbers of Indonesians to whom President
Sukarno wished to speak but could not for lack of conventional facilities."
Projecting a future scenario where "the situation would arise in which an
outside state could develop an audience which was denied to the television
studios within that country," D'Arcy recalled that TV program exchanges in
Europe had, by the end of the 1950s, produced a situation where the nations
now most involved in program exchange are "those who, because they are
less developed, are greatly in need of program content." This meant that
"many countries would be forced to rely in large part on programs beamed
via satellite. Countries unable to satisfy audience demand by local programming would in effect be open to propaganda and commercial advertising by
outside states, thus opening up long-term domestic and economic effects
beyond their control."[15] Although D'Arcy's concerns did not emerge during
the 1960s, his observations proved incredibly accurate in the long term for
our contemporary world of twenty-first century global television.

On August 20, 1964, INTELSAT was formed as a consortium of eleven nations. President Lyndon Johnson called the occasion "a cause of gratification"

as outer space became "a medium for international communications."[16] One of the first INTELSAT decisions settled questions of satellite orbits. Rather than a constellation of low-orbit and medium-orbit nongeosynchronous satellites dependent on advanced terrestrial switching techniques as envisioned by AT&T with Telstar, INTELSAT chose a system of geosynchronous satellites. This choice ensured the possibility of direct round-the-clock satellite feeds independent of advanced terrestrial switching with extant telecommunications networks such as AT&T (in other words, a geosynchronous satellite does not periodically "disappear" over the horizon, thus necessitating a switching of signal reception to a new satellite "appearing" over the horizon). Instead, a single large earth station (receiving dish) could simply be continuously aimed at a single geosynchronous satellite for any national network interested in receiving an INTELSAT signal feed. Soon after, during the 1964 Tokyo Summer Olympics in October, a NASA experimental geosynchronous satellite (Syncom III) relayed live television coverage of the Olympic Games to the United States, despite not being originally designed for television transmission. With assistance from the Defense Department, the television signal went via microwave relay from Tokyo to Kashima (about 50 miles from Tokyo and the location of the Japanese uplink station). The signal was downlinked at the Pacific Missile Range at Point Mugu, California, and then microwaved to Los Angeles for standard television network distribution.[17]

In 1965, INTELSAT launched Early Bird, its first commercial geosynchronous satellite designed for television transmission. Early Bird, unsurprisingly, served the transatlantic route and had a capacity for up to 240 voice relay circuits, or one two-way television channel. Transatlantic television transmission began on May 2 and approximately 127 hours of transatlantic television transmission had been logged by July 25: roughly 71 hours from Europe to North America, and roughly 56 hours from North America to Europe. Early transatlantic TV events included 6 hours and 49 minutes of Pope Paul VI on his visit to the United States and the UN; 10 hours and 12 minutes on various Gemini space program missions; 9 hours and 24 minutes on news and public affairs, and 7 hours 8 minutes on sports events. One hour of television transmission during nonpeak hours (U.S. Eastern time zones weekdays 5 A.M.–7 A.M., 4 P.M.–9 P.M., and weekends 5 A.M.–9 P.M.) was billed at $3,400 for a one-way feed; peak hours cost $5,400.[18]

Early Bird: Spring, 1965 Transatlantic TV Flows

North America to Europe ≈ 56 hours
Europe to North America ≈ 71 hours

Early Bird: Examples of 1965 Transatlantic TV Events

Pope Paul VI visit to United States: 6 hours 49 minutes
USS *Wasp* (astronaut splashdown and recovery): 8 hours 2 minutes
Gemini space program: 10 hours 12 minutes
Sports: 7 hours 8 minutes
News and public affairs: 9 hours 24 minutes

Despite these program hours, COMSAT was looking at a future of red ink, based on this kind of commercial demand for transatlantic satellite communications. COMSAT had yet to show a profit and none could be foreseen, at least for the short term. Jack Valenti advised President Johnson in September 1965 that "Comsat might be heading for trouble . . . sales estimates simply have not been met due to apathy on the part of hoped-for European customers" and weak sales seriously threatened the patience of stockholders in moving rapidly forward on building out a single worldwide communication satellite system. The 1964 stock prospectus for COMSAT set a recommended original price of $20.00 per share and forecast that international communications would be a principal source of revenue.[19]

However, military and defense revenue for COMSAT as a part of its routine operations was now off-limits. In 1964, the Johnson administration had decided against pursuing Defense Department and similar military communications contracts with COMSAT. Such arrangements, though lucrative for the corporation, nevertheless muddied world opinion on the global and open policy of a single shared satellite communications system. Put another way, world citizenship and national security were, so to speak, techno-discursively incompatible in a single American global satellite communications system, and therefore military satellites and commercial satellites had to be developed on their own separate tracks.[20] Along with Special Assistant to the President for Telecommunications J. D. O'Connell, Valenti advised Johnson that COMSAT could be financially revivified if NASA awarded the communications service contracts for their upcoming Apollo missions to COMSAT rather than to the Defense Department. That would allow COMSAT to "move ahead quickly with global communications satellite service" while assuaging stockholder fears of slow growth. In turn, this created opportunities to reduce the costs of extending satellite communications to the developing world and could be an advantage in INTELSAT relations. Estimating the NASA contract would use about 50% of COMSAT's capacity, Valenti believed that even more valuable than increased revenue was the new satellite and earth station construction needed to satisfy the NASA contract, which would "give Comsat a wider global range because of the satellites to be launched to handle the NASA requirement."[21] O'Connell added that low demand from European partners, particularly in telephone, telegraph, and data traffic, stemmed from those partners finding "their financial interests are better served by the continued use of cable systems in which they have larger ownership participation." Failure to grow COMSAT and INTELSAT would strengthen the hands of European nations in determining the future of INTELSAT. Playing the Soviet threat for good measure, O'Connell believed the NASA-COMSAT arrangement could forestall Soviet efforts to help "lesser developed nations attain communications by satellite. Early action by the United States is necessary to preclude this possibility."[22]

Thus the COMSAT and the Apollo moon program became intertwined and mutually supportive. COMSAT communications services for the Apollo missions not only provided much-needed revenue to COMSAT, the contract requirements also justified new construction, and opened opportunities to bring more nations of the world—especially in Asia, Africa, and Latin America—under the American umbrella of satellite communications. This arrangement also meant that global publicity for American space missions, such as live international TV coverage, was good for COMSAT, good for Apollo, and good for the global image of America.

Interest in satellite communications and lesser-developed countries had earlier emerged during the Kennedy administration. Leland Johnson proposed in a 1962 RAND report that "educational television, current events, television, and telephone service" were the key services for lesser-developed nations, and even the Eisenhower-era Sprague Committee report about the global image of America had recommended educational television in lesser-developed nations as a prestige application of American science.[23] Even though the RAND report argued that worldwide educational television could be accomplished with or without satellite communications, "current events television" into lesser-developed nations would be greatly enhanced by the instantaneity of global satellite distribution, further disseminated by local microwave relay distribution. In 1965, the Hughes Corporation adopted a bombastic tone supporting its plans for educational television via satellite, labeling this technology "at least as important as the atomic potential in weaponry" that could "secure for the United States an historic premier position in world education . . . [and] prevent Communist capture of the initial installations in what must be an ultimate use of communications satellites."[24]

USIA Director Leonard Marks had already brought educational television to American Samoa, and during a presidential visit in 1965, Lyndon Johnson inspected the educational television facilities in Pago Pago.[25] The Pago Pago facilities were one of several initiatives by the Johnson administration toward globalizing education via satellites, television, and electronic information. Marks chaired the Task Force on Educational Television in Less Developed Countries, reporting in 1967 that Southeast Asia and Latin America were both excellent venues for educational television.[26] Television and education as a component of nation building in South Vietnam began with USIA and USAID (U.S. Agency for International Development) assistance in February 1966.[27] Even more ambitious was Networks for Knowledge, an early attempt to globally disseminate computer-based, or in the vernacular of the day, machine-readable information. In February 1968, Hewson Ryan drafted a Networks for Knowledge proposal suggesting a "pilot international project which will enable other nations to share the knowledge of this nation." This proposal called for an integrated global demonstration of multiple communications technologies in action. Ryan pushed for "the latest technology *in use,* excluding the obsolescent as well as the visionary, and avoiding any promotional promises of universal 'go-power' panaceas of the kind associated with breakfast cereals, acupuncture, and Marshall McLuhan." The report promised a worldwide Networks for Knowledge demonstration would confirm that no other nation "matches the U.S. in overall technical competence, in the willingness to share its capabilities with others, or in promoting educational programs among the masses of the world."[28]

In 1952, UNITEL envisioned global microwave TV relay contributing to American security by creating "wideband linkage." RAMAC at the 1959 Moscow Exhibition answered questions about the global image of America and tracked Soviet curiosity, all via an IBM computer. The 1968 Networks for Knowledge proposal demonstrates the discursive shift to globalization in visions of computer networking albeit while panning Marshall McLuhan, who coined the term "global village" in 1962. Despite efforts to distinguish between military and civilian systems, there are still military applications lurking in the background of Networks for Knowledge. As Paul Edwards notes, the American military in Southeast Asia had operation Igloo White in place by 1968, deploying thousands of electronic sensors on the Ho Chi Minh Trail that sent data to a command center in Thailand, and processed that data to coordinate aviation strikes against the enemy.[29] ARPANet sent its first computer-to-computer message in October 1969. Nevertheless, as was the case in separating COMSAT from U.S. military satellite corporations, Networks for Knowledge represents a separation of computer-based communications into distinct spheres for security and for globalization. Both the technology trails—microwave-relay global TV to film and tape-based program exchanges to a single global satellite system for live American global television, and wideband linkage to RAMAC to Networks for Knowledge as steps forward in American information diplomacy—signify the contours of technological trails along discursive lines, promoting globalization as the public face of American science and using American science to promote something of that sense of world citizenship.

By the mid-1960s, one major source for programming global television with sounds and images of American science was the space program. As the INTELSAT network grew to include both Atlantic and Pacific satellites, so did the global dissemination of live television coverage of American space missions: from launch in Florida to mission control in Houston to splashdown and astronaut recovery on aircraft carriers such as the *Wasp* or *Hornet*. Although the intent to globally televise the image of America through American space science was certainly genuine on the part of the program creators, the global programmers and audiences had also indicated a willingness to accept this programming—in part because American space science was perceived, accurately or not, by more than a few national networks as politically benign. Such was the case, for example, in Indonesia, where the USIA reported in 1967 that USIA-supplied TV news clips and documentaries "are being used increasingly in otherwise meager TV fare here. Space films [are] especially popular, probably a continuing hang-over from days when that was the only material they dared use. [It is] still too soon for use of controversial political clips."[30] A global preference for American science was also evident at the World's Fair in Montreal, Expo '67. The American exhibit at Expo '67 offered a theme of "creative America" that included an emphasis on Hollywood and displayed such memorabilia as Judy Garland's ruby red slippers from *The Wizard of Oz*. However, onsite public opinion polling found that attendees only gave substantial praise to the Buckminster Fuller–designed geodesic dome, and the display on outer space. Over half of the respondents found the Creative America display "trivial" with an overemphasis on "movie stars."[31]

Even though American science emerged as a program theme that was either popular or unobjectionable for global audiences, questions remained on reaching global audiences with a single shared communications satellite system. INTELSAT satellite deployment during 1967 reached most of the world, leaving the Indian Ocean (and the potential for live TV transmission to much of East Africa and the Indian subcontinent) as the only area not yet reached by INTELSAT satellites. However, for many nations, the satellite above could not be accessed without their own earth stations for their national TV network and, by extension, for educational technology applications using satellite communications. In 1966, the NSC recommended assistance in satellite communications for lesser-developed nations a policy in the national interest, and in January 1967, the White House Working Group on Educational Uses Abroad of Communications Satellites recommended an "active program" linking international education, American geopolitical goals, and satellite communications. Beyond educational and instructional television, the working group also recommended "a special study of the factors involved in overseas extensions of the proposed U.S. national information-retrieval network, utilizing satellite and other transmission means."[32] The State Department and the AID also recommended financial support for constructing earth stations in lesser-developed nations and regions, including Central America, Colombia, Chile, Brazil, Nigeria, Ethiopia, Kenya, Tanzania, Uganda, Turkey, Pakistan, India, Thailand, Philippines, and Korea (although Iran was later preferred over Turkey). The State Department initiated seminars on uses of earth stations in 1966 and had found that to make "the satellite communications system an operable one, the major effort remains, however, the rapid emplacement of earth stations so that the satellites can be put to use as they become available."[33]

The White House Working Group on Educational Uses Abroad of Communications Satellites also returned to the electronic borders of the Iron Curtain. With Western Europe and Japan involved as profitable trade routes, and lesser-developed nations involved through government policy and targeted assistance, the Soviet world remained the only major region not yet envisioned for direct interface with an American-led single global communication satellite system. Discussions on TV program exchanges between the United States and USSR dated back to the Eisenhower administration, satellites had been informally discussed in the Dryden-Blagonravov science discussions of the early 1960s, and direct negotiations regarding the possibility of Soviet involvement in global communications satellites began in 1964.[34] An early Soviet objection concerned the importance given to intercontinental telephone traffic; the Soviets proposed that satellite circuitry for telephony should be decreased and circuitry for television distribution should be increased.

A formal invitation to join INTELSAT was offered to the Soviets and Eastern Europe by President Johnson in 1967, but the Kremlin remained ambivalent into 1968, arguing for greater UN control and for cooperation with Molniya, the emergent Soviet domestic communications satellite system. The State Department's Bureau of Intelligence and Research surmised it "doubtful that the Soviets ever seriously considered breaking out of a regional framework and mounting a self-sufficient world hookup competing across-the-board with INTELSAT." Conceding the Soviets had at one point gone "through motions consistent with such a policy," and at the same time, experimented in TV program exchange with Paris via their own Molniya communication satellite system, despite the fact that Molniya was originally designed for domestic Soviet communications. The French presumably cooperated in this venture because it created conditions for "dramatizing the Paris-Moscow dialogue and advertising the French SECAM process." Having both Molniya and INTELSAT access might end up being "the best of both worlds for the USSR, securing the advantages of INTELSAT service without the drawbacks of INTELSAT membership. Moscow could stay out of what it may feel is a U.S.-operated club, yet at the same time plug MOLNIYA into a world hookup and accordingly enhance its international standing and earnings."[35]

The Soviet Union also believed internal friction within INTELSAT on the eve of the 1969 meetings to make the interim INTELSAT agreements permanent decisions might work in their favor, particularly with France. France argued strongly for the ability to make separate regional agreements in its own interests rather than always having policy for INTELSAT aimed at a single global system. The American Embassy in Paris reported in May 1968 that the political aims of a French-led global satellite system "completely elude the cool, patient, statistical study of the growth in world communications and its extension to probable future needs." Speculating that "France fears television broadcasts directly from satellites into her sphere of political interest with as much passion as she yearns to beam broadcasting into that area from her own satellites," this was not the time to expect "objectivity" in French communication satellite policy.[36]

Instead of joining INTELSAT, the Soviets proposed to the world their own global communications satellite system, Intersputnik. Avoiding the weighted voting (based on investment and trade) of INTELSAT and instead operating on a one nation, one vote policy, Intersputnik stood as an alternative satellite consortium of the Socialist world. Eugene Rostow, then chairing a Presidential Task Force on Communications Policy, told Soviet Ambassador Anatoliy Dobrynin in August 1968 that Dobrynin was welcome to discuss Soviet participation in global satellite communications with Rostow or other American representatives. Rostow confided that he was the person in the Johnson administration who "had these matters on his plate."[37]

Whatever Rostow had on his plate for Soviet INTELSAT cooperation spilled all over the floor a few days later, as the Soviets invaded Czechoslovakia. The invasion not only made discussion between the Americans and Soviets regarding Soviet participation in INTELSAT unfeasible, it led to a chilly reception for Intersputnik at a UN Outer Space Conference in Vienna, with one Italian delegate commenting: "So this is what they mean by 'one-nation, one-vote' procedure."[38] The shadow of the Cold War also fell in September 1968 upon preparations for the 1969 conference leading to permanent INTELSAT agreements, particularly—shades of 1947 and the ITU conference in Atlantic City—what constituted a "member state" for INTELSAT. A provision allowing membership for "all states" would on the one hand be the most open and global provision possible, but at the same time theoretically opened the door for such Cold War problem children as East Germany, North Korea, and Communist China, which could in turn rankle some allies as well as certain members of Congress. North Korea was still not yet admitted to the ITU, for example. Secretary of State Dean Rusk chose "ITU membership" instead of "all states" as the policy decision for the permanent INTELSAT agreements, thus preventing internecine conflict on both fronts.[39] Along with opposition to INTELSAT governance based on usage rather than nationality, the Soviets could now represent Intersputnik as the only global satellite system open to all states, not just ITU members. The fact that only a few Intersputnik nations were not ITU members, and all of those were Communist, was less important than the symbolism.

Despite not joining INTELSAT, the Soviet relationship with the United States and the free world regarding global communications satellites was, by the last years of the 1960s, cordial more often than not. Moments of rancor were few, and bellicose confrontations so typical of the early 1950s were now infrequent. Starting with IGY and Sputnik, the superpowers had engaged in a race to lead world public opinion regarding science and technology. That race was run on a curious track: not along the older track of security and national sovereignty, but along what then was a new track of world citizenship and extraterritoriality, now recognized in the twenty-first century as a track of globalization. The mileposts included the Limited Test Ban Treaty of 1963 and the Outer Space Treaty of 1967. Lyndon Johnson saw the 1967 treaty as a "hopeful sign" that "national rivalry is not a permanent barrier to international understanding." Signaling the superpower experiences that led to the 1967 treaty, Johnson also observed that "the first decade of the Space Age has witnessed a kind of contest. We have been engaged in competitive spacemanship. We have accomplished much, but we have also wasted much energy. . . . The next decade should increasingly become a partnership—not only between the Soviet Union and America, but among all nations under the sun and stars." Dobrynin shared in the spirit of world citizenship but also centered his comments regarding the 1967 treaty squarely on Soviet accomplishments and Marxist-Leninist scientific orthodoxy, noting that the public announcement of ratification took place on Sputnik's tenth anniversary: "This occasion has special significance, since it coincides with the tenth anniversary of the historic experiment of the launching of the first Sputnik . . . within the spirit of time, extremely short compared with the history of civilization, mankind has acquired hands which are able to stretch out millions of miles from this cradle and has learned to work with his hands; has acquired new eyes which are able to see what has always been hidden from man, and has acquired a new idea capable of uniting the thoughts of people all over the earth."[40] Not only had the superpowers deterritorialized and desovereignized outer space since the launch of Sputnik, they had accomplished the same in Antarctica—which was often used by the superpowers as a template for outer space treaties.[41] Additional mileposts signifying the linkage of science and world citizenship included the geosynchronous orbit, limiting weapons of mass destruction, and global networks for communications satellites. Both superpowers used science and technology as a limit on sovereignization in these extraterritorial regions, denying themselves and thereby denying all others the opportunity to extend national sovereignty beyond the limits of the habitable planet. As such, they learned to live with successful resolutions of extraterritorial tensions and even learned that accomplishing resolutions regarding extraterritorial tensions could be advantageous to the geopolitical strands of both superpowers, even if one led while the other lagged in world public opinion.

At the end of the day—or, in the case of this story, by the end of 1969—science had become a sovereign of extraterritoriality for planet Earth and outer space. Of the two sciences of the two superpowers, American science clearly won the science race. This race was refereed by global public opinion and increasingly covered by television. Championship conferred globalization upon its victor. American science could claim, on behalf of world citizenship, the South Pole, the geosynchronous orbit, the first global satellite system, the new territory of ARPANet and Networks for Knowledge now called the Internet and cyberspace, and the moon as the ultimate prize. Along with Cold War debates over the electromagnetic spectrum, challenges to the magnetosphere posed by aboveground and high-altitude atomic weapons testing and concern over natural resources, wildlife conservation, the purity of air and water, open access to outer space, and the depoliticization of Antarctica, these extraterritorialities all represent tensions and resolutions between the two superpowers. Extraterritorial spaces were part of the planetary environs. At the same time, they became seen as locales or arenas that somehow transcended the governance, security, and diplomacy traditionally and heretofore contained within and among inhabited landmasses and politically organized into nation-states. Thus, the activities and negotiations resolving these extraterritorial tensions played out in ways such as melding science with geopolitics, psychological warfare with information diplomacy, consumer interests with global public opinion, and television with world citizenship.

American science crossed the finish line just nineteen days after INTELSAT III, the final satellite in the single global system, became operational over the Indian Ocean. The successful linkage of INTELSAT III into the INTELSAT global satellite constellation now meant that, for the first time, live worldwide television programming was a reality, relayed through INTELSAT and subsequently distributed, as Tedson Meyers had foreseen just before the launch of Telstar, via national TV networks. The first big blockbuster must-see TV program for world audiences was an all-American production. Millions around the world watched on television as Neil Armstrong transformed a small step into a giant leap. At that moment, other vicarious participants in the Cold War story of the globalization of American science, technology, and global electronic communications certified their own world citizenship by watching, courtesy of American TV networks, NASA, and INTELSAT, coverage of the moon mission telecast on their own national networks. In so doing, they also participated in the American-led transformation of psychological warfare to information diplomacy, of East-West security to globalization, and of television from a new global electronic communication technology to the dominant form of global media.

* * *

In the immediate aftermath of the Second World War, American leaders first faced the question of global television as a "facet of east-west problems." The opening moments of Cold War television in Berlin and elsewhere led some American observers to argue "anyone with a Western mind would consider this kind of spectacle as stupid," and later, in the wake of Sputnik and the battle for global public opinion, for still others to argue "the key to many of these countries is not the mud hut population." "A group of angry young intellectuals" from foundations, universities, Madison Avenue, and elsewhere agreed that "we can give the world a vision of America" but this vision needed an expansive and inclusive view that, among other things, centered on American science and aimed to turn global viewers into vicarious participants. The early success of this approach with ordinary Soviets at the 1959 Moscow Exhibition led one analyst to conclude the sheer number of encounters possible through machine-based information diplomacy represented "a record of some kind in the history of international communication." By the dawn of the 1960s, electronic information networks, particularly live global television, could claim to represent "something of that sense of world citizenship." By the 1969 moon landing, American leadership had finally succeeded in its Cold War quest regarding a commanding presence in global television, satellite constellations, and multiple electronic information networks by transmitting live and across the entire planet "a new idea capable of uniting the thoughts of people all over the earth." That new idea was Cold War globalization, offered in an American variant and designed, like the visions of Cold War security which preceded it, to project a global image of America that served the nation's interests as the most powerful geopolitical entity on—and beyond—the small blue-green orb known as Earth.

Epilogue:
"To Speak with a Single Voice Abroad"

As we read the pages of history, we find those pages strewn with
the wreckage of great civilizations in the past who lost their leadership just at the time that they were the richest, and at the time
when they had the capability of being the strongest. They lost their
leadership because their leader class failed to meet the responsibilities and the challenges of the times. They, in other words, turned
away from greatness. They grew soft. They did not welcome the opportunity to continue to lead, which was their destiny at that time,
and those civilizations are forgotten except as they are read about
in the pages of history.

—Richard Nixon, "Salute to a President" remarks, November 1971

When elected to the College de France in 1970, Michel Foucault said he
wished he could have "slipped imperceptibly" into opening his inaugural
lecture, "enveloped in words, borne way beyond all possible beginnings."[1]
Labeling this a "desire to be freed from the obligation to begin," after conducting this research, I have the polar opposite: a desire to be freed from the
obligation to conclude. For it is very difficult, in ways intellectual, political,
professional, and personal, to speak about Cold War television, electronic
information networks, psychological warfare, information diplomacy, and
the global image of America from 1946 to 1969 as an American living in the
present moment of world history. This difficulty stems from the tumultuous
events of the first years of the twenty-first century: the 2000 presidential
elections, the tragic events of September 11, the exponential expansion of
government secrecy, the Patriot Act, the War in Iraq, the Abu Ghraib and
Guantanamo Bay prisons, the worldwide expansion of terrorism, extraor-
dinary renditions of persons, transit bombings in London and Madrid, and
responses built on concepts such as military intervention, or transformative
diplomacy. We seem to suddenly live in a world not marked by globalization,
but instead marked by globaphobia.

The global image of America is a complex and contested historical construct that is one of the continuing responsibilities of American diplomacy. Preserving, projecting, and promoting global images of America in the national and strategic interests of the United States is a core component of American diplomacy. In this regard, one may look back upon the past and ask whether lessons learned from 1946 to 1969 regarding the global image of America still endure in twenty-first-century American diplomacy, or instead are those lessons seemingly lost on our current leaders.

Occupied Germany and Occupied Iraq

> ... the U.S. Government requires a coordinated means to speak with a single voice abroad.
> —*Report of the Defense Science Board Task Force on Managed Information Dissemination,* October 2001

As was the case at the dawn of the Cold War with occupied Germany, the United States now finds itself going through the occupation and reconstruction of another sovereign nation: Iraq. Though exact numbers were vague, estimates suggest at any given moment there were between 1,500 and 3,000 public information officers working in the American zone of Germany during the occupation period. When James Conant arrived in occupied Germany from the presidency of Harvard University to become the new U.S. ambassador, he remarked he had more people working in public information under him now than he had in the combined total of faculty and staff he had left at Harvard. Furthermore, a number of these individuals working in public information services in occupied Germany became prominent figures in government and private sectors after their return to the United States. For example, several of the highest-level officers in the international programs division of the Ford Foundation during the 1950s and 1960s had previously served as public information officers in occupied Germany.

* * *

> The United States did not run from Germany and Japan following World War II. We helped those nations to become strong and decent, democratic societies that no longer waged war on America. And that's our mission in Iraq today.
> —George Bush, remarks to New Hampshire Air National Guard, October 2003

In comparison, the current situation in Iraq does not show evidence of the same, or similar, scale and scope of commitment to public information officers on site, nor to a serious effort to indigenously rebuild Iraqi media around democratic values. Despite the claim of the president, the cases are scarcely, if at all, comparable. Rather than working at local levels and emphasizing the rebuilding of broadcast outlets and the reestablishment of newspapers, as was the case in the occupation of Germany, the flagship project by American diplomacy for Iraqi media, a TV service called Al-Hurra, is programmed out of Washington and beamed via satellite for transmission in Iraq. Joining Al-Hurra were Radio Sawa and *Hi!* magazine, all begun by the U.S. government as single-voice media outlets in conjunction with the invasion and occupation of Iraq. Al-Hurra, Sawa, and *Hi!* are not projects aimed to build new indigenous Iraqi media systems, nor are they projects designed to decentralize preexisting Iraqi media outlets. Al-Hurra, Radio Sawa, and *Hi!* have little to nothing to do with rebuilding Iraqi media. Rather, all three have everything to do with the 2001 recommendation of the Defense Science Board that the United States have a coordinated means to speak with a single voice abroad.

Understanding versus Ignoring New Global Media Technologies

> If anyone here lived in the Middle East and watched a network like Al-Jazeera day after day after day, even if you were an American you would begin to believe that America was bad. . . . Quite honestly, I do not get up in the morning and think that America is what's wrong with the world. The people that are going on television, chopping off people's heads is what's wrong with the world.
> —Donald Rumsfeld, quoted in "Rumsfeld: Al-Jazeera Over Iraq," June 2005

As the chapters of this book have demonstrated, understanding new global media technologies and their relationships to security, psychological warfare, information diplomacy, world citizenship, and the global image of America from 1946 to 1969 was difficult, frustrating, time-consuming, laborious, and expensive. However, as can be seen from the vantage point of the early twenty-first century, failing to do so is perilous for the global image of America.

American diplomacy at the start of the Cold War was uninformed about the global growth of television, particularly from the late 1940s through the middle of the 1950s. Almost all of the early thinking about the global growth of television in the 1940s and into the early 1950s was for the most part not directed by high-level officials from the State Department, the Pentagon, the White House, Capitol Hill, or elsewhere inside the federal government. Instead, thoughts rose up from local embassy initiatives and similar questions from lower- and mid-level career civil servants, foreign service officers, military personnel, and private individuals. Embassies did not routinely receive worldwide circulars from Washington instructing them to monitor global TV growth until about 1957. The first efforts as such simple tallies were aimed only at Communist nations and did not become worldwide roundups until 1960 or so. Until the mid-1950s, U.S. embassies did not routinely have TV sets unless embassy officers brought them over when they were posted—in fact, much of what the State Department learned about Soviet TV from 1946 to 1955 is only because a few Moscow Embassy officers had brought TV sets with them when they were posted to Moscow, and on their own initiative wrote up reports and reviews describing Moscow TV programs. In terms of live global television programming, Soviet live TV transmissions first reached audiences across all of Europe in April 1961, with televised celebrations of Yuri Gagarin's pioneering space flight. U.S. live TV transmissions did not reach Europe until July 1962, with the transmission relays of Telstar, the first American TV-capable satellite. In the global media world of the twenty-first century, this is almost mind-boggling: a similar situation might be if Al Jazeera had a sixteen-month lead over CNN as a global news network.

Yet, by the end of the 1960s, Americans led the way in global television, both in terms of technology and content. As a part of the recalibration of the global image of America during the Cold War, global television joined a conceptual set of signifiers connoting something then occasionally called *world citizenship*. This list of signifiers included the global sharing of television content; concern for animal wildlife, natural resources, and atmospheric and oceanic purity, or what would now be called environmentalism; space and polar exploration; and limiting the weapons of mass destruction, most notably aboveground and high-altitude atomic weapons testing. In short, to be a *world citizen* meant having some sort of awareness and discursive familiarity with these and other extraterritorialities of the Cold War. Understanding that television and satellites were fundamental to the global image of America did, by the 1960s, mean that television, satellites, and electronic information networks became foundational for promoting an American-led vision of world citizenship, for example, through TV coverage (and subsequent global dissemination of that coverage) of the American space program. American astronauts provided global TV program content through their various space missions, and the United States simultaneously led the momentum to build INTELSAT (including funding INTELSAT through NASA contracts). INTELSAT was the world's first communications satellite network that proved upon completion to be the first global communications network capable of live worldwide delivery of a television program. Going into the final two decades of the Cold War, the global image of America had finally become informed by the difficulties, challenges, and opportunities of new communications technologies. To not do so would have been perilous, as proven during the 1980s by the fate of the other superpower that had failed to rise to the difficult task of understanding new global communications technologies and then adapting to those complex conditions.

Yet in the aftermath of the Cold War, and especially in the realities of global conflict and the ordinary soldier in the twenty-first century—no matter the nationality, no matter the battlefield—the second Bush administration appears to have chosen the perilous route of ignoring new global communication technologies, messages, and consequences, claiming to have no understanding or prior knowledge of the situation or environment leading to thousands of GI photos showing American abuse of Iraqi prisoners, for example. One cannot find a conflict anywhere in the world after the Cold War where ordinary soldiers are not routinely carrying cameras, both still and video. Nevertheless, the second Bush administration acts as if the ubiquity of cameras, computers, and digital images among the military rank-and-file of all global combatants is a great unknown. The second Bush administration also appears to not know that the number of TV sets in the world doubled from 1989 to 1994, and then doubled again from 1994 to 2004, and most of that growth is outside of North America, Western Europe, and Japan. This suggests the American electorate is a minority audience for any twenty-first-century presidential TV sound bite, due to global dissemination. The second Bush administration seems to have, at best, only a hazy understanding of the rate of personal computer growth, Internet growth, and electronic networking in the world beyond the borders of the United States. By ignoring new global communications technologies and their complex tapestry of messages, the second Bush administration seems to think that media consumers in Asia, Africa, Latin America, and the Middle East are still stuck at very remedial levels of consumption and understanding of media technologies and content that were more or less the norm a generation ago, but are by no means the norm today. Today, these worldwide media consumers are no longer remedial consumers, but are mature and sophisticated consumers of media form and content, as shown by their incredible indigenous expansion of both the technology and content of both old and new electronic communications during the past two decades. The evidence is everywhere, but the second Bush administration shows few, if any, signs it remembers the Cold War lesson that the hard work of paying attention to the complexities of global media growth is in the interests of the global image of America. Instead, it appears the second Bush administration has chosen to take the easy path and neglect this issue, thus placing the global image of America in peril.

Rather than recognize a complex, mutative world of multiple audiences and sophisticated media literates, twenty-first-century American foreign policy consistently posits an unfounded assumption of simple, unchanging audiences and remedial media literates. The single voice of twenty-first-century American diplomacy is crafted and aimed at a global audience imagined to be incapable of mutation to anything more subtle or sophisticated than a basic, unified position of support or opposition to the global image of America. American diplomacy in the twenty-first century believes in a single voice with no mutations as the route toward recrafting the global image of America.

Single Voice, No Mutations, and the Unexpected Outcome of the Cold War

The promulgation of the global image of America during the Cold War was a key factor in spurring an American-led discourse on extraterritorialities and world citizenship, or what is identified in this book as a particular American-led discourse of globalization. This leads to a question regarding the differences and similarities between globalization and Americanization. Are globalization and Americanization different phenomena, or are they the same? Adding to the debate are the contested origins of globalization, with arguments advanced that variously lay claim to globalization's origins in the beginnings of human migrations, in the rise of European capitalism, in the latter half of the nineteenth century, or in the formal institutionalized emergence of the postwar international system circa 1945. This particular study, a global history of Cold War television, was not designed to deeply explore the contested roots of globalization's history; that would be a quite different book. Put another way, the aim of this book has not been to argue that American Cold War diplomacy invented and operationalized the theory and practice of globalization, all on its own, and without historical precedent. In that sense, Americanization and globalization are not one and the same.

If the question of Americanization and globalization during the Cold War is posed on different historical terms, however, the affinity between the two terms is stronger. Instead of asking the question in terms of the history of globalization, what happens if the question is posed in terms of the discursive formation, or the historical articulation, of the concept of globalization? Put another way, instead of asking when did globalization start, what happens to the comparison of Americanization and globalization when this question is asked along the lines of intellectual and discursive history: when did people start talking about globalization, thinking about globalization, and especially using the concepts and articulation of globalization (or equivalent phrases) as a way of viewing the world, shaping decisions, and exercising power? When did this emergent discursive formation of what we now call globalization take shape and form for articulation, dissemination, and expansion into a global discourse? How was that global discourse taken beyond the dialogue of its crafting interlocutors and into public conversation, spreading into a global dialogue? What were the examples, the arguments, and the reasons advocated for initiating a particular American-led global dialogue cast along the lines of what we now call globalization?

Asking these questions—basically, a set of questions not about the history of globalization's origins, but instead about the history of globalization's discursive formation into a global dialogue—leads to the formulation of American diplomacy in the latter 1950s and early 1960s that advocated a global image of America defined along the lines of inclusive science and technology; recast superpower rivalries along competing visions of consumer society; viewed international communications, environmental issues, and outer space as global rather than national issues of interest; and partially transformed psychological warfare into information diplomacy. Constantly gauged, supported, and rearticulated through the social-scientific measurement and analysis of global public opinion, this formulation of American diplomacy along the concepts of globalization opens a second articulation, or a second way of framing, the Cold War world that stands as an alternative to East-West security, although it is deeply intertwined with that earlier articulation. Although the historical origins of globalization are, as they should be, open to lively dispute, a close analysis of the global growth of Cold War television and electronic information networks with American diplomacy suggests that the historical origins of an American-led discourse of globalization and a global dialogue employing that discourse are intimately tied to the Cold War diplomacy of the United States. In this discursive sense, Americanization and globalization are very closely related. The United States did not originate or invent globalization. However, Cold War American diplomacy did initiate and promulgate a particular global dialogue about globalization as a way of promoting the global image of America through a constructed discourse about extraterritorialities and world citizenship that was spread through American-led television and electronic information networks. This was crafted in a manner that linked the globalization discourse and American diplomacy to advance the national interests of the United States.

Even though the American-led discursive formation of a global dialogue about globalization in a Cold War world was a successful campaign, to analyze this campaign solely from the hegemonic power of public and private American policymakers would be an incomplete analysis. The American turn toward globalization as a discursive alternative to East-West security and superpower conflict was not taken from a position of overwhelming strength, but rather from a condition brought about by some perceived weaknesses in American global stature and leadership. One wonders, for example, whether the same or a similar discursive articulation would have been reached without the Soviet advances in science and technology during the 1950s, without Sputnik, or without the work of the BBC in networking the Soviet Union into Eurovision, bringing live Soviet television into all of Europe while live American transatlantic television remained but a future dream. In this sense, perceived problems in world public opinion regarding the global image of America were a spur in conceptualizing and advancing the discourse of globalization. The values placed by people around the world on that particular dialogue were subject to constant testing and measurement. Some of the impetus for the articulation of a globalization discourse stemmed from frustrations and problems of wedging global television and global media into the earlier Cold War conceptual framework of East-West security and superpower conflict. Thus the American formulation of a discourse about globalization did not emerge solely from a position of asserting unquestioned American strength in geopolitics, media technologies, and world public opinion, but rather as a crafted response to potential American weaknesses in earlier Cold War frameworks as well as in certain facets of extraterritorial geopolitics and world public opinion. The American Cold War discourse about globalization did not simply impose itself, so to speak, upon an inarticulate global public, but rather was designed to include that global public and assist world citizenship. The dialogue helped budding world citizens articulate an American-inspired discourse of globalization (by becoming vicarious participants in world citizenship through American media technologies and the message of freedom through American science) as a part of the ongoing conversation about modern life on a shared habitable planet understood through both traditional nation-states and new extraterritorial concepts. As measured through public opinion polling, many world citizens embraced the new discourse.

To borrow a methodological approach from literary studies, it might be said that millions of world citizens accepted the preferred reading of the American-led discourse of globalization during the Cold War, as evidenced by public opinion polls, attendance at USIA exhibits, the embracing of science and technology in the service of a consumer society, and watching live American television distributed globally via satellite. To continue with this methodological metaphor, however, many other world citizens instead chose to read against the grain of the preferred reading for the American-led globalization discourse. What might be called reader-response, alternative, or resistant readings did not show up so much in social-scientific public opinion measurement results or USIA exhibit comment books as they did in Vietnam War protests, calls for superpower disarmament, arguments for national self-determination, and questions regarding living conditions in the vast poor areas of the world.

In this respect, the discursive power of the Americanized globalization discourse eventually proved somewhat beyond the control of its crafters. The American formulation of a discourse on globalization and its dissemination into a global dialogue was successful beyond its original terrain, the terrain of the Cold War. However, over time the power of that discourse took on a life of its own, no longer controllable in the same ways known in the late 1950s and the 1960s. As the Cold War wound down from 1989 to 1991, the discourse of globalization grew in complexity and became more potent than ever, outliving its original intent and mutating into complex discourses of potential power for people the world over. One might even say that, beyond all the science and technology, beyond consumer culture, and beyond political freedom, the American-led discourse of globalization was the most valuable legacy or gift that came out of the Cold War world. Globalization became a malleable political and intellectual discourse that people the world over recognized, and a discourse all people in the world could attempt to rearticulate and remake on their own terms in forming their own brand of authenticity, power, citizenship, justice, and identity. There was even a bonus: the means of communication necessary for this American campaign—a global communications satellite system, Networks for Knowledge, support for earth stations in developing nations, massive flows of information, live global television networking capabilities—all of these were adaptable by the newly empowered and increasingly independent voices in the globalization dialogue. Everyone was already globally connected, because Cold War America had made it so. Out of the legacy of the Cold War came both a powerful and adaptable discourse along with the proven ability to not just look and to listen, but also the latent ability to speak and to show.

In the 1970s and 1980s, the growing uncontrollability of the globalization discourse was a challenge, but not really an insurmountable problem for American diplomacy. Yes, there were many embarrassments and more than a few outright disasters: Vietnam, Cambodia, Cuba, and Chile, for example. However, the Cold War itself was a sort of compass or guidepost for the extension and the limits of the American-led globalization discourse, because the earlier precepts of East-West security and superpower conflict had not been replaced by a discourse of globalization but continued to function in relationship with a discourse of globalization.² As long as the main target of Cold War globalization discourse could be demonstrated by American foreign policy (through public opinion measurement, spin doctoring, news management, carefully placed interviews, press conferences, development projects, and so forth) as combating, containing, or "détente-ing" Communism, particularly in Eastern Europe and the USSR, then the ancillary and often uncomfortable uses of the globalization discourse beyond original American intents could be grudgingly accepted or conveniently ignored, more often than not through marginalization.

When the Berlin Wall came down in 1989—live, unrehearsed, and unedited on global television—and in the aftermath leading to the dissolution of the USSR in December 1991, the original policy aim of the American-crafted globalization discourse vanished. Yet the discourse, like its companion discourse of security, remained and, in the case of globalization, even flourished in mutation. Spurred along mightily in the 1980s by issues and factors including deregulation, privatization, liberalization, multinational corporations, financial markets, the "new media" of the era (fax, video recorders, cable, direct satellite TV, personal computers, networking, new telephone services, and similar), expanded global travel, refugees, environmentalism, and higher education, globalization at first seemed poised to absolutely thrive as the uncontested ideology of a post–Cold War world. However, the end of the Cold War was also something akin to a hurricane, typhoon, or perfect storm. Like a hurricane, the end of the Cold War destroyed many ideas, ideologies, and institutions; left many other ideas, ideologies, and institutions still standing, but with lingering questions about their strength, relevance, and durability; and revealed yet other ideas, ideologies, and institutions that had been effectively buried beneath the edifices of the Cold War itself.

The 1990s did bear witness to genuine steps in nuclear disarmament, a long run of prosperity for the wealthy nations of the world, an incredible build out of telecommunications and information technology infrastructure, the end of apartheid in South Africa, a relaxing of authoritarianism in China, and other manifestations of what was referred to as a peace dividend from the end of the Cold War. Simultaneously, that same decade saw the violent dissolution of Yugoslavia; the rise of the Taliban; conflict in the Persian Gulf; genocides in Africa; the development of extraordinarily effective tactics for producing death and terror among the peoples of the Middle East; an attack on the World Trade Center in New York City; an attack on a federal government building in Oklahoma City; the assassination of the Israeli prime minister by a disaffected Jew; a sarin gas attack on the Tokyo subway system; a brutal war in Chechnya; fatwas against satellite television; increased attacks on American military bases overseas; and an indiscriminate global wave of bombings and violence (sometimes by governments, more often by adherents of opposing faiths) against churches, synagogues, temples, mosques, and other buildings, statues, and symbols of all organized religions everywhere on the planet. All of which hurled the geopolitical extraterritoriality of violent religious extremism back into global consciousness with a vengeance. What were once obscure meetings of government ministers and business officials—the gatherings of the World Trade Organization, World Bank meetings, Davos summits—became focal points for spirited and, on occasion, disruptive protests. Although a few of these events arguably represent the pushing of a global dialogue built on an American Cold War discourse of globalization to its extreme but ultimately recognizable limits, many others simply do not match up well with that particular discourse of globalization.

American foreign policy in the post–Cold War world at first generally responded to these phenomena in a manner akin to the responses about perceived excessive Cold War articulations of globalization. These initial responses in the 1990s aimed at marginalization, even denunciation perhaps; they articulated perceptions that these were a series of isolated and abhorrent events, extreme cases that did not collectively signify systemic and structural problems in world citizenship and extraterritorial understandings. Lulled by relative prosperity, swayed by the allure of market forces as a substitute for policy decisions, and seduced by the passions of domestic partisan politics bitterly waged over issues having little if anything to do with world leadership, all the while relentlessly marketed to the world at large according to the commercial dictates of a voracious global 24–hour wall-to-wall news cycle rather than the considered deliberations that are recognized as the hallmark of careful statecraft, American diplomacy in the 1990s began to drift and unravel. The foundational moorings of Cold War visions were gone, for both better and for worse. It would not be fair to say no one cared any more about thoughtful diplomacy, wise American statecraft, or careful global leadership. However, not enough people with the means and motivation to make a difference seemed to care enough to come together and find ways to transcend the superficial issues and petty spats that so recently obsessed the United States to distraction. It was almost as if there was an unspoken consensus that diplomacy, statecraft, and leadership would simply happen, simply take care of itself without the need for transcending these superficial issues and petty spats. Turning American politics and governance into a lively entertainment spectacle was the more important goal of the day, because passionately performing in these political melodramas became equated with, among other things, electoral power. The twentieth century ended with the political equivalent of a televisual end-of-the-season cliff-hanging spectacular worthy of *Dallas* and "Who shot J.R.?" in the 2000 presidential elections, an election that, no matter your preferred candidate, no sensible person can claim was a shining moment in American history.

Then came September 11.

In the twenty-first century, American foreign policy is now currently blinkered into a singular, stultifying worldview. One searches for evidence of the vision in contemporary American foreign policy, statecraft, and diplomacy signifying the wisdom of a diplomacy that, like its Cold War ancestor, is able to maintain a secure world while also looking beyond the question of security for additional ways of persuading the world to accept the values of American leadership. The American-led discourse of globalization was an important component of Cold War American diplomacy and foreign policy, a discourse that proved incredibly effective. Conceived and carried out with great skill, and carefully introduced into a global dialogue, this discourse had all the earmarks of a perfect public relations campaign. However, it also had something else, something that does seem to be unfortunately missing from contemporary American foreign policy in the twenty-first century. Despite all the propaganda, persuasion, psychological warfare, public opinion management, and information diplomacy, the American-led Cold War globalization discourse had a very small but genuine kernel of truth, a tiny sense of trust, about it.

The promulgation of the Cold War globalization discourse did depend on this tiny sense of collective trust: the implicit admission of possible American weaknesses in some areas of global leadership, combined with what genuinely was, particularly for the developing nations of the world, an increased attention on their thoughts and opinions as represented by opinion polling, was just enough to convey this small sense of collective trust, this tiny sense that the United States was, by the recognized parameters of the era, conveying truthfulness. This was larded with great manipulation, massive deception, and an unceasing spinning, packaging, and endless delivery of the message constantly laden with bells and whistles, with bows and ribbons. Nevertheless, a sizable majority of those beyond the shores of the United States who aspired to and believed in American concepts of world citizenship and extraterritorialities did come to endorse and eventually articulate that very discourse for themselves, because that discourse was designed, as best as could be accomplished by the established and agreed-upon methods of the era, to confirm that one of the many things American diplomacy was doing was listening as well as speaking. To use a computer programming metaphor, the globalization discourse was written with a very small bit of truth, trust, and interactivity in its source code. Planting these few bits and bytes creating a small kernel of truth and trust in the source code of the American-led Cold War globalization discourse was the final, and most important, bit of wisdom in this discursive formation.

By today's twenty-first century standards of discursive formations, political freedoms, social science measurements, public relations practices, new electronic communication technologies, global networking, and media flows, the Cold War globalization discourse for American diplomacy is quaint and outdated. No one could use these same Cold War methods of the 1950s and the 1960s today and craft a diplomacy that would be taken seriously for its persuasiveness, sophistication, wisdom, and sincerity. Even though these Cold War discourses of security and globalization can and should be maintained, nurtured, and improved, a continued articulation of these discourses is not enough, because we are no longer in a Cold War world. Both of these Cold War discourses, by nature of the historical conditions of their design, are missing something from their source code that twenty-first-century American diplomacy needs: a small interactive kernel of trust that positively recognizes and appreciates the globally multitudinous realities of both identity and difference. The post–Cold War world must be seen as a multiverse, not a universe; and this multiverse must be seen as a valuable, rather than problematic, outcome of the end of the Cold War.

Binary Concepts of Identity and Difference in the DNA of Cold War Geopolitics

The end of the Cold War was imagined by the crafters of Cold War discourses to also be the end of identity and difference. The Cold War world was a world of binary choice. The end of the Cold War, it was supposed, would eliminate the binarism by leading the post–Cold War world into ultimately binding to and then living in only one of two possible new worlds. To return to the metaphor of biology, DNA, and the double helix from the introduction to this book, the ideologues of the Cold War had faith that, in the future, the superpower double helix would unravel. Then, only one of the two superpowers would lead, thus eliminating global difference and reshaping a new world after the Cold War. When the superpower double helix finally unraveled, one superpower would win the race to become the leading strand, launching a continuous synthesis with the waiting world more quickly, and thus be the first to reconstitute with the world at large a new double helix to its own dictates. The losing superpower would suffer the fate of the lagging strand, trailing behind the other in the race to reconstitute a new double helix and taking longer to discontinuously synthesize with the waiting world. The outcome of this race to unzip the Cold War superpower double helix and become the leading strand continuously synthesizing with the waiting world would then bring about what some once called the end of history. When America was victorious, the ideologues of freedom would succeed in creating what Richard Kerry called a Star-Spangled Mirror: the United States would be able to look out at the rest of the world and see itself reflected by the image that the rest of the world "ought" to display.[3]

However, there was an unexpected outcome. The world after the unwinding of the superpower double helix and the reconstitution of two new double helixes did not behave according to the anticipated results. The new world instead quickly became a world of greater difference and mutation than the Cold War world it replaced. It was almost as if after the superpower double helix finally unwound and began reconstitution into two new double helixes, no leading strand emerged, but instead two lagging strands emerged. Both superpowers were slower to reconstitute, and both were less able to reconstitute to their own dictates. Both therefore found themselves discontinuously synthesizing with the waiting world and facing greater risk of mutation, because the rest of the world had become more complex and therefore more capable of introducing mutation in the process of reconstitution. Perhaps in this case of the superpower double helix and the waiting world, even winning the race to unravel and become the leading strand was not a guarantor of mutation-free continuous synthesis into a new double helix. In short, the waiting world proved more complex and more mutative than had been anticipated for both the victor and the loser of the superpower double helix race.[4]

History had not ended after all. The Star-Spangled Mirror became a sort of *vexierspiegel*, a distorting mirror more akin to a haunted house than a carnival. Thus, for the ideologues that imagined the end of the Cold War would bring about the end of binarism, a singular world without mutations, and even the end of history, the Cold War itself had an unexpected ending: more rather than less complexity, multiple voices rather than a single voice, a mutating world rather than a world of no mutations. The Cold War ended with both a victory and a defeat. As anticipated, the United States won the race to be the leading strand in reconstituting with a post–Cold War world. However, the unanticipated outcome of that victory—discontinuous synthesis with a world of greater complexity and mutation—meant that history would not end. Civilizations would clash. The Star-Spangled Mirror would fail to reflect the image it "ought" to reflect. The dreamlike world with one universal identity and zero difference had instead turned out to be a nightmarish world with uncountable multiversal identities and infinite difference. The geopolitical DNA of the post–Cold War world was complex and mutative beyond all plans, goals, visions, and expectations.

The challenge, then, for American diplomacy in the twenty-first century will be to find ways to effectively lead a new global dialogue in recognition of this unanticipated mutation of geopolitical DNA. The choice is acceptance or rejection of the unanticipated outcome of global complexity and mutation. For those who are willing to embrace greater global difference, American diplomacy now needs to open its source code and find ways that convey and promote to the world a small kernel of collective truth, trust, and interactivity. This small interactive kernel of collective truth and trust needs to symbolize that the United States sincerely believes in a new, albeit unexpected, world that recognizes and respects the valuable possibilities of difference. American diplomacy in the twenty-first century needs a new message: Americans envision a world that is a better world not because the end of the Cold War eliminated difference, but a world that is a better world because the end of the Cold War enhanced difference. This message needs to be somehow interdependently written into the extant and now antiquated source codes of security and globalization currently articulating the global image of America.

Unfortunately, evidence mounts daily to suggest that what is at hand in the diplomatic toolkit will be insufficient to maintain a projection of the global image of America that embraces greater global difference. Given the activities of the second Bush administration, rebuilding the global image of America in respect and recognition of greater global difference now appears a monumental challenge for many years to come. Fifty-plus years of building the global image of America have been squandered by actions in the aftermath of September 11. The United States is now back to the ad hoc and circumstantial responses, to the unfounded accusations and untested assumptions, to the failure to listen as well as to speak, to forgetting that a small kernel of truth about one's weaknesses and shortcomings can be highly beneficial, and to the perilous ignorance of the world of global communications, all of which so poorly served the global image of America during the bleakest days of the Cold War. Should the present moment be sustained indefinitely, then the global image of America could someday become what Richard Nixon once described as a "wreckage of great civilizations in the past" for many years in the future.

Despite the potential pessimism of those who advocate a world of greater difference, many still do hope that American diplomacy and the global image of America will not eventually symbolize the wreckage of a great civilization in the past. Instead, the hope is that American diplomacy will remember and rearticulate its own past through leadership that tests assumptions before acting upon them, makes deep and full commitments to civic societies everywhere, and invests in understanding and wisely using global media technologies despite the difficulties and expenses of such undertakings. In this way, the global image of America might someday show that the world after the Cold War is not the globaphobic world of twenty-first century American foreign policy. Rather than the present globaphobic moment where the global image of America is dedicated to the representation of fear, mistrust, unfounded accusations, untested assumptions, unbridled power, and disdain for allies, friendships, and difference, the global image of America needs to transcend this globaphobia. The global image of America in the twenty-first century needs to find ways to show America believes the world after the Cold War is a better world precisely because it is a world of greater, not lesser, difference than the world we used to live in.

Yet this idea that the world after the Cold War is a better world precisely because it is a world of greater, rather than lesser, difference seems to be an anathema to the architects of twenty-first-century American foreign policy. Evidence grows daily to suggest they have chosen the path of opposition against greater global difference, complexity, and mutation. Instead, they imagine a world after the Cold War the way it was "supposed" to be: a world without difference from America, a world that reflects back the image of America it ought to reflect, and a world without mutations of any American-led discourses of security, globalization, freedom, or democracy. Rather than build twenty-first-century American foreign policy and a global image of America supporting the unexpected outcomes of the Cold War, the second Bush administration is building twenty-first-century American foreign policy to block the unexpected outcomes of the Cold War. This means stopping the complexity and mutation of the geopolitical genome, shutting down the embryonic adaptations and mutations of the globalization discourse evident in the aftermath of the Cold War. It even means setting out to reengineer the geopolitical genome so it is resistant to mutation. In this sense, the transformative diplomacy of the second Bush administration seeks to transform the global information revolution of the last two decades of the twentieth century into a clash of civilizations for the first two decades of the twenty-first century. This is not a discursive formation in the name of globalization, but rather it is in the name of globaphobia.

Although globaphobia can be understood as irrational reactions to the Asian currency crisis of the mid-1990s; or as a catch-all negative label for anyone who opposes institutions such as the World Trade Organization; or even as a loose coalition of tree-hugging environmentalists, local market shoppers, and New Age ideologies, globaphobia can also be understood as a known strategy for the production of discourse. The strategy of globaphobia as a production of discourse is in keeping with what Michel Foucault outlined in his 1970 College de France lecture: "In every society the production of discourse is at once controlled, selected, organized, and redistributed according to a certain number of procedures, whose role is to avert its powers and its dangers, to cope with chance events, to evade its ponderous, awesome materiality."[5] Globaphobia, as seen through the vision of a single voice, with no mutations, does these things as a discourse: controls, selects, organizes, redistributes, copes with chance events—all the while masking its own powers and dangers to evade awareness of its own ponderous, awesome materiality. In this way, globaphobia as a discursive formation is in keeping with the discursive formations of other disciplines, in that it creates a space, or set of boundaries, to enhance ideas that are, to use Foucault's phrase, "within the true" of its own discipline, but also cordoning off the potential for "the truth" to enter into dialogue from beyond globaphobia's own disciplinary boundaries.

However, globaphobia, when compared with other discursive formations of modernity, seems to also have a special quality, something along with building the boundaries that tell us what is, and what is not, within the true. This special quality of globaphobia, a quality that can be found in the emergent discursive formation of twenty-first-century American foreign policy, is bound up in what Foucault called the difference between reason and folly:

> From the depths of the Middle Ages, a man was mad if his speech could not be said to form part of the common discourse of men. His words were considered null and void, without truth or significance, worthless as evidence, inadmissible in the authentification of acts or contracts, inescapable even of bringing about transubstantiation—the transformation of bread into flesh—at Mass. And yet, in contrast to all others, his words were credited with strange powers, of revealing some hidden truth, of predicting the future, of revealing, in all their naiveté, what the wise men were unable to perceive. They either fell into a void—rejected the moment they were proffered—or else men deciphered in them a naïve or cunning reason, rationality more rational than that of a rational man.[6]

Globaphobia is the discursive formation that allows folly to be truth and the words of a madman to have strange powers even though those words are not part of the common discourse of men. Globaphobia is discursively dependent upon a core audience that has already been fed on, and developed a continuous appetite for, fear, mistrust, paranoia, and xenophobia. All these qualities allow the core audience to reject the modern boundaries of disciplines designed to tell us that which is within the true, as well as to be permeated by the truth, and to replace those boundaries with the distinct, confining, falsely secure, unchanging, impermeable, and exclusive boundaries that contain the territory only within the true of globaphobia. These discursive boundaries of globaphobia are strong, for living within the true of globaphobia requires simultaneously living outside the boundaries of truth for all the other disciplines. Globaphobia becomes a geopolitically discursive extraterritoriality that denies the credence of all other discursive disciplines and extraterritorial possibilities. Globaphobia rewards its core audience and its crafters with strange discursive powers, credits itself with revealing hidden truths and predicting the future, and reveals to those who believe in the discourse of globaphobia all that all the wise men were themselves unable to perceive, thus producing a rationality more rational than that of a rational man, or what might be called by those outside of these discursive borders an irrationality.

It is, of course, extraordinarily difficult to believe that the most powerful nation in the world could truly be in the midst of developing an irrational discourse for its own foreign policy. Thus the difficulty in concluding, a difficulty I mentioned at the beginning of this epilogue. Yet as much as I try to position American foreign policy after September 11 with its Cold War legacy from security to globalization within the true of all possible discursive boundaries—after looking at the evidence of secrecy, of mistrust, of manipulation, of false accusations, of unfounded assumptions, of ignoring global complexities and denying global differences—no matter where I look for evidence of the discursive formation of twenty-first-century American foreign policy, at this moment, what I find is a continuous synthesis of strange powers at work building a globaphobic discourse through a single voice with no mutations.

Notes

Introduction

1. Schwoch, "Global Dialogues, Paradigmatic Shifts, and Complexity," 133–52.

2. Abbas, *Hong Kong.*

3. The *Oxford English Dictionary* traces the etymology of *globalization* to Marshall McLuhan's concept of the global village in the early 1960s and reports one of the first published uses of the actual term *globalization* occurred in 1962: "1960 CARPENTER & MCLUHAN *Explorations in Communication* p. xi, Postliterate man's electronic media contract the world to a village or tribe where everything happens to everyone at the same time: everyone knows about, and therefore participates in, everything that is happening the minute it happens. Television gives this quality of simultaneity to events in the global village." 1962 M. MCLUHAN *Gutenberg Galaxy* 31 The new electronic interdependence recreates the world in the image of a global village . . . 1962 *Spectator* 5 Oct. 495 Globalisation is, indeed, a staggering concept." (OED online, 2005; 2nd ed., 1989.)

4. "Scientists Set Transmission Record."

5. Max Jordan, report on League of Nations International Institute of Educational Cinematography meeting, Nice, 16 April 1935, National Broadcasting Company (hereafter NBC) Collection, box 102, folder Television Institute (Rome), 1935, State Historical Society of Wisconsin (hereafter SHSW).

6. Farrier, "Report on Television Observations in Europe," 15 July 1937, NBC Collection, box 102, folder Report on TV Observations in Europe, SHSW.

7. Thomas Hutchinson to John Royal, 8 September 1938, NBC Collection, box 102, folder TV in Europe, SHSW.

Chapter 1: "A Facet of East-West Problems"

1. Memo to Truman, author unknown, 5 July 1945, Truman Presidential Papers, box 1370 494 A (1951)—498 Contributions (N), folder #495, Truman Library. Emphasis in original.

2. See, for example, Uricchio, "Introduction to the History of German Television, 1935–1944"; Hempel, "German Television Pioneers and the Conflict Between Public Programming and Wonder Weapons"; Hoff, "German Television (1935–1944) as a Subject and Medium of National Socialist Propaganda"; Elsner et al., "Early History of German Television"; and Kohntopp and Ziclinksi, "*Der Deutsche Rundfunk* and Television."

3. Some of these studies are cited below.

4. See, for example, Drummond and Paterson, eds., *Television in Transition;* Drummond, Paterson, and Willis, eds., *National Identity and Europe;* Price, *Television, the Public Sphere, and National Identity.*

5. See the roundtable on "The American Occupation of Germany in Cultural Perspective," with articles by Petra Goedde, Jessica C. E. Gienow-Hecht, Uta G. Poiger, Rebecca Boehling, and Rob Kroes; see also Gimbel, *Science, Technology, and Reparations.*

6. Geniow-Hecht, *Transmission Impossible,* 177–78.

7. LaFeber, "Technology and U.S. Foreign Relations," 2. See also Dizard, *Digital Diplomacy.*

8. For a summary of American foreign policy and ITU activities in the first four decades of the twentieth century, see Schwoch, *American Radio Industry,* esp. chap. 3.

9. See Winkler, "Wiring the World."

10. Schwoch, *American Radio Industry,* chap. 3.

11. PHOTINT issues are discussed at greater length in chapters 7 and 8.

12. Secretary of State Byrnes to Ambassador Harriman, American Embassy, Moscow, 11 October 1945, record group (hereafter RG) 59, 574.WTC/10-1145; Harriman to Byrnes, 31 October 1945, National Archives (hereafter NARA), RG 59, 574.WTC/10-3145; both NARA. All NARA documents cited herein were deposited at Archives II, College Park, Maryland, at the time of writing.

13. Byrnes to Harriman, 29 January 1946, RG 59, 574.WTC/10-1546, NARA.

14. For proceedings, see *Documents of the Moscow Telecommunications Conference, 1946* (Bern: Bureau of the International Telecommunications Union, November 1946), in RG 59 574.WTC; see also Dean Acheson to Harriman, 14 August 1946, RG 59, 574.WTC/7-2946; Francis Colt De Wolf (Chair, U.S. delegation to 1946 Moscow conference) to Kelchner, "World Telecommunications Conference," office memorandum, 4 September 1946, RG 59, 574.WTC/9-446 CS/A; all NARA.

15. Smith (Moscow) to State Department, 9 October 1946, RG 59, 574.WTC/10-946; Acheson to Moscow embassy, 10 October 1946, RG 59, 574.WTC/10-446; Durbrow (Moscow) to State Department, 11 October 1946, RG 59, 574.WTC/10-1146; Acheson to De Wolf (Moscow), 12 October 1946, RG 59, 574.WTC/10-1146 CS/V; De Wolf to Otterman (State Department), 19 October 1946, RG 59, 574.WTC/10-1946; De Wolf to Byrnes, 21 October 1946, RG 59, 574.WTC/10-2146; all NARA. This final document is De Wolf's summary of the conference proceedings.

16. Note from Soviet Foreign Office to Moscow embassy, 20 December 1946, RG 59, 574.WTC/12-2046; Tomlinson to De Wolf, office memorandum, 20 December 1946, RG 59, 574.WTC/12-2046; Soviet Foreign Office to Moscow Embassy, 4 January 1947, RG 59, 574.WTC/9-1646; all NARA.

17. American Legation, Bern, memo on Universal Postal Union and Baltic States, 31 March 1947, RG 59, 574.WTC/3-3147, NARA. The Soviet Union also tried, and failed, to get a UN seat for Karelia.

18. Acheson to American Legation, Bern, 11 April 1947, RG 59, 574.WTC/3-2747, NARA.

19. In ITU deliberations regarding new uses of the electromagnetic spectrum, the ITU allocates bandwidth for new services, and then various national governments assign frequencies within that bandwidth to new users. Despite the global nature of electronic communications in the early twenty-first century, this process is basically the same today. Additionally, for various reasons, including imperial history, the ITU has three "regions" consisting of the Western Hemisphere, Europe and Africa, and Asia. On occasion, these three regions do exercise autonomy over frequency allocations and assignments. Differing allocations for cellular telephony across the three regions, for example, has created the familiar situation where many cellular telephones are not globally compatible (or why an older American-made cell phone typically will not work in Europe).

20. These acronyms eventually emerged to describe the three major television systems currently in use, although these acronyms were not used at the time under examination. These standards describe the number of lines in a single TV frame or image. The NTSC is the current American standard, with 525 lines per frame; PAL is the U.K. standard, with 625 lines per frame, and SECAM is the French standard, with 819 lines per frame. Having said that, I also note this is a simplification in many ways. The PAL standard apparently owes as much to the efforts of the Netherlands as to those of the United Kingdom. Additionally, another complicating factor is the lack of global standards for electrical current. Electric current is cycled and distributed at either 50 or 60 cycles and at either 110/120 or 220/240 volts. Even here, local power plant decisions have some small variation. Variations in electric power supply can cause significant interference in television signal reception, so (unlike radio broadcasting transmissions) local electric power supply has a significant bearing on the choice of technical standards for television. See Crane, *Politics of International Standards* for more on the emergence of NTSC, SECAM, and PAL as color systems.

21. Memorandum by Otterman, 15 August 1949, RG 59, 800.7501/8-1549, NARA.

22. See, for example, State Department to Van Der Pol (Geneva embassy), 14 November 1949, RG 59, 574.Study Group/11-1449, NARA.

23. De Wolf to Kelchner, memorandum, 11 April 1950, RG 59, 399.20 ITU/4-1150, NARA.

24. Edward Allen, report of the Chairman of the U.S. Delegation to Study Group XI on Television, 15 September 1952, RG 59, 399.20–ITU/9-1552, NARA. Two of these systems were already scheduled for future shutdown but were still operating. Some of the differences were not in the number of lines per frame (625 was becoming somewhat of a standard) but in the bandwidth of the signal, varying from 6 to 8 megacycles.

25. Ibid.

26. Murphy (Berlin Embassy) to State Department, 5 August 1948, RG 59, 576.Copenhagen/8-548, NARA. See also Otterman to DeWolf, 11 July 1948, RG 59, 574.Stockholm/7-1148; Otterman to De Wolf, 22 July 1948, RG 59, 574.Stockholm/7-2248; U.S. Secretary of State Marshall to Burton, Copenhagen, 6 August 1948, RG 59, 576.Copenhagen/7-3148; all NARA.

27. Marshall to Caffrey (Paris Embassy), 6 August 1948, RG 59, 576.Copenhagen/8-648, NARA. I have quoted at length from this strongly worded document as it provides a concise summary of many of the major issues.

28. Murphy to State Department, 24 August 1948, RG 59, 576.Copenhagen/8-2448, NARA.

29. De Wolf to State Department, 16 June 1948, RG 59, 576.Copenhagen/6-1548, NARA.

30. Parker to U.K. High Commission in Germany, 1 May 1953, Foreign Office (hereafter FO) 1056/409, British Public Records Office (hereafter PRO-UK).

31. Marvel (Copenhagen Embassy) to State Department, 13 September 1948, RG 59, 576.Copenhagen/9-1148; Marvel to State Department, 16 September 1948, RG 59, 576. Copenhagen/9-1648; both NARA.

32. Otterman to Hooker, Office memorandum, 16 September 1948, RG 59, 574/9-1648, NARA. Documents spell this name as both "Fortoushenko" and "Fortushenko."

Chapter 2: "A Western Mind Would Consider This Kind of Spectacle as Stupid"

1. Williams, *Broadcasting and Democracy in West Germany*, 3.

2. Noam, *Television in Europe*, 77. This book has a very good overview of German broadcasting in its chapter on Germany. For a capsule summary, see also Smith, ed., *Television*, 46–47.

3. Theodore Striebert, Oral History (10 December 1970), 1, Eisenhower Library.

4. "Future of Control of German Information Media," memo, 14 October 1947, RG 59, lot file 55D371, box 7, folder Mr. Wisner's File, NARA.

5. Florence Kelly, State Department, memorandum, 24 November 1950, RG 59, 399.20–ITU/11-2450, NARA. The United States opposed the admission of North Korea; that admission to the ITU did not take place until 1975.

6. Lewis to Olson, 27 November 1950, RG 59, lot 55D371, box 9, folder Top Secret, NARA.

7. HICOG to State Department, 16 November 1950, RG 59, 399.20–ITU/10-2450; De Wolf to Blumberg, memorandum, 2 February 1951, RG 59, 399-20–ITU/2-251; both NARA.

8. De Wolf to Blumberg, memorandum, 2 February 1951. The historical residue has been wiped clean on the ITU Web site, which lists Germany as a charter member from 1 January 1866, and Japan as a member since 29 January 1879.

9. Adenauer to Allied High Commission, 15 December 1952, FO 1056/409, PRO-UK.

10. Otterman to Allison, memorandum, 24 April 1952, RG 59, 399.20–ITU/4-2452, NARA. Unless otherwise indicated, the discussion and quotes in the next few pages draws from this document.

11. FM operates in the same frequency bandwidth as VHF television, so this also has great potential impact on television frequencies. RADAR operates here as well, as do many military and aviation communication systems, particularly during this period. Otterman specifically mentions threats to field tactical units and the point-to-point relay system into West Berlin as military assets at risk, noting he expects the Soviets to specifically request assignments for East Zone television that will interfere with military communications linking West Berlin with West Germany. The 1948 blockade and airlift also raised lingering questions about the security of fixed or wire-based electronic communications between

Berlin and the British, French, and American occupation zones, thereby heightening the strategic value of wave-based (radio) electronic communications for the three German occupiers.

12. Medium wave is better known as AM radio in North America.

13. See State Department to HICOG, Bonn, 23 April 1952, RG 59, 399.20–ITU/4-2152; HICOG to American consul, Geneva, 24 April 1952, RG 59, 399.20–ITU/4-2152; De Wolf (Geneva) to State Department, 21 April 1952, RG 59, 399.20–ITU/4-2152; all NARA.

14. De Wolf (Buenos Aires) to State Department, 10 October 1952, RG 59, 399.20–ITU/10-1052, NARA.

15. State Department to HICOG, 23 April 1952, RG 59, 399.20–ITU/4-2152, NARA.

16. Connors to Smith, memo on RIAS, 28 May 1953, RG 59, lot file 62D333, Executive Secretariat, PSB Working File, 1951–1953, box 8, folder Luncheon Meetings, NARA.

17. G. Turner to I. C. Edwards, 29 November 1950, FO 1056/409, PRO-UK.

18. Noam, *Television in Europe*, 76–78.

19. HICOG to State, 8 July 1950, RG 59, 962B.44/8-1650, NARA.

20. On low-power transmission for West Berlin, see Turner to Edwards, 30 December 1950, FO 1056/49, PRO-UK. On the ECA, see Bernhard, *U. S. Television News and Cold War Propaganda*, 125.

21. See Gimbel, *Science, Technology, and Reparations*, 16, 30, 100, for information on RCA and the "intellectual reparations" activities of American corporations in occupied Germany. RCA representatives in the spring of 1945 tracking down Telefunken engineers for the U.S. government first cabled their results directly to RCA without going through authorized government channels (16). On the price of East German TV sets, see Meade Brunet, RCA, to De Wolf, 2 January 1951, RG 59, 962B.44/1-251, NARA.

22. HICOG to State, 28 January 1952, "Television in the Soviet Zone of Germany," RG 59, 962B.44/1-2852, NARA.

23. HICOG to State, 21 April 1953, "Soviet Zone Television," RG 59, 962B44/4-2153, NARA.

24. HICOG to State, 30 January 1953, "Eastern Television," RG 59, 962B.44/1-3053, NARA.

25. HICOG to State, 13 November 1952, "Television in East Germany," RG 59, 962B.44/11-1352, NARA.

26. HICOG to State, 25 August 1953, "Sovzone Television," RG 59, 962B.44/8-2553; HICOG to USIA, 20 November 1953, "East Zone Television," RG 59, 962B.44/11-2053; HICOG to State, 2 August 1954, inventory of East Zone broadcast transmitters, RG 59, 962B.40/8-254; all NARA.

27. Herbert Jacobson, HICOG, to Sylvester Weaver, 10 July 1953, NBC Collection, box 122, folder Weaver, 1953: International TV, SHSW. Jacobson added, "this has been the biggest boost to television in Germany since the Coronation." The international televising of the Coronation of Elizabeth II in 1953 is discussed in further detail in chapter 5.

28. Fekete, "Television in East and West Germany," 7.

29. On broadcasting (radio) in the British zone, see Tracey, *Decline and Fall of Public Service Broadcasting*, chaps. 7 and 8.

30. Heide Fehrenbach found a similar "zonal dialogue" in her research on postwar cinema in Germany. See *Cinema in Democratizing Germany*, 69–75.

31. Schivelbusch, *In a Cold Crater,* chap. 5.

32. "Potential Penetration of Free World Countries by Soviet Orbit Television," 6 December 1955, IRI Intelligence Survey Summary, RG 306, USIA Office of Research, Classified Research Reports, Briefing Items to Briefing Notes, box 3, NARA.

33. "Overseas Television Developments Quarterly Report," 30 March 1956, RG 306, Office of Research, Intelligence Bulletins, Memorandums and Summaries, 1954–56, box 2, NARA.

34. "Potential Penetration of Free World Countries by Soviet Orbit Television."

35. "Communist Propaganda Activities in Western Europe During 1955," 1 March 1956, RG 306, Records of the USIA, Office of Research, Intelligence Bulletins, Memorandums & Summaries, 1954–1956, box 7, folder IS-2–56, NARA.

36. Romney Wheeler, "Television in Europe," 10 April 1956; McAndrew to Weaver, 29 March 1956; both NBC Collection, box 126, folder Weaver, 1956: Foreign (Wheeler) and Weaver, 1956: International TV (McAndrew), SHSW.

37. Nelson, *War of the Black Heavens,* 93.

38. Wilbur Schramm, "Report of the Chairman on Fourth Annual Conference on US Broadcasting to the Soviet Orbit," no date, conference held 9–13 September 1957, U.S. President's Committee on Information Activities Abroad (hereafter Sprague Committee), box 1, folder Radio and Television #'s 1, 3, 5, 14, 26 (2), Eisenhower Library.

39. "Overseas Television Developments October 1–December 1 1959 and Year-End Roundup for 1959," USIA report, Sprague Committee, box 1, folder Radio and Television #'s 1, 3, 5, 14, 26 (2), Eisenhower Library; "Potential Penetration of Free World Countries by Soviet Orbit Television," USIA IRI Intelligence Summary, 6 December 1955, RG 306, Classified Research Reports, box 3, folder Series Reports—Intelligence Summary (15)—1955, NARA.

40. "Overseas Television Developments," 1 June 1960, R-39-60, RG 306, "R" Reports, 1960–63, box 2, NARA.

41. See chapter 7 for a discussion of live Soviet TV programming to all of Europe in celebration of the Yuri Gagarin spaceflight in April 1961.

42. Enden et al., *Yleisradio 1926–1996,* 133–36. Salokangas (who wrote this section) adds that the British Ambassador was briefed of these developments in 1954. Germany had originally planned to televise the canceled 1940 Helsinki Olympics. Despite ostensibly being the first telecasters, by the 1960s, Estonians were faithful watchers of Finnish TV, and a somewhat common linguistic base allowed for general verbal comprehension by the Estonians. In 1956, the USIA reported that the USSR intended to use the Tallinn station to broadcast some programs in Finnish; see "Current Developments in the Soviet Bloc," 4 June 1956, RG 306, Classified Research Reports, box 1, folder CD/BR—Sov/Sat—MarJune 1956, NARA. The Helsinki—Tallinn TV situation is also discussed in chapter 7.

43. While traveling in the former GDR in 1997, I immediately noticed the orientation of rooftop TV antennae—always to the west. Dresden, the only major city in the former GDR beyond the signal range of Western television, was sardonically referred to during the final years of the Cold War as the "valley of the clueless."

44. See Schwoch, *American Radio Industry.*

Chapter 3: "The Key to Many of These Countries Is Not the Mud Hut Population"

1. See, for example, Shulman, *Voice of America,* esp. epilogue.

2. Sidney Souers, "Central Intelligence Group, Survey of the Function of Monitoring Press and Propaganda Broadcasts of Foreign Powers," 25 February 1946, U.S. Department of State, Office of the Historian, Foreign Relations, 1945–1950, Emergence of the Intelligence Establishment, CIA Historical Files HS/HC-276, Non-Record Material, NARA.

3. See, for example, Simpson, *Science of Coercion;* Glander, *Origins of Mass Communications Research.* See also Rawnsley, ed., *Cold War Propaganda in the 1950s.*

4. For an analysis of Project Troy, see Needell, "Project Troy and the Cold War Annexation of the Social Sciences," 3–38. For a copy of the Project Troy final report (which still had some sanitized sections when I read it in 1997) see RG 59, lot 52-283, International Information Agency, Records Relating to Project Troy 1950–1951, box 1, NARA.

5. Howland Sergeant to James Webb, 27 December 1950, RG 59, lot 52-283, (Project Troy), box 1, NARA.

6. Project Troy report, vol. 1, p. vii, RG 59, lot 52-283, box 1, NARA. Quotations in original.

7. Webb to Frederick J. Lawton, 12 March 1951, RG 59, lot 52-283, (Project Troy), box 1, NARA.

8. Putnam to Gray, 1 November 1951, "Notes on a Grand Strategy for Psychological Operations," Truman Presidential Papers, Staff Member and Office Files (hereafter SMOF): Psychological Strategy Board Files, box 14, folder 091.411 Agenda for PSB meetings, 1951–1952, Truman Library. The bombastic rhetoric is not particularly unusual for PSB documents.

9. Ochenkowski to Truman, 22 July 1951, Truman Presidential Papers, box 1285, folder #427, Truman Library. Some on Madison Avenue would likely have argued there was great propaganda value in circulating American brand names; see, for example, Wagnleitner, *Coca-Colonization and the Cold War.*

10. "America's Campaign of Truth," text of Edward Barrett speech at the Centennial Conference on Communications, Northwestern University, 12 October 1951, RG 59, Subject Files Relating to National Security Policy 1950–1957, lot # 62D385, box 3, NARA.

11. "Are We Winning the War of Words?" *The Northwestern University Reviewing Stand,* transcript of WGN Radio broadcasts, 17:8 (14 October 1951). A copy is found with the Barrett speech cited in the note above.

12. Raymond Allen, Closing Lecture of the Psychological Warfare Seminar, University of North Carolina, 15 August 1952, Truman WHCF, box 31, Folder Psychological Strategy Board [correspondence, 1951–52], Truman Library.

13. "Use of American Influences in Support of U.S. Objectives in Vietnam, Cambodia, and Laos," 6 July 1953, RG 59, lot file 62D333, box 6, folder PSB D-46, NARA. The summary herein is taken from this document.

14. Gray to Truman, 22 February 1952, box 1656, Office File Papers of Harry S. Truman 1289 (1951)—1295 (1948), folder Psychological Strategy Board 1290–D, Truman Library. In his oral history, Gray described PSB as "the necessary, although wobbly, precursor to OCB." Gray, Oral History, 18 June 1973, p. 56, Truman Library.

15. For an excellent and thorough analysis of American propaganda during the Eisenhower presidency, see Osgood, *Total Cold War.*

16. MacDonald, "Communist Exploitation of Western 'Cultural Imperialism,'" 16 May 1952, Truman Presidential Papers, SMOF: Psychological Strategy Board Files, box 9, folder 091—Russia File #2 [of 2], Truman Library. Lloyd Free had warned at an ITU conference in 1948 that American principles were being attacked by Soviet charges of "cultural imperialism"; see his essay "What Can Be Done Through High Frequency Broadcasting for Freedom of Information," NBC Collection, box 284, folder High Frequency Broadcasting Conference, SHSW.

17. On the Canada TV market, see Malcolm, confidential memo, 3 October 1952, FO 953/1261, PRO-UK. On the British cabinet, see draft, no date, "Television—Establishment of an Overseas Television Service," FO 953/1261, PRO-UK. For an example of British interest in Berlin television, see Turner, memo to Information Services Division, "Television in Berlin," 21 January 1952, FO 1056/49, PRO-UK.

18. Hubbell to Sylvester Weaver, NBC (copy of Hubbell's testimony), 18 May 1953, NBC Collection, box 122, folder Weaver, 1953: International TV, SHSW.

19. For two recent studies of American-European intellectual activities during the Cold War, see Berghahn, *America and the Intellectual Cold Wars in Europe;* and Saunders, *The Cultural Cold War.*

20. USIA exhibits are discussed in greater detail in chapter 6.

21. "Discussion at the 235th Meeting of the National Security Council, Thursday, February 3, 1955," Dwight D. Eisenhower Papers as President of the United States (Ann Whitman Files) (hereafter Eisenhower Presidential Papers), NSC Series, box 6, folder 235th Meeting of the NSC, Eisenhower Library.

22. Ibid.

23. Both Simpson, *Science of Coercion,* and Glander, *Origins of Mass Communications Research,* have extensive discussions of Schramm and Pool in their roles as influential advisors to American psychological warfare. My discussion of Schramm and Pool in this chapter is mainly limited to archival documents in which they are the authors of the document or mentioned in the document. Nevertheless, this is a convenient moment to point out that Schramm built both the Institute of Communication Research at the University of Illinois, and later the Department of Communication at Stanford University, largely on the largesse of classified USIA contracts. Pool, associated with the Center for International Studies (CENIS) at MIT, was appointed by the Ford Foundation to establish ways of determining the effectiveness of messages and their impact on audience attitude research. The 1953 planning committee recommending Ford Foundation funding of an international communications unit in CENIS stated, "the term 'international communication' in the sense intended . . . does not mean mechanical, electronic, or other physical means of conveying information across frontiers. What it means is the interchange of words, impressions, and ideas which affect the attitudes and behavior of different peoples toward each other." *Research in International Communication: An Advisory Report of the Planning Committee,* MIT: CENIS, 1953. A copy is found in Jackson, C. D.: Records, 1953–1954 (hereafter C. D. Jackson Records), box 6, folder Rostow, Walter W. (4), Eisenhower Library.

24. Dickson, *Sputnik,* 3.

25. "Discussion at the 339th meeting of the National Security Council, Thursday, October 10, 1957," Eisenhower Presidential Papers, NSC Series, box 9, folder 339th Meeting of the NSC, Eisenhower Library. Unless otherwise indicated, subsequent discussion of this meeting herein is based on this document.

26. Based on the entire document, I believe the "interference" question has to do with telemetry, ground control, and remote reading of satellite-based instruments. On the prestige question, Eisenhower's comment reminds me of this 1955 observation:

> As man reaches upward to the outer atmosphere, new political problems arise, the nature of which we are as yet unable to grasp. Heretofore, the relations between nations and military forces were determined by the geometry of a spheroid's curved surface. . . . Henceforth, international relations will be geared to the more difficult geometry of the interior of a large spheroid enveloping at its core a smaller and impenetrable spheroid, the earth. But even more confusing, the radius of the outer spheroid—symbolizing the aerospace of the altitude which man had reached at any given time—is expanding. The technologically most advanced nations will operate within the highest aerospace, while the spheroids circumscribing the aerial capabilities of the more backward nations will have shorter radii. Hence, in the future, the geometry of power will be described by several enveloping spheroids of different sizes. . . . Truly, a new *Weltbild* is emerging.

Stephan T. Possony and Leslie Rozenzweig, "The Geography of the Air, 1955," quoted in Ploman, *Space, Earth and Communication,* 9.

27. This passage recounting the comments of Arthur Larson is a near-verbatim quote from the summary of the previously cited NSC meeting of 10 October 1957. Because it is not clear in the documents that this is a verbatim quote from Larson, or instead is simply the recorder's summation of Larson's statement, I have not placed the statement in quotation marks, to avoid unintentionally implying that this long passage is a verbatim quote from Larson. I have taken a similar procedure throughout these NSC documents in reporting the lengthier comments of participants, although I do use quotation marks for single words and short phrases.

28. "Discussion at the 347th Meeting of the National Security Council, Thursday, December 5, 1957," Eisenhower Presidential Papers, NSC Series, box 9, folder 347th Meeting of the NSC, Eisenhower Library.

29. A final version of NSC 5814 is included in Logsdon, ed., *Exploring the Unknown.* A working draft of NSC 5814 is included in the document cited in the next note of this chapter.

30. "Discussion at the 371st Meeting of the National Security Council, Thursday, July 3, 1958," Eisenhower Presidential Papers, NSC Series, box 10, folder 371st Meeting of the NSC, Eisenhower Library. For an overview of space policy in the Eisenhower administration, see Callahan and Greenstein, "Reluctant Racer," 15–50.

31. "Discussion at the 415th Meeting of the National Security Council, Thursday, July 30, 1959," Eisenhower Presidential Papers, NSC Series, box 11, folder 415th Meeting of the NSC, Eisenhower Library.

32. "The USIA Survey Operation," Leo Crespi, USIA, to Social Science Research Group, USIA, 22 July 1955, RG 306, Office of Research, Special Reports, 1953–1963, box 10, NARA.

33. Larson comments in transcript, "The Open Mind," WRCA-TV 26 October 1958, NBC Collection, box 248, folder October 26, SHSW.

34. This summary of the formation of the Sprague Committee is taken from the finding guide to Sprague Committee materials at the Eisenhower Library, accessible online in PDF format at http://www.eisenhower.utexas.edu/listofholdingshtml/listofholdingsU/ USPRESIDENTSCOMMITTEEONINFORMATIONACTIVITIESABROAdSPRAGUE-COMMITTEERECORDS1959l.PDF.

35. Waldemar Nielsen is a key figure in this study, and he is discussed further in chapter 4. Nielsen wrote for the *New Yorker,* worked on the Marshall Plan, and served as a cultural affairs officer with the American occupation forces of Germany and HICOG. See, for example, Edward Gruskin to Nielsen, memo on American Forces Radio Network, 3 April 1950, RG 469, Records of the US Foreign Assistance Agencies, 1948–1961, Office of the Special Representation in Europe (1948–1953), Information Division Country Files, 1948–1950, Austria-Germany, box 10, folder Germany—P&I—Special Media, NARA. For much of the 1950s, Nielsen worked closely with Shephard Stone, crafting Ford Foundation programs and initiatives in Europe. See Berghahn, *America and the Intellectual Cold Wars in Europe.* As discussed in chapter 4 of this study, Nielsen, along with Lou Cowan, coined the idea of the Presidential Freedom Awards, originally spun as an American counterweight to the Lenin Prize. Starting in the mid-1960s, Nielsen then embarked on a very long career as a consultant to virtually every major American foundation. For his own account of these activities, see, for example, *Inside American Philanthropy.*

36. Cowan to Nielsen, 1 May 1960, Sprague Committee, box 1, folder Radio and Television #'s 1, 3, 5, 14, 26 (15), Eisenhower Library.

37. "The Impact of Achievements in Science and Technology Upon the Image Abroad of the United States," committee meeting, 20 June 1960, Eisenhower Presidential Papers, Sprague Committee, box 6, folder Science and Technology #23 [file #3] (9), Eisenhower Library. Unless otherwise indicated, discussion of this meeting herein is based on this document.

38. Beckler worked in the President's Office for Science and Technology, headed by George Kistiakowsky.

39. Again, as with the NSC documents previously cited, it is difficult to determine between the verbatim quotes of participants and the comments as written by the recording secretary. I have stuck very closely to the language of the recording secretary throughout my discussion of this meeting, using quotation marks as I can best determine appropriate.

40. This section of the final report can be found in Eisenhower Presidential Papers, Sprague Committee, box 22, Eisenhower Library. Hereafter cited as Sprague Final Report, "Image of American Science and Technology."

41. Sprague Final Report, "Image of American Science and Technology," I-1.

42. Ibid., I-4.

43. Ibid., IX-1–IX-2. Coming on the heels of the McCarthyism of the early 1950s, one surmises that the views of the Sprague Committee had an unsettling effect on American science policy planners. On McCarthyism and American science, see Wang, *American Science in an Age of Anxiety.*

44. "Public Opinion Abroad and US and Soviet Science and Technology," 15 April

1960, RG 306, Office of Research, Research Notes, 1958–62, box 3, NARA. Quotations in original.

45. This account of the case of Edward Yellin is drawn from the following: draft of NSF memorandum to Members of the Executive Committee, National Science Board, 15 June 1961; Lee White to Kennedy, 8 June 1961; David Beckler to Lee White, 6 July 1961; Alan Waterman to Jerome Wiesner, President's Office for Science and Technology, 30 June 1961; Alan Waterman memo, 21 June 1961; all in Papers of Lee C. White, box 12, Kennedy Library.

46. NSF memorandum, 15 June 1961 (see n. 45).

47. For three recent studies addressing American Cold War propaganda and domestic audiences, see Bernhard, *U.S. Television News and Cold War Propaganda*; Sproule, *Propaganda and Democracy*; Curtin, *Redeeming the Wasteland*.

48. Der Derian, *Virtuous War.*

49. Pool to Eugene Skolnikov, 29 April 1960, Eisenhower Presidential Papers, Sprague Committee, box 6, folder Science and Technology #23 [file #2] (6), Eisenhower Library. C. D. Jackson apparently had a close relationship with one of Pool's mentors at MIT, Walt W. Rostow. Jackson and Rostow carried on a regular correspondence and helped each other draft speeches. See Rostow to Jackson, 18 August 1953, C. D. Jackson Records, box 6, folder Rostow, Walter W. (2), Eisenhower Library.

Chapter 4: "A Group of Angry Young Intellectuals"

The epigraph to this chapter is drawn from Nielsen, Oral History, 5 October 1972, Ford Foundation Archives (hereafter FFA), 27.

1. Nielsen, Oral History, p. 2; Ford Foundation Press Release, 1 October 1953; both FFA.

2. See http://www.nytimes.com/2005/11/04/nyregion/04nielsen.html?pagewanted=all for brief biographical information. Nielsen wrote a number of books on philanthropy, including *Big Foundations* (1972), *The Endangered Sector* (1979), *Golden Donors* (1985), and *Inside American Philanthropy* (1996).

3. I do not mean to inadvertently suggest that no one has heard of Nielsen or has prior knowledge of the interactions between American philanthropy and Cold War global media culture; rather, I see this as an understudied topic.

4. Simpson, *Science of Coercion*, 28.

5. Berghahn, *America and the Intellectual Cold Wars in Europe*, 143–44.

6. See Berghahn, *America and the Intellectual Cold Wars in Europe*, esp. chap. 6. A similar discussion, albeit with overly sensational tones, can also be found in Saunders, *Cultural Cold War*, 139–40.

7. See Berghahn, *America and the Intellectual Cold Wars in Europe*, chap. 6; Donald G. Marquis, Oral History, 27 October 1972, pp. 10–14, FFA. At this time, a significant amount of activity took place at the foundation's Pasadena offices, in close proximity to RAND at Santa Monica.

8. Donald Marquis recalled that Project Troy meetings were "very cloak-and-daggerish. We met in an underground, windowless building in Lexington and I'd go home weekends." Marquis, Oral History, pp. 20–21, FFA.

9. Paul Hoffman to MIT President James Killian, 7 August 1952, Grant Number PA05600104, microfilm reel R1194, FFA.

10. Excerpt from the "Settlement to the Docket" for the Board of Trustees Meeting, 15 July 1952, Grant Number PA05600104, microfilm reel R1194, FFA. Despite officially needing a top secret clearance to read the Project Troy report until declassified in 1997, foundation trustees were briefed about Project Troy in 1952.

11. Speier and Marquis to Gaither, 5 May 1951, "Institute of International Communications." This report is attached, along with similar materials, in Speier to James Young, 23 January 1952, all Grant Number PA05600104, microfilm reel R1194, FFA. According to Donald Marquis, Rowan Gaither and perhaps others at Ford originally believed Hans Speier would leave RAND to run CENIS at MIT (which Speier did not do). Marquis, Oral History, pp. 10–14, FFA.

12. My phrase "decision by Speier" is not based on any known direct correspondence from Speier regarding this issue, but rather from previously cited material. Put another way, available evidence indicates that Speier apparently reached this decision.

13. In his oral history—although it is not clear Marquis is also talking about CENIS, but instead is explaining why he declined an offer to run the Ford Behavioral Science Program—he observes: "I made a lot of strange decisions in that period which were based on the assumption that I wanted to stay in close relationship to research—the carrying out of research and this [a directorship] was one step removed. And for the same reason I turned down deanships and provost offers at Stanford and Pittsburgh and so on . . . I was snowed by the idea of using the established scientific method in a new field and it just got perverted into trivia." Marquis, Oral History, pp. 37–41, FFA.

14. Not listed in microfilmed materials examined; it is possible that not all materials from this meeting were microfilmed and, if so, may not have been preserved by the Ford Foundation.

15. For background on Pool (in addition to his own extensive works) see Simpson, *Science of Coercion;* Glander, *Origins of Mass Communications Research.*

16. David de Sola Pool was a prominent figure in New York City; for example, he appeared and spoke on the inaugural telecast of WPIX on 15 June 1948. See Gould, "Television Station WPIX has Premiere," *New York Times,* 20 June 1948; for a brief discussion of this telecast, see Desjardins, *Recycled Stars.*

17. Memo to Nielsen, with stamped date 24 December 1952, with cover note stating, "Wally—-This is it—from Barney," Grant Number PA05600104, microfilm reel R1194, FFA. Parenthetical material in original. Harold Lasswell is discussed further in this chapter. Nathan Lietes was an émigré whose father was a revolutionary purged by the Bolsheviks; Laswell and Lietes worked together during World War II in the Division for the Study of Wartime Communications. On Lietes, see Kuklick, *Blind Oracles,* 32.

18. See Douglas Ensminger to John Howard, 2 April 1954; and Howard to Carl Spaeth, 11 April 1954; both Grant Number PA05600104, microfilm reel R1194, FFA.

19. Relevant correspondence for the 1958 Stanford grant, including proposals drafted by Schramm comparing the Stanford program with CENIS and MIT, may be found in Grant Number PA05800374, microfilm reel R0347, FFA.

20. The 1953 planning committee that put together CENIS stated, "the term 'international communication' in the sense intended . . . does not mean mechanical, electronic,

or other physical means of conveying information across frontiers. What it means is the interchange of words, impressions, and ideas which affect the attitudes and behavior of different peoples toward each other." *Research in International Communication: An Advisory Report of the Planning Committee,* MIT: CENIS, 1953. A copy is found in C. D. Jackson Records, box 6, folder Rostow, Walter W. (4), Eisenhower Library.

21. These issues are discussed further in chapter 3 of this study.

22. Nielsen to Senator Bourke Hickenlooper, 23 March 1953, Papers of Bourke Hickenlooper, Foreign Relations Committee Subject and Individual (hereafter Hickenlooper Foreign Relations Papers), box 86, folder Foreign Relations Committee Subject and Individual Overseas Information Subcommittee, 1953, March–April, Hoover Library. In this letter, Nielsen recaps his testimony before the committee on 16 March 1953. Emphasis in original. Some of these hearings were televised; see, for example, Kathryn Ellis Nowak (residing in Hempstead, N.Y.) to Hickenlooper, 15 May 1953, Hickenlooper Foreign Relations Papers, box 86, folder Foreign Relations Committee Subject and Individual Overseas Information Subcommittee, 1953, March–April, Hoover Library. Mrs. Novak had watched these hearings on TV and completely supported the Voice of America and other overseas information activities. She asked Hickenlooper to see to it that "those men working on the program are *loyal* Americans" and added that New York City was "still permeated with Communists." Emphasis in original.

23. The following account of USIA funding of Williams and Farmer at the 1955 Second International Congress of Cinema and Television School Directors in Cannes is, unless otherwise indicated, from USIA Intelligence Memorandum, "Statements of Dr. Don G. Williams, Participant in the Second International Congress of Cinema and Television School Directors," 29 June 1955, RG 306, IRI Intelligence Memorandum, Office of Research, box 9, NARA.

24. The distribution of the memo included the following federal agencies: USIA, State Department, Department of Defense, CIA, and OCB, the successor psychological warfare planning agency to PSB.

25. "Target: The World," memo, 31 August 1956, RG 59, subject files of the Bureau of Intelligence and Research (INR) 1945–1960, lot 58D776, box 1, folder USIA, NARA.

26. Discussed further in chapter 3 of this study.

27. Chapter 6 of this study examines the 1959 Moscow Exhibition in detail. See also Marling, *As Seen on TV,* chap. 7.

28. The direct approach was also used in arts and performance. An example is overseas tours of U.S. military bands and orchestras. See also Von Eschen, *Satchmo Blows Up the World.*

29. Nielsen memo, 24 March 1961, "A Plan for the Creation of an Annual President's Honor List" and attached note from Walt W. Rostow of 26 March 1961; both Presidential Papers of John F. Kennedy, National Security Files (hereafter Kennedy NSC), box 297, folder Ford Foundation 3/8/61–3/26/61, Kennedy Library. Unless otherwise noted, discussion herein is based on these documents.

30. Murrow to Sorenson, 19 July 1961, RG 306, USIA Files: FRC 68 A 1415, Policy and Plans-General/61, NARA. FRUS JFK #127. Murrow asked to "get the word around" to drop terms such as *under-developed countries, undeveloped countries, backward countries,* and similar terms, advocating *developing* or *modernizing* as preferable substitutes. He also

suggested finding new terms to replace *East-West, Cold War, pro-West,* and *pro-American,* preferring to find ways to articulate concepts such as *peaceful world community* or *world of free choice.*

31. Berghahn, *America and the Intellectual Cold Wars in Europe,* esp. chap. 9.

32. Cowan to Slater, 22 December 1962; Cowan to Slater, 21 December 1962; both in Papers of Joseph E. Slater (hereafter Slater Papers), box 34, folder 352 Organizations: International Broadcast Institute (IBI) Correspondence: Louis Cowan, FFA.

33. Cowan to Slater, 21 December 1962. Cowan added these parochial and national tendencies were "a full-blown exposition of the advertising credo: 'I'm not worried about the war in Bolivia—I'm worried about my waistline.'"

34. Ibid. Quotations in original.

35. Cassirer, a nephew of Ernst Cassirer, was a director of TV news at CBS during the Second World War. See Mike Conway, "Telecasting the News: A TV Pioneer's Period Writings on the 1940s-Era," conference paper, Broadcast Education Association, Las Vegas, N.V., April 2003.

36. IRTI is also often referred to in relevant correspondence as the International Broadcast Institute (IBI). See the following, all in Slater Papers, FFA: no title, handwritten date 3/14/66, notes on Bellagio meeting, box 35, folder 364 IBI: Meeting: Bellagio Reports; "Certificate of Incorporation of International Broadcast Institute," 29 July 1966, box 34, folder 349 Organizations: IBI Charter; notes by Arthur Morse on Bellagio Conference, box 35, folder 364 IBI: Meeting: Bellagio Report; D'Arcy to Slater, 15 August 1966, box 34, folder IBI Correspondence: memoranda miscellaneous.

37. No title, handwritten date 3/14/66, notes on Bellagio meeting, box 35, folder 364 IBI: Meeting: Bellagio Reports, Slater Papers, FFA.

38. Thornton, no date (document has his name handwritten on first page), box 35, folder 364 Organizations: IBI Meeting: Bellagio Reports, Slater Papers, FFA.

39. Notes by Arthur Morse on Bellagio Conference, no date, box 35, folder 365 Organizations: IBI Meetings: Bellagio Reports, Slater Papers, FFA.

40. No title, handwritten date 3/14/66, notes on Bellagio meeting, box 35, folder 364 IBI: Meeting: Bellagio Reports, Slater Papers, FFA.

41. Ibid.

42. The American quest for live transatlantic television and the development of communication satellites in the 1950s and 1960s is discussed in detail in chapters 5, 7, and 8 of this study.

43. "Background Papers for Forthcoming Outer Space Talks in New York," 29 August 1966, Papers of Presidential Aides—Joseph Califano (hereafter Califano Papers), box 71, folder Celestial Bodies Treaty Negotiating History—1 SECRET, Johnson Library. The rise of satellites culminating in the negotiation of this 1967 treaty is discussed in chapter 8.

44. Unusual in part because of the diatribes Bundy leveled at the Ford Foundation while he was the NSC director in the Kennedy administration. Bundy told John McCloy on 4 April 1962 that the foundation was "overadministered," and they found it "almost as hard to terminate programs as a university does." Criticizing both the Ford Foundation and Harvard University for failing to act together "in the grand manner," Bundy suggested large-scale projects for overseas development. He added on 25 June 1962 that "university people are a cantankerous and self-righteous lot" and the way to solve this was "direct negotiations between a Ford Foundation Vice-President and a Harvard Dean." Bundy to

McCloy, 4 April 1962 and 25 April 1962, both Kennedy NSC, box 297, folder Ford Foundation 4/4/62–5/7/62, Kennedy Library.

45. Stone to Bundy, 10 August 1966, box 12, folder IBI Early Ford Foundation Proposal 8–10–66—Shep Stone, Papers of Sig Mickelson (hereafter Mickelson Papers), SHSW.

46. "The Social Planetarium," in Lasswell to Slater, 25 August 1966, box 37, folder 403 Communications, International, Slater Papers, FFA. The 1967 Eurovision "Our World" program reminds me of this Lasswell passage; see Parks, *Cultures in Orbit,* 21–46.

47. In addition to Simpson, *Science of Coercion,* Kuklick, *Blind Oracles,* and Glander, *Origins of Mass Communications Research,* on the durability of this network of experts in the arena of domestic communications policy in the 1960s and 1970s, see Light, *From Warfare to Welfare.*

Chapter 5: "We Can Give the World a Vision of America"

1. Byrnes to Truman, 19 July 1946, Truman Presidential Papers—Official Files, box 533, folder OF 85–U, Truman Library.

2. See chapters 1 and 2 of this study.

3. There are, of course, some exceptions. National Socialist Germany had introduced the fixed-frequency set—basically, a set that was not tunable—as a low-cost radio set for the masses that could not be tuned to anything other than Nazi stations. The USSR, and to a lesser extent some areas of Eastern Europe, still made extensive use of wired loudspeakers rather than tunable sets—a majority of Soviet listeners were on wired loudspeakers rather than tunable sets until about 1970. The United States, the United Kingdom, and France introduced an extensive FM radio system into occupied Germany: in part to counter the Nazi experience, in part to counter Soviet propaganda. However, the general observation of universal radio reception holds.

4. State Department to Van Der Pol (Geneva Embassy), November 14, 1949, RG 59, 574.Study Group/11-1449, NARA.

5. *Tele-Tech,* December 1952; found in Holthusen Papers, box 10, folder Television: Worldwide Network Plan—Printed Matter, Hoover Library.

6. In February 1928, British TV experimenter John Baird did send a crude TV signal across the Atlantic via shortwave. From about 1936 to 1939, and again after signal resumption from 1946 to the early 1950s, a BBC-TV signal was occasionally picked at the RCA facilities at Riverhead, New York (discussed later in this chapter). Similar to the earliest days of radio broadcasting, the earliest days of telecasting saw a number of reports detailing reception over extraordinarily long distances, including intercontinental over-the-air reception. The growth of stations worldwide contributed to attenuation—the tendency for signals to interfere with each other and thereby lessen the distance they travel—and the sunspot cycle of the 1950s further aggravated long-distance TV reception. Long-distance TV reception, often known as "TV DX," remains as an amateur hobby.

7. Karl E. Mundt, "We Can Give the World a Vision of America!," *Baltimore Sun,* 19 November 1950; found in RG 59, Records Relating to International Information Activities, 1938–1953, lot # 53D11, box 88, folder Television, NARA.

8. Karl E. Mundt, text of "The Vision of America" speech, on 5 June 1950, 81st Cong., 2nd sess., *Congressional Record* 96, pt. 110: 8130–39.

9. Mundt, "We Can Give."

10. Senator Hickenlooper of Iowa, speaking for himself, Mr. Knowland, Mr. Wiley, Mr. Mundt, Mr. Fulbright, Mr. Green, Mr. Gillette, and Mr. Hill, "To strengthen the foreign relations of the United States by establishing a Commission on International Telecommunications," on 27 June 1953, S.J. Res. 96, 83rd Cong., 1st sess. in Papers of Bourke B. Hickenlooper, Senate Foreign Relations Committee (hereafter Hickenlooper Papers—Senate—Foreign Relations), box 89, Hoover Library.

11. *Television Opportunities,* July–Aug 1953; found in Holthusen Papers, box 10, folder Television: Worldwide Network Plan—*Television Opportunities* 1953–55 and undated, Hoover Library.

12. Ibid.

13. Sarnoff to Coy, 22 December 1948; Sarnoff to Forrestal, 30 November 1948; Sarnoff to Truman, 30 November 1948; Sarnoff, "Outline of Proposal," 30 November 1948; all in Truman Presidential Papers, White House Central Files (hereafter WHCF): Confidential File, State Department Correspondence File, 1948–49, box 39, folder State Department, Correspondence, 1948–49 [5 of 6 . . .], Truman Library. The description of Ultrafax and its potential for television in the main text of this study, unless otherwise noted, is from these documents.

14. Sarnoff to Truman, 30 November 1948; "Outline of Proposal," 30 November 1948 (see preceding n. 13.)

15. "Ultrafax: A million words a minute," RCA pamphlet, 21 October 1948, NBC Collection, box 596, folder Ultrafax; White to Sarnoff, 6 July 1953, NBC Collection, box 566, folder Transatlantic TV; both SHSW.

16. David Sarnoff, statement to UN Forum on Freedom of Information, 10 December 1949, Holthusen papers, box 10, folder Television: Worldwide Network Plan—Sarnoff Speeches 1950, Hoover Library; David Sarnoff, "Our Next Frontier . . . Transoceanic TV," *Look,* 12 September 1950, Holthusen Papers, box 6, folder Television: Worldwide Network Plan Clippings 1950–1958 and undated, Hoover Library. The 1949 UN conferees awarded Sarnoff with a certificate of appreciation for his "advocacy of concepts of freedom to listen and freedom to look as fundamental expressions of Freedom of Information." Sarnoff did not also advocate freedom to speak and to show, and instead merely settled for freedom to listen and to look, thus preserving the elite speaker—mass listener dichotomy at the heart of twentieth century mass culture.

17. Sarnoff, "Our Next Frontier . . . Transoceanic TV."

18. In addition to documents cited in this study, see also Osgood, *Total Cold War,* part 1, for a thorough discussion of the formation of the USIA and attendant American propaganda activities.

19. "International Information Administration 10th Semiannual Report of the Secretary of State to Congress on the International Information and Educational Exchange Program," July–December 1952, in Hickenlooper Papers—Senate—Foreign Relations, box 88, folder Information Program Subcommittee, International Information Administration, General, 1953, Hoover Library.

20. The brief biography of Holthusen in this paragraph is based on the finding guide to the Henry Holthusen collection in the Hoover Library at http://www.ecommcode2 .com/hoover/research/historicalmaterials/other/holthuse.htm.

21. Holthusen to Daniell, 5 May 1952; Daniell to Holthusen, 22 May 1952; both in Hol-

thusen Papers, box 6, folder Television: Worldwide Network Australia, 1952, Hoover Library.

22. "The UNITEL Relay Network Plan," October 1952, C. D. Jackson Records, box 6, folder S, Eisenhower Library.

23. *Look,* 27 January 1953, reprint, illustration, found in Holthusen Papers, box 6, folder Television: Worldwide Network Plan Clippings 1950–1958 and undated, Hoover Library.

24. Halstead, "New York—London Television Microwave Link vs. Coaxial Cable," 27 May 1952; found in Holthusen Papers, box 3, folder Medium-Wave Radio 1951–60 and undated, Hoover Library.

25. "A Report on Radio Broadcasting and Intercity Telecommunication Services in the Republic of Turkey, With Recommendations for Future Development, Including the use of Television and Microwave Relay Network Facilities," (hereafter "1951 Turkey Telecommunication Services Report"), prepared by Henry Holthusen, William S. Halstead, and Walter Duschinsky, in Holthusen Papers, box 11, folder Worldwide Network Plan—Turkey Holthusen Report, 1951, Printed Copy, Hoover Library. This is a bound volume running about three hundred pages in length.

26. Partner, *Assembled in Japan.* Chapter 3, "The Vision of America: Bringing Television to Japan" (71–106) is an excellent discussion of NTV and Holthusen based on Japanese documents, with an analysis of postwar Japanese television in the context of Cold War geopolitics. See also *Pacific Stars and Stripes* 9:222, 1 September 1953, Holthusen Papers, box 9, folder Television: Worldwide Plan—Japan Clippings, 1952–59 and undated; *Tokyo Evening News,* 28 August 1953, and undated photo, Hickenlooper Papers—Senate—Foreign Relations, box 89, folder Information Programs Subcommittee International Telecommunications Nippon Television Network, 1952–54; all Hoover Library.

27. On the Canadian TV market, see Malcolm, confidential memo, 3 October 1952, FO 953/1261, PRO-UK. On the British cabinet, see draft, no date, "Television—Establishment of an Overseas Television Service," FO 953/1261, PRO-UK.

28. Taylor to Weaver, "Live TV From Europe," 14 September 1951, NBC Collection, box 277, folder NBC Taylor Europe; Hanson to Denny, "Transoceanic Television," 27 February 1952, NBC Collection, box 278, folder NBC Taylor Transoceanic Television; both SHSW.

29. M.A. Robb, memo, 3 June 1953, FO 1056/409, PRO-UK.

30. Fraser to Nixon, March 3 1952, NBC Collection, box 278, Folder NBC Taylor Transatlantic Television, SHSW, discussed the funeral of George VI; "God Save the Queen," no date but before 2 June 1953, NBC Collection, box 279, folder Foreign Contacts, SHSW, analyzes media coverage of the 1937 coronation. The archbishop of Canterbury and duke of Norfolk, in consultation with three female guests of the royal family, spent the evening of the 1937 coronation in a private projection room screening newsreel rush footage of the ceremony and clearing or censoring footage for public release.

31. McAndrew to Taylor, 21 October 1952; Wheeler to Taylor, 21 October 1952; both NBC Collection, box 278, folder Coronation: Astral, SHSW. Romney Wheeler added, "Ah, for a nice simple Election to cover!"

32. CBS Television Coronation Souvenir, no date but after 3 June 1953; Sig Mickelson Papers, box 1, folder Coronation 1953, SHSW.

33. Based on Nielsen reports. See *Radio-TV Daily,* 7 July 1953, NBC Collection, box 279, folder Coronation—General, SHSW.

34. CBS Coronation Souvenir.

35. "Looking Ahead," *National Planning Association Monthly Report* 2:7, October 1954. A clipping may be found in Holthusen Papers, box 6, folder Television Worldwide Network Plan clippings, 1950–58 and undated, Hoover Library.

Chapter 6: "A Record of Some Kind in the History of International Communication"

Epigraph to chapter 6 is drawn from "Inventory of Resources Presently Available for Psychological Operations Planning," report, Col. Charles McCarthy, Psychological Strategy Board, 5 January 1952, RG 59, lot file 62–D-33, box 4, folder PSB D-19, NARA. Emphasis in original. This remarkable document lists hundreds of "resources" that might be mobilized as a part of American psychological strategy and tactics for the Cold War and targets research programs at many American universities, including Yale, Johns Hopkins, Columbia, Harvard, Stanford, Cornell, Washington, Princeton, MIT, Chicago, Illinois, Virginia, and the New School for Social Research, as well as every major newspaper and wire service and scores of civic organizations.

1. The descriptive term of the time used in the USIA reports is "Negro" and direct quotes herein taken from USIA reports will use this term.

2. See Hixson, *Parting the Curtain,* esp. chaps. 6 and 7, for a full and informed discussion of the 1959 Moscow Exhibition.

3. See Hixson, *Parting the Curtain;* Haddow, *Pavilions of Plenty;* Marling, *As Seen on TV.*

4. The 1956 Space Unlimited exhibit is discussed further in chapter 7.

5. "Draft Script for 'PEOPLE'S CAPITALISM,'" 14 October 1955; speech extract of 'People's Capitalism' delivered by Theodore Repplier, President, Advertising Council of America; "Capitalism—This is America" reprint from editorial in *Collier's Magazine,* 6 January 1956; circular memo on People's Capitalism exhibit to all USIS posts, 12 June 1956; all in RG 306, Multi Area (World) Project Files, 1953–63, box 1, NARA. Hixson, *Parting the Curtain,* 133–45, and Osgood, *Total Cold War,* 270–75, offer detailed discussions of People's Capitalism.

6. "Draft Script for PEOPLE'S CAPITALISM."

7. "People's Capitalism in the U.S.A.," brochure produced for Washington exhibit, 14–22 February 1956, RG 306, Multi Area (World) Project Files, 1953–63, box 1, NARA.

8. "Monthly Report on People's Capitalism for August 1957," no date, RG 306, Multi Area (World) Project Files, 1953–63, box 1, NARA.

9. Memo on meeting with the vice president, 2 June 1959, RG 306, Records Relating to the American National Exhibition, Moscow, 1957–59, box 4, NARA.

10. Abbott Washburn later recalled that Nixon "stayed in the Soviet Union for a couple of weeks . . . went around to a number of points in the country and visited plants and dams, and when he came back, he did something that no top official of the government had ever done in the Soviet Union: he went on television . . . it was a singularly appropriate,

effective, and appealing, moving talk . . . it was one of Nixon's high points." Washburn, Oral History, January 1968 volume, p. 88, Eisenhower Library.

11. "RAMAC and Model C on Moscow Mission," *IBM World Trade News*, July 1959, found with RG 306, Records Relating to the American National Exhibition, Moscow, 1957–59, box 5, RAMAC memo, 29 August 1959, NARA.

12. Memo from P. R. Matheny, IBM, to USIA, 29 August 1959, RG 306, Records Relating to the American National Exhibition, Moscow, 1957–59, box 5, NARA.

13. In another use of machines to collect Soviet public opinion data, exhibition attendees were encouraged to vote for their favorite exhibit on voting machines. See "Shoup Voting Machine Poll," 29 August 1959, RG 306, Records Relating to the American National Exhibition, Moscow, 1957–59, box 5, NARA. However, of the 2.7 million attendees, only about fifteen thousand used the voting machines, or less than half of the total number of questions answered by RAMAC (about 37,000 answers). About two thousand individual entries were written in comment books located throughout the exhibition grounds. See "Report on American Exhibition in Moscow," USIA Office of Research and Analysis report P-47-59, 28 September 1959, RG 306, Records Relating to the American National Exhibition, Moscow, 1957–59, box 7, NARA.

14. "The RAMAC Experience," USIA Office of Research and Analysis report R-28-60, 4 May 1960, RG 306, "R" Reports 1960–63, box 2, NARA. The discussion of RAMAC in the next few paragraphs is taken from this report.

15. Bird, *Better Living.*

16. "Some Notes Concerning the U.S. Exhibit in Moscow," Hadley Cantril, Yale University, 22 January 1959, RG 306, Records Relating to the American National Exhibition, Moscow, 1957–59, box 7, NARA.

17. USIA Director Edward Murrow to Kennedy, "First Effort to Measure 'World Opinion,'" 10 July 1963, RG 306, Multi Area (World) Project Files, 1953–63, box 8, NARA.

18. "Communist Bloc Scientific and Technological Achievements and Prospects Over the Next Decade," no date, probably 1959, Sprague Committee, box 6, folder Science and Technology #23 [file 31] (8), Eisenhower Library.

19. "Agenda Item No. 7," 29 June 1959, RG 59, Executive Secretariat Records Relating to the National Aeronautics and Space Council, 1959, box 1, NARA.

20. On Soviet computing and the debate regarding cybernetics, see Gerovitch, "'Russian Scandals'"; Gerovitch, "'Mathematical Machines' of the Cold War"; and Gerovitch's book, *From Newspeak to Cyberspeak.* See also Erlichigoity, *Planet Management;* Edwards, *Closed World;* and Conway and Siegelman, *Dark Hero of the Information Age,* esp. part 3, on the Cold War, computers, and cybernetics.

21. Graham, *What Have We Learned,* esp. pp. 34–42.

22. Basically, Lysenkoism used Marxist-Leninist scientific theory building to deny the existence of the gene and thus influence agricultural policy. Promulgated in the 1930s with ultimately disastrous results for both agriculture and the environment, Lysenkoism was fully rejected by the 1960s, in large part due to the eventual diffusion of the 1953 work of Francis Crick and James Watson on DNA (which eventually earned them the Nobel Prize) into Soviet scientific literature. See Graham, *What Have We Learned,* 22–30.

23. See Callahan and Greenstein, "Reluctant Racer."

24. "Soviet Curiosity about America," USIA Office of Research and Analysis report R-15-60, 9 March 1960, RG 306, "R" Reports 1960–63, box 1, NARA.

25. Ibid.

26. Many thanks to Susan Courtney for giving me this description of RAMAC as a benign American liberal in response to a conference presentation at the Center for Twentieth Century Studies in 1999.

27. Pool to Eugene Skolnikov, 29 April 1960, Sprague Committee, box 6, folder Science and Technology #23 [file #2] (6), Eisenhower Library.

28. Memo to Ruth Erbb, 3 August 1959, RG 306, Records Relating to the American National Exhibition, Moscow, 1957–59, box 1, NARA.

29. "Overseas Television Developments October 1–December 31, 1959," 3 February 1960, USIA Office of Research and Analysis report R-3-60, RG 306, "R" reports 1960–63, box 1, NARA.

30. Leslie Brady, U.S. Embassy (Moscow) to State Department, "Three Weeks of Sokolniki," 20 August 1959, RG 306, Records Relating to the American National Exhibition, Moscow, 1957–59, box 7, NARA.

31. Ibid.

32. Leslie Brady, U.S. Embassy (Moscow) to State Department, "Six Weeks of Sokolniki," 11 September 1959, RG 306, Records Relating to the American National Exhibition, Moscow, 1957–59, box 7, NARA.

33. Brady, "Three Weeks of Sokolniki."

34. "Soviet Counter Moves to American Exhibition in Moscow," USIA Office of Research and Analysis Research Note 72–59, 15 May 1959, RG 306, Records Relating to the American National Exhibition, Moscow, 1957–59, box 7, NARA. On Soviet exposure to American consumer society, see also Ponomarkeno, "Out of the Kitchen." Ponomarkeno also discusses the 1959 Moscow Exhibition and RAMAC.

35. Brady, "Three Weeks of Sokolniki."

36. For a comparative table of the U.S.-USSR space race, including much data on unmanned satellites, see Harford, *Korolev*, 324–39.

37. Leslie Brady, "Post Mortem on Sokolniki," 6 October 1959, RG 306, Records Relating to the American National Exhibition, Moscow, 1957–59, box 7, NARA.

38. See also Osgood, *Total Cold War,* esp. pp. 275–80.

39. For a comprehensive study of the USIA written by a former USIA officer, see Dizard, *Inventing Public Diplomacy.*

40. "Report on American Exhibition in Moscow," USIA Office of Research and Analysis report P-47-59, 28 September 1959, RG 306, Records Relating to the American National Exhibition, Moscow, 1957–59, box 7, NARA. Emphasis in original. The following discussion is based on this document.

41. Ibid.

42. "Comparative Summary of Soviet Coverage of the Vice President's Visit," USIA report S-47-59, 8 September 1959, RG 306, Special Reports, 1953–63, box 17, NARA.

43. "Overseas Television Developments," 3 February 1960, R-3-60, RG 306, "R" Report, 1960–63, box 1, NARA.

44. "Soviet TV, September and October, 1951," John McSweeney, Moscow Embassy, to State Department, 14 November 1951, RG 59, 961.44/11-1451, NARA. Knox and Stines, as

discussed further, wrote many of the first detailed reports about Soviet television. Mc-Sweeney reported in this memo that a second TV set arrived in the embassy in October 1951, an RCA-Victor brought over and converted to local standards by Embassy Counselor Elim O'Shaughnessy. He also reported the British Embassy had also recently purchased its first TV set; one American newspaper correspondent, Thomas Whitney, had a TV set; the Swedish Embassy counselor had a TV set; and although the Venezuelan Embassy was the first to have a TV set in 1949, that set had been given by the ambassador to his private secretary when he left Moscow in 1950. Regarding the British Embassy, the British legation reported to London in December 1954 that the embassy TV sets "are in constant use" by the laundry ladies and chancery servants, which made attentive monitoring by embassy personnel difficult. C. C. Parrott, Moscow Embassy, to Earl Jellicoe, Foreign Office, London, 3 December 1954, FO 953/1491, PRO-UK. For an overview of American diplomacy in Moscow, see Mayers, *The Ambassadors and America's Soviet Policy.*

45. Stines to State Department, 18 November 1950, RG 59, 961.44/11-1850, NARA.

46. "Moscow Television Program November 16, 1950," Collins to State Department, 25 November 1950, RG 59, 961.44/11-2550, NARA.

47. "Stalin Prize Winners on Moscow Television," Knox to State Department 2 April 1951, RG 59, 961.44/4-251, NARA. On Stalinist popular culture and "speaking Bolshevik" in the 1930s, see Kotkin, *Magnetic Mountain.*

48. "Moscow Television Center Increases Program Schedules; Comments on Past Performance," Knox to State Department, 12 April 1951, RG 59, 961.44/4-1251, NARA. Emphasis in original.

49. "Moscow Television Developments, April-June, 1951," Stines to State Department, 26 June 1951, RG 59, 961.44/6-2651; "Soviet Railroad Day on Moscow TV," Stines to State Department, 16 August 1951, 961.44/8-1651; "Moscow TV Programs, July-August 1951," Stines to State Department, 31 August 1951, 961.44/8-3151; "Anniversary of Stalingrad Power and Irrigation Project," Stines to State Department, 4 September 1951, RG 59, 961.44/9-551; "Soviet Tank Day on Moscow TV," Stines to State Department, 10 September 1951, RG 59, 961.44/9-1051; "Anniversary of Turkmen Canal Project on Moscow TV," Stines to State Department, RG 59, 961.44/9-1351; all NARA.

50. "Soviet Performers at Berlin Youth Festival on Moscow TV," Stines to State Department, 14 September 1951, RG 59, 961.44/9-1451, NARA.

51. "Soviet Television Developments: November and December, 1951 and January, 1952," John McSweeney to State Department, 26 January 1952, RG 59, 961.44/1-2652, NARA.

52. "Number of Television Sets in Moscow Area," McSweeney to State Department, 21 March 1952, RG 59, 961.44/3-2152, NARA. At about this time, the State Department informed the Moscow Embassy that its television reports were of value and interest in Washington and asked for short summaries of as much of the programming schedule as possible. Thus the embassy reports changed to short lists of program titles typical of guides in American newspapers, which unfortunately eliminated the richly detailed textual analyses of Moscow TV from embassy staffers typical of 1950 and 1951.

53. "TV Roundup," Elim O'Shaughnessy to State Department, 16 December 1952, RG 59, 961.44/12-1652, NARA.

54. "Moscow Television Programs for 1953," Jacob Beam to State Department, 12 February 1953, RG 59, 961.44/2-1253, NARA.

55. Pat Murrin to Taylor, 7 July 1953, NBC Collection, box 279, folder Foreign Contacts, SHSW.

56. C. C. Parrott, Moscow Embassy, to Earl Jellicoe, Foreign Office, London, 3 December 1954, FO 953/1491, PRO-UK.

57. "Report on Third Annual Conference on U.S. Broadcasting Into the Soviet Orbit," 13–17 August 1956, RG 306, Classified Research Reports, box 3, folder Research Report 95-31-56—1956, NARA. Wilbur Schramm chaired this conference.

58. "The RAMAC Experience," USIA Office of Research and Analysis report R-28-60, 4 May 1960, RG 306, "R" Reports, box 2, NARA.

59. "Soviet Curiosity About America."

60. Ibid. Emphasis in original.

61. "Report on American Exhibition in Moscow," USIA Office of Research and Analysis report P-47-59, 28 September 1959, RG 306, Records Relating to the American National Exhibition, Moscow, 1957–59, box 7, NARA. In this report a "communication unit" was operationalized as one American answering one Soviet question, with units generated per question determined by how many Soviets received the answer. For example, one American answer received by thirty Soviets generated thirty communication units.

62. Brady, "Post Mortem on Sokolniki."

63. Pool, "Public Opinion and the Control of Armaments," 1 May 1960, Sprague Committee, box 13, folder Consultants (2), Eisenhower Library.

Chapter 7: "Something of That Sense of World Citizenship"

1. See Gerald Beadle, "Global Television—A Force for World Unity," speech at the Waldorf-Astoria Hotel to the New York Chapter of the Academy of Television Arts and Sciences, 5 October 1961; BBC press release, no date, "BBC TV Triumphs at Montreax"; both Papers of Newton Minow (hereafter Minow Papers), box 6, folder British Broadcasting Corporation 1961, Mar–May, 1963, SHSW. Unless indicated, the following account of the BBC and its role in achieving live all-European television transmission is based on these documents.

2. "Planning for Future Information Activities," 8 August 1960, Sprague Committee, folder PCIAA 43, Eisenhower Library.

3. Difficult at the time because of the distance between Helsinki and Tallinn, as well as the technical conversions required. By 1959, Helsinki established a microwave link with Stockholm for TV program exchange via the Aaland Islands and Turku, thus networking Finland to the television landscape of Western Europe and Eurovision. "To be in contact with the other neighboring countries, a temporary 7GHz link connection between Tallinn in Estonia and Porkkala in Finland was installed in 1961. This connection was first used to transmit the May Day parade in Moscow to Eurovision. Some weeks earlier Yleisradio had helped to pass on an important news item from Moscow to the Eurovision network. The world's first cosmonaut, Yuri Gagarin, was received in Moscow, and the TV transmission from Tallinn was received on the roof of the Pasila water tower using an ordinary TV set and the signal was fed via a microwave link to Eurovision." Enden, et al., *Yleisradio 1926–1996*, 255. Porkkala, a peninsula in the Gulf of Finland, had been occupied by the Soviets in 1944 by renegotiating a prior Soviet lease of the Hanko peninsula; the

Soviets withdrew military forces in 1956. Pasila, the location of the water tower with the TV antenna, is a Helsinki neighborhood.

4. Beadle, "Global Television—A Force for World Unity."

5. Ibid.

6. "British Public Opinion on Space Leadership," Office of Research, Research memorandums, 1963–1982, RG 306, M-36-70, 4 December 1970, box 12, NARA.

7. Sprague Committee, "The Impact of Achievements in Science and Technology Upon the Image Aboard of the United States," part III, p. 1, draft 9 June 1960, box 7, folder Science and Technology #23 [file #4] (2), Eisenhower Library.

8. Office of Strategic Services, Research and Analysis Branch, R&A #2775, "The World-Wide Intelligence Photographic Documentation Project," National Archives Microfilm Publication M1221, #2775, RG 59, NARA. The USSR is curiously excluded from this project, despite covering the rest of the world, including all the other wartime allies. Perhaps OSS photoreconnaissance plans for the postwar USSR were compartmentalized outside of this particular global project. The USSR had also not participated in the 1944 Chicago conference that organized the International Civil Aviation Organization; signatories had promised, among other things, overflight rights for civil aircraft, and perhaps the OSS took signatories into account in preparing this study. The question of international overflight, though not explicitly discussed in this book, was crucial to many satellite decisions by presidential administrations in the 1950s and 1960s; for Eisenhower, one of the bright spots about Sputnik was that the Soviets de facto established the principle of worldwide satellite overflight with their Sputnik orbit, thus negating any future Soviet attempts to protest U.S. satellite overflights of the USSR.

9. For overviews, see, for example, Day, Logsdon, and Latell, eds., *Eye in the Sky;* Richelson, *Wizards of Langley* on CORONA; and for a popular treatment tied to science and IGY, see Bergaust and Beller, *Satellite!*

10. Bergaust and Beller, *Satellite!*, 21.

11. Ibid., 132–33.

12. "The U.S. 'Space Unlimited' Exhibit at the Berlin Fair, 1956," report no. A-3, series no. 3, 24 October 1956, Research Staff, Office of Public Affairs, American Embassy (West Germany), RG 59, decimal file location unknown, NARA.

13. The discussion of U.S. satellite activity herein centers on publicly announced and declassified satellites used for scientific and similar purposes. This discussion does not, for the most part, include classified satellite launches, rocket soundings, unmanned suborbital probes, balloons, rocket stage and equipment testing, and similar activities. In terms of communications and signals research, several experiments (some classified, others unclassified) using suborbital balloons as passive reflectors were carried out during this era, as well as experiments using the moon, and experiments using meteor tails (meteor burst communications), employing both natural phenomena as passive reflectors for communications relay. Meteor burst communications, which are of longstanding interest to some amateur radio enthusiasts, had a research revival in the 1980s under the Strategic Defense Initiative, and explorations of commercial applications for meteor burst communications have recently emerged.

14. Now better known by its acronym DARPA, for Defense Advanced Research Projects Agency.

15. "United States Aeronautics and Space Activities, January 1–December 31 1958, Year One of the Space Age," no date, probably February 1959, RG 59, Executive Secretariat Records Relating to the National Aeronautics and Space Council, 1959, lot 65–D-464 (hereafter lot 65–D-464), box 2, NARA.

16. Dickson, *Sputnik,* 191–202 discusses Project SCORE, and the quoted phrase is found on p. 200. Dickson also reproduces Eisenhower's SCORE message.

17. "Discussion at the 392nd Meeting of the National Security Council, Tuesday, December 23, 1958," Eisenhower NSC Papers, box 10, folder 392nd Meeting of NSC, Eisenhower Library.

18. Dickson, *Sputnik,* 207–9.

19. See E. C. Ezell and L. N. Ezell, *Partnership* at http://www.hq.nasa.gov/office/pao/ History/SP-4209/ch2–3.htm#explanation2, for a capsule summary. West Ford was also known as Project Needles.

20. Although transatlantic radio telephony had begun in 1927, transatlantic phone conversations prior to the laying of the first transatlantic telephone cable (TAT 1) in 1956 were often unreliable, as Arthur Clarke recounts: "Today, when you call a friend on the far side of the Atlantic, you seem to be talking quietly together—not, as was too often the case in the old days, shouting over a high wind during a thunderstorm." Clarke, *Voice Across the Sea,* 17.

21. Even Telstar in 1962 was not usable at all hours for a transatlantic link, as shall be discussed later.

22. Jerome Weisner, memorandum for the President, 27 April 1963, Kennedy NSC Papers, box 284, Kennedy Library.

23. Walt Rostow to McGeorge Bundy, "OCB Functions," 27 January 1961, Kennedy NSC Papers, box 284, folder Operations Coordinating Board General 1/27/61–7/27/61 and Undated, Kennedy Library. Rostow noted that "a group of cats and dogs appears to have fallen, out of normal Washington history, into the OCB: the Antarctic; exhibits, educational exchanges, radio and television; and disaster relief. Also certain aspects of the outer space business. For these, homes—probably other homes—must be found."

24. Kennedy Executive Order 10995, "Assigning Telecommunications Management Functions," 17 February 1962, Kennedy NSC Papers, box 283a, Kennedy Library.

25. See the report of the Task Group on the Survivable Communications Requirements of the President and Top Civil Leaders, 20 August 1962, Kennedy Presidential Papers NSC, box 283a, Kennedy Library, which, among other things, calls for a wide range of temporary systems: "under many circumstances, particularly in international communications, there is no point in providing for highly survivable circuits to people in extremely soft environments . . . designers of the survivable system should carefully consider the extent to which the needs . . . can be met by restorable rather than survivable communications. . . . The President must have the capability to reach on short notice the top leadership of a small number of selected allies . . . [and] the means for communications with the leadership of nuclear capable enemy powers immediately before, during, and after attack on this country." West Ford, if it could be made reliable, is a good example of a restorable system quickly adaptable to global communication in crisis conditions.

26. A presumption on my part as the name of the authoring agency and report under

discussion is still classified in the document from which this account is taken, although the classification appears consistent with classification protection afforded to the CIA and other intelligence agencies.

27. Wiesner to Kennedy, 25 October 1962, National Security Files, Meetings and Memoranda Series, NSAM no. 201, box 339, Kennedy Library. U.S. State Department, *Foreign Relations of the United States, Kennedy Administration*, vol. 25, *Organization of Foreign Policy; Information Policy; United Nations; Scientific Matters* (hereafter FRUS JFK) #436.

28. Memorandum from the Chairman of the Subcommittee on Communications of the National Security Council (Orrick) to the Executive Committee of the National Security Council, May 21, 1963, National Security Files, Meetings and Memoranda Series, NSAM no. 201, box 339, Kennedy Library. FRUS JFK #442.

29. Strictly speaking, no treaties to this day explicitly protect satellites, although the 1963 Limited Test Ban Treaty, the 1967 Outer Space Treaty, the 1972 ABM agreements and subsequent SALT (Strategic Arms Limitation Talks) agreements, and the 1997 Anti-Theater Missile Defense Agreements all offer implicit partial protection to satellites.

30. Thompson to Rusk, 21 February 1962, Kennedy NSC Papers, box 190a, folder US/USSR Television Exchange Broadcast, Kennedy Library.

31. This cable message came from Kennan while he was in Belgrade, but came through Paris. The citation on this document may be a bit confusing: Bundy to Sorenson (this is handwritten at top) received at State Department 23 February 1962, Kennedy NSC Papers, box 190a, folder US/USSR Television Exchange Broadcast, Kennedy Library. Eisenhower had also mulled the possibility of exchanged TV speeches with Khrushchev; see "Memorandum of Conference with President Eisenhower," 5 August 1959, Eisenhower Library, Whitman File, DDE Diaries. U.S. State Department, Foreign Relations of the United States, Eisenhower Administration, vol. 10, pt. 1: *Eastern Europe Region, Soviet Union, Cyprus*, #106.

32. Charles Bohlen to Bundy, 9 March 1962, Kennedy NSC Papers, box 190a, folder US/USSR Television Exchange Broadcast, Kennedy Library.

33. Newton Minow to Kenneth O'Donnell, 26 June 1962, Kennedy Presidential Papers, WHCF, box 247, Kennedy Library. Minow added, "as you can see, the White House is becoming familiar territory all over the world."

34. Nielsen News (press release), 21 March 1962, Kennedy WHCF, box 654, folder OS 4 3-1-62–3-31-62, Kennedy Library. The Glenn flight of 20 February 1962 had the largest American daytime TV audience to that date and drew slightly more viewers than either the Democratic or Republican nominating conventions of 1960. My parents kept me out of school that day (a rare occurrence!) so our family could watch the Glenn events live on TV.

35. Meyers to Ralph Dungan, "International Broadcasting," 24 May 1962, Minow Papers, box 18, folder International Communications 1961–1963, SHSW. Meyers later served as director of educational broadcasting projects overseas for the U.S. Peace Corps.

36. Ibid., 1–3.

37. Ibid., 4.

38. Ibid., 4–8.

39. Ibid., 8–9.

40. Ibid., 14. Meyers then went on to ask what has become a perennial (and still unresolved) question in presidential administrations: whether a single agency should be charged with international communications, and if so, which agency.

41. These events can be seen in the 1962 AT&T documentary *Behind the Scenes of Telstar,* which is still in distribution on both DVD and videocassette by several commercial film and video distributors. For a memoir of this telecast by an AT&T engineer, see Eugene O'Neill, "Commentary on the Telstar Project," 13 July 1991, at http://www.smecc.org/ eugene_0%27niell_-_telstar.htm. O'Neill recalls requesting of the AT&T managers an opportunity for in-house testing: "To my horror they vetoed this and arranged that the very first transmissions would be covered on nationwide TV." In 1964, Lyndon Johnson awarded Kappel the Presidential Medal of Freedom; John Kennedy had acted upon Nielsen and Cowan's suggestion in 1963 and inaugurated the Medal of Freedom awards.

42. Colella to Kennedy, 26 July 1962, Kennedy Presidential Papers, White House Central Subject Files, box 991, folder UT 1 11-1-61–4-17-62, Kennedy Library.

43. Price to Johnson, 24 July 1962; Gardner to Johnson, 1 August 1962; Myers to Johnson, 27 July 1962; Wykoff to Johnson, 12 July 1962; the Walter Van Broock family to Johnson, 16 July 1962; Rogers to Johnson, 11 July 1962; all Vice-Presidential Papers of Lyndon Johnson, box 183, folder Science Space and Aeronautics Telstar, Johnson Library.

44. Office of Research, Research memorandums, 1963–1982, "British Public Opinion on Space Leadership," M-36-70, 4 December 1970, RG 306, box 12, NARA.

45. For a discussion of high-altitude nuclear tests, satellites, and the "culture of reliability" in Cold War electronics research, see Jones-Imhotep, "Disciplining Technology," 125–75. Canada's first satellite, specifically designed for upper ionospheric (topside ionogram) measurements, was launched in the fall of 1962 amid questions of electronic reliability in highly radiated ionospheric conditions; this article also explores different attitudes regarding electronic reliability in military and commercial Cold War applications. On high-altitude tests and EMPs, see also testimony of George W. Ullrich, Deputy Director, Defense Special Weapons Agency, at House of Representatives Hearings on Threats Posed by Electromagnetic Pulse to U.S. Military Systems and Civilian Infrastructure, July 16, 1997 House Military Research & Development Subcommittee at http://www.fas.org/ spp/starwars/congress/1997_h/h970716u.htm.

46. On the damage to Telstar by Starfish Prime, see Barth, Dyer, and Stassinopolis, "Space, Atmospheric, and Terrestrial Radiation Environments," 466–82, esp. 470, which observes Telstar received one hundred times the radiation dose it was designed to withstand due to Starfish Prime. See also Early, "Telstar I—Dawn of a New Age." Also damaged was the U.K. Ariel 1 satellite, launched 26 April 1962 for ionospheric research. Ariel 1 experienced partial systems failure. Telstar's Pacific leg of its orbit did bring it fairly near to Johnson Island, but was also near its apogee of approximately 3,500 nautical miles.

47. Jones-Imhotep, "Disciplining Technology."

48. DuPont, "Nuclear Explosions in Orbit."

49. Corona, the American photo surveillance satellite system of this era, ejected an exposed film pod that was plucked mid-air by an airplane. Zenit, the Soviet counterpart, returned the entire satellite, film intact, to Soviet territory. On Corona, see Day, Logsdon, and Lattell, *Eye in the Sky;* on Zenit, see Harford, *Korolev.*

50. Unless otherwise indicated, the summary in this paragraph is based on Rusk to U.S. UN Delegation, 6 June 1963, Kennedy NSC Papers, box 308, Kennedy Library.

51. Radiation risk to satellites has most likely returned in the twenty-first century. The Defense Threat Reduction Agency (DTRA) forecast in 2001 that "the Low Earth Orbit (LEO) will likely be targetable by more 'rogue' regimes in the 21st century . . . the residual effects of a 10–50 kiloton nuclear weapon detonated at 120–300km altitude could disable, in a matter of weeks, all LEO satellites not explicitly hardened to absorb a total radiation dose 3–4 magnitudes of order greater than natural background levels." DTRA, *Twenty-First Century Threat Reduction*.

52. "Treaty Banning Nuclear Weapons Tests in the Atmosphere, in Outer Space and Underwater," art. 1, ¶ 1(b).

53. U.S. Atomic Veterans, Cecil R. Coale, Ph.D., at Atomic Veterans History Project Web site, http://www.aracnet.com/~pdxavets/cecil-co.htm. The magnetometer tests were run to measure any possible changes in the earth's magnetic field, and Coale recalled, "the strip chart recorders hummed loudly as soon as the flash occurred. Wow, was there a big change in the earth's magnetic field! Welcome to the electromagnetic pulse!" On Hawaii hotel rooftop parties, see also DuPont, "Nuclear Explosions."

54. Early, "Telstar I."

55. Ibid. Early states: "Unanticipated by the planners, and unknown to them, I believe, was that a hydrogen bomb was to be exploded in the upper atmosphere [the 'Starfish Prime' test] on July 9, 1962. The Telstar launch was scheduled for the early hours of July 10, 1962. Both launches went per schedule. The bomb fired and Telstar worked. The bomb, however, gave rise to enormous numbers of high energy electrons and ions, a substantial fraction of which went into the van Allen belts. These swamped completely the normal van Allen belt populations, and caused noticeable radiation damage. Loss of control of the satellite repeater occurred first in August. Painstaking and brilliant analysis by the circuit and system engineers identified the specific point of failure and provided revised commands which effectively bypassed the failed circuit, thus restoring control and usefulness of the satellite until continuing radiation damage caused final failure a few weeks later."

56. A. C. Dickieson, interview with Ed Sharpe, date unknown, Southwest Museum of Engineering, Communications, and Computation, at http://www.smecc.org/a_ _c_ _dickieson.htm.

57. NSSDC Master Catalog: Spacecraft, "Telstar 1," at http://nssdc.gsfc.nasa.gov/database/MasterCatalog?sc=1962–029A.

58. Martin, *Communication Satellites*.

59. Calculation of temporal and longitudinal approximations are by the author. In addition to DuPont, and the Early and Dickieson interviews, data for these tables is drawn from the following: "Operation Dominic" at http://www.hmm-364.0rg/dominic.html; "Chronological Listing of Above Ground Nuclear Detonations, 1962" at http://www.johnstonsarchive.net/nuclear/atest62.html; and "NASA-NSSDC Telstar 1" at http://nssdc.gsfc.nasa.gov/nmc/masterCatalog.do?sc=1962–029A.

60. "U.S. Nuclear Tests Infogallery" at http://www.radiochemistry.org/history/nuke_tests/dominic/.

61. Satellite and manned mission count tabulated from chronologies in Gunther's Space page Web site at http://www.skyrocket.de/space/

62. The South Atlantic Anomaly is roughly ovoid; the following description is a generalization based on landmasses. Above earth, the northern end of its ovoidal perimeter is near the mouth of the Amazon River, and its southern end is near the Falkland Islands. The anomaly curves down from above the mouth of the Amazon and curves up from the Falklands across the Atlantic to the southern tip of Africa, and westward nearly to the Galapagos Islands. The anomaly also fluctuates and drifts slightly westward over time.

63. For various images of the South Atlantic Anomaly, see http://visibleearth.nasa .gov/view_rec.php?id=192 or http://www.ngdc.noaa.gov/stp/GOES/image/uosat_t.gif. For orbital paths of Sputniks 1, 4, and 6 in relation to the South Atlantic Anomaly, see http://www.sputnikbook.net/images/gallery/orbit5.jpg, http://www.astrolink.de/pics/ m056/m056001/tk/m056001_002.jpg, or http://www.astrolink.de/pics/m056/m056004/ tk/m056004_001.jpg. For the John Glenn (Friendship 7) orbital path of 1962, see "Results of First Manned Orbital Space Flight, February 20, 1962," p. 6, at http://www-pao.ksc.nasa. gov/kscpao/history/mercury/ma-6/docs/ma-6–results.pdf.

Chapter 8: "A New Idea Capable of Uniting the Thoughts of People All Over the Earth"

1. National Aeronautics and Space Council, Policy Document, Communication Satellites, 7 July 1961, Lyndon Johnson Vice-Presidential Papers, box 117, folder Science—Space and Aeronautics Council—Communication Satellite Program [2 of 2], Johnson Library. Quotations in original.

2. Pierce, "Communication Satellites" *Scientific;* see also Glover, "NASA Experimental Communication Satellites, 1958–1995."

3. Kappel to E. C. Welch, 20 June 1961, Johnson Vice-Presidential Papers, box 117, folder Science—Space and Aeronautics Council—Communication Satellite Program [2 of 2], Johnson Library. For an analysis in defense of the AT&T position, see Whalen, *Origins of Satellite Communications.*

4. "Report to the Congress from the President of the United States, United States Aeronautic and Space Activities 1961," 31 January 1962, Kennedy NSC Papers, box 307, Kennedy Library.

5. Dutton to Kennedy, 13 November 1961, Kennedy WHCF, box 653, folder OS 2 Aeronautical and Space Vehicles 1961, Kennedy Library.

6. Gardner to Blumenthal, "U.S. Policy on the Organization of Global Satellite Communications," 4 October 1962, RG 59, IO/OES files lot 68D379, NARA, FRUS JFK #435. Unless otherwise indicated, the following discussion of this policy memorandum is based on this document.

7. Ibid., quotations in original.

8. David Bruce (London Embassy) to State Department, 8 May 1963, RG 59, lot 68D379, K-11, NARA. FRUS JFK #440.

9. "Aide-de-Memoire from the Government of the United States to the Governments of the United Kingdom and France," 26 June 1963, RG 59, lot 68D379, K-11, NARA. FRUS JFK #443.

10. E. C. Welch to Johnson, 13 March 1963 (recounts conversation between Welch and Sarnoff), Johnson Vice-Presidential Papers, box 192, folder Communication Satellite, Johnson Library. Welch added, "there is merit in Sarnoff's proposal . . . the nature of the business does not make competition the most effective condition for performing the services required." This is especially true when the "services required" are a single worldwide system rather than competing systems on the most lucrative international telecommunications service routes.

11. "Establishment of Intergovernmental Agency for Satellite Communications," 22 November 1963, RG 59, lot 68D379, K-11, NARA. FRUS JFK #448.

12. "Communication Satellites—Report of Plenary Meeting of European Conference on Satellite Communication, Rome, November 26–29, 1963," RG 59, lot 68D379, K-11, NARA. FRUS JFK #449.

13. For a good overview, see Slack, "Brief History of Satellite Communications," 7–20. See also Whalen, "Billion Dollar Technology."

14. "Outer Space," airgram from U.S. UN mission to State Department, 8 November 1963, RG 59, lot 68D379, K-11, NARA. FRUS JFK #447.

15. Ibid.

16. Papers of Horace Busby, box 43, folder Global Commercial Communications Satellites Comm.—Aug 20, 1964, Johnson Library.

17. COMSAT, *Communications Satellite Corporation Report Pursuant to Section 404(b) of the Communications Satellite Act of 1962, Report for 1964* (Washington, D.C.: Government Printing Office, 1965); a copy may be found in Johnson Presidential Papers, White House Central Files EX FG (hereafter Johnson WHCF EX FG), box 421, folder FG 806 Communications Satellite Corporation 8/14/64–3/17/66, Johnson Library.

18. Ibid. Two-way monochrome or one-way color charges were 150 percent of these rates. Readers should bear in mind that although several American TV stations were already offering 24–hour daily programming by 1965, 24–hour daily TV programming was largely unknown at that time in Europe.

19. *Prospectus, 10,000,000 Shares, Communications Satellite Corporation, Common Stock*; a copy is in Johnson Presidential Papers, WHCF (hereafter Johnson WHCF), box 421, folder FG 806 Communications Satellite Corporation 11/22/63–8/13/64, Johnson Library.

20. On the decision for separate American military and commercial satellite systems, see: Memorandum from the Deputy Secretary of Defense (Vance) to President Johnson, 13 March 1964, Johnson Library, National Security file, (hereafter Johnson NSC), subject file, Communications (Nat'l Communications Systems, COMSAT, etc.), Vol. 1 [2 of 2]; "Communication Satellites," in U.S. State Department, *Foreign Relations of the United States, Johnson Administration*, vol. 34, *Energy, Diplomacy and Global Issues* (hereafter FRUS LBJ), #64; Memorandum from the Legal Adviser (Chayes) (drafted by Leonard Marks) to the Under Secretary of State (Ball), 16 March 1964, RG 59, Records of the Department of State, Central Files, 1964–66, TEL 6, NARA, FRUS LBJ #65; Letter from the Chairman of the Military Operations Subcommittee of the House Committee on Government Operations (Holifield) to President Johnson, 13 May 1964, Johnson NSC, Communications (Nat'l Communications System, COMSAT, etc.), vol. 1., FRUS LBJ #67; Memorandum from the President's Special Assistant for Telecommunications (O'Connell) to Secretary

of Defense McNamara, 10 July 1964, Johnson NSC, subject file, Communications (Nat'l Communications System, COMSAT, etc.), vol. 1 [1 of 2], FRUS LBJ #70.

21. "Mr. President Comsat May be Heading for Trouble," undated letter, Johnson Presidential Papers, White House Confidential Files (hereafter Johnson Confidential), box 41, folder FG 806 Communications Satellite Corporation, Johnson Library. I have attributed this memo to Valenti because it is the cover memo (although a rough draft and unsigned, in the typical form of cover memos from aides to LBJ) attached to O'Connell to Valenti, 21 September 1965, a memo from O'Connell arguing for NASA contracting of Comsat services for the Apollo missions; as well as an earlier memo from O'Connell (7 May 1965) on lack of demand, and possible European resistance, to Comsat.

22. O'Connell to Johnson, 21 September 1965, Johnson Confidential, box 41, folder FG 806 Communications Satellite Corporation, Johnson Library. See also O'Connell to Special Assistant to the President W. Marvin Watson, 7 May 1965, "Policy Concerning U.S. Assistance in the Development of Foreign Communications Satellite Capabilities," Johnson Confidential, box 41, folder FG 806 Communications Satellite Corporation, Johnson Library.

23. Leland Johnson, "Communications Satellites and Underdeveloped Countries," January 1962, RAND, Memorandum RM-2985–NASA; a copy may be found in Papers of S. Douglas Cater (hereafter Cater Papers), box 46, folder Communications Satellite Service for Less Developed Countries (1), Johnson Library. On the Sprague Committee report, see chapter 3 of this study.

24. Hughes Corporation, "The Educational Satellite System," no date (1965), Cater Papers, box 46, folder Hughes Aircraft (2) [Educational Television Satellites], with cover memo to Cater dated 20 October 1965, Johnson Library. Norman Sherman of the White House staff advised Cater that "Hughes seems involved in the current struggle to break the Corporation's role as the chosen instrument . . . the ComSat Corporation could be asked to come forward with a proposal as to how this project might best be carried out . . . it could be farmed out to a neutral research outfit like Stanford Research Institute, Rand, etc. for study and recommendation."

25. Leonard Marks, Oral History, 15 June 1970, p. 41, Johnson Library.

26. Joseph Califano to Johnson, 11 October 1967, Johnson WHCF, box 363, folder FG 600/Task Force/Educational TV in LDC's, Johnson Library.

27. Loren Stone, "Television in Vietnam 1966—A Report," Papers of Leonard Marks (hereafter Marks Papers), box 29, folder Report on Vietnam, Johnson Library.

28. Hewson Ryan, "Network for Knowledge," 4 April 1968, Marks Papers, box 28, folder Network for Knowledge, Johnson Library. Emphasis in original. See also Andrew Aines to W. DeVier Piersen, 11 March 1968, background paper on Networks for Knowledge, Johnson WHCF, box 306, folder FG 600/Task Force/Networks for Knowledge, Johnson Library.

29. Edwards, *Closed World*, 3.

30. "USIS Program Indonesia," no month (probably August), 1967, Marks Papers, box 25, folder NSC, 1967, Johnson Library.

31. "The US Exhibit at Expo '67," December 1967, Marks Papers, box 22, folder Expo '67 Opinion Survey, Johnson Library. The call for science was met by the USIA at Osaka '70, with outer space accomplishments highlighted in a pavilion architecturally influenced by the moon.

32. "Foreign Educational Uses of Communications Satellite," 14 January 1967, memorandum by Douglass Cater, Johnson Library, National Security file, Charles E. Johnson files, COMSAT—Educational Purposes, NSAM 342 (Domestic and Foreign), #3, box 12. FRUS LBJ #92.

33. "Communications Satellite Earth Station Construction in Less Developed Countries—NSAM 342," 31 December 1966, RG 59, Department of State, NSAM files, lot 72 D 316, NARA. FRUS LBJ #91.

34. Chayes to Rusk, 30 March 1964, RG 59, Central Files, 1964–66, TEL 6, NARA; FRUS LBJ #66; U.S. Embassy, Bern, to State Department, 16 June 1964, RG 59, Central Files, 1964–66, TEL 6, NARA; FRUS LBJ #68. See also Dizard, *Digital Diplomacy,* 44–54.

35. Hughes to Rusk, 25 March 1968, RG 59, Central Files, 1967–69, TEL 6, NARA. FRUS LBJ #100.

36. American Embassy (Paris) to State Department, 13 May 1968, RG 59, Central Files, 1967–69, TEL 6, NARA. FRUS LBJ #101.

37. Rostow, memorandum of conversation, 19 August 1968, RG 59, Central Files, 1967–69, TEL 6. FRUS LBJ #105. For a discussion of this task force, see Comor, *Communication, Commerce, and Power,* esp. chaps. 3 and 4.

38. American Embassy, Vienna, to State Department, 21 August 1968, RG 59, Central Files, 1967–69, SP 6 UN, NARA; FRUS LBJ #106; Rusk to Johnson, 3 September 1968, RG 59, Central Files, 1967–69, TEL 6, NARA; FRUS LBJ #107.

39. Read to Rusk, 27 September 1968, RG 59, Central Files, 1967–69, TEL 6, NARA. FRUS LBJ #108. See also "The Soviet Statsionar Satellite Communications System: Implications for INTELSAT," April 1976, CIA Interagency Intelligence memorandum, Records of the Central Intelligence Agency, RG 263, National Intelligence Estimates, box 20, NARA. Intersputnik was purchased by Lockheed Martin in 1997.

40. "Remarks of the President at the Ceremony on the Outer Space Treaty"; "Remarks of his Excellency, Anatoly F. Dobrynin, Ambassador of the USSR to the United States, at the Ceremony of the Outer Space Treaty"; both press releases 10 October 1967, both in Johnson NSC, box 36, folder Outer Space Treaty, Johnson Library.

41. On the precedent of Antarctica in negotiating the 1967 treaty, see "Negotiations on Celestial Bodies—Outer Space Treaty," State Department, 22 June 1966; "Background Papers for Forthcoming Outer Space Talks in New York," 29 August 1966; "Proposal to USSR for agreement on Celestial Bodies," memo by Leonard Meeker, 23 June 1959; and "Position Paper for US Participation in Legal Subcommittee of UN Committee on the Peaceful Uses of Outer Space," 15 July 1960; all in papers of Joseph Califano, box 71, folder Celestial Bodies Treaty Negotiating History—SECRET, Johnson Library. The 15 June 1960 background paper observes, "there is a virtually universal interest in outer space . . . through sponsoring and facilitating programs of affirmative international cooperation, the United States can give a sense of meaningful participation to a number of countries that might otherwise be standing on the sidelines in frustration and growing hostility. By such initiatives the United States can induce very favorable comparisons with the attitude and policies of the Soviet Union. . . . It is in the United States interest to take measures to preclude claims to sovereignty over celestial bodies on the analogy of the recent Antarctic Treaty."

Epilogue

The four epigraphs are drawn from: (i) Richard Nixon, remarks at a "Salute to the President" dinner, New York City, 9 November 1971. See http://www.presidency.ucsb.edu/ws/index.php?pid=3212 for text. (ii) U.S. Department of Defense, Office of the Under Secretary of Defense for Acquisition, Technology, and Logistics, *Report of the Defense Science Board Task Force on Managed Information Dissemination,* October 2001. (iii) White House, Office of the Press Secretary, 9 October 2003, press release, remarks by the President to New Hampshire Air National Guard, at http://www.whitehouse.gov/news/releases/2003/10/20031009–9.html. (iv) "Rumsfeld: Al-Jazeera Promotes Terrorism," AP newswire, 4 June 2005.

1. Foucault, "Discourse on Language," 215.
2. To borrow and adapt from Jeremi Suri, détente became the practiced and crafted resolution of global tensions built up in the interplay of power and protest. Suri, *Power and Protest.*
3. Kerry, *Star-Spangled Mirror,* esp. preface and chap. 1.
4. As Bruce Kuklick argues, defense intellectuals of the Cold War era "were creatures of this culture and its beliefs and never offered advice that transcended the culture." Kuklick, *Blind Oracles,* 223.
5. Foucault, "Discourse on Language," 217.
6. Ibid.

Selected Bibliography

Archival Sources

Busby, Horace. Papers. Lyndon B. Johnson Presidential Library. Austin, Tex.

Califano, Joseph. Papers. Lyndon B. Johnson Presidential Library. Austin, Tex.

Cater, Douglas S. Papers. Lyndon B. Johnson Presidential Library. Austin, Tex.

Eisenhower, Dwight D. Presidential Papers. Dwight D. Eisenhower Presidential Library. Abilene, Kans.

Ford Foundation. Records of Grant Numbers PA05600104 and PA05800374. Microfilm. Ford Foundation, New York.

Gray, Gordon. Oral History (18 June 1973). Harry S. Truman Presidential Library. Independence, Mo.

Hickenlooper, Bourke. U.S. Senate Papers, Foreign Relations Committee Subject and Individual. Herbert Hoover Presidential Library. West Branch, Iowa.

Holthusen, Henry. Papers. Herbert Hoover Presidential Library. West Branch, Iowa.

Jackson, C. D. Records. Dwight D. Eisenhower Presidential Library. Abilene, Kans.

Johnson, Lyndon B. Presidential Papers. Lyndon B. Johnson Presidential Library. Austin, Tex.

———. Vice-Presidential Papers. Lyndon B. Johnson Presidential Library. Austin, Tex.

Kennedy, John. Presidential Papers. John F. Kennedy Presidential Library. Boston, Mass.

Marks, Leonard. Oral History (15 June 1970). Lyndon B. Johnson Presidential Library. Austin, Tex.

———. Papers. Lyndon B. Johnson Presidential Library. Austin, Tex.

Marquis, Donald. Oral History (27 October 1972). Ford Foundation Archives. New York.

Mickelson, Sig. Papers. State Historical Society of Wisconsin. Madison.

Minow, Newton. Papers. State Historical Society of Wisconsin. Madison.

National Broadcasting Company. Records. State Historical Society of Wisconsin. Madison.

Nielsen, Waldemar. Oral History (5 October 1972). Ford Foundation Archives. New York.

Records of the British Foreign Office. British Public Records Office. Kew Gardens, London, United Kingdom.

Records of the Central Intelligence Agency. Record Group 263. National Archives. Washington, D.C.

Records of the U.S. Department of State. Record Group 59. National Archives. Washington, D.C.

Records of the U.S. Information Agency. Record Group 306. National Archives. Washington, D.C.

Slater, Joseph E. Papers. Ford Foundation Archives. New York.

Streibert, Theodore. Oral History (10 December 1970). Dwight D. Eisenhower Presidential Library. Abilene, Kans.

Truman, Harry S. Presidential Papers. Harry S. Truman Presidential Library. Independence, Mo.

———. Staff Member and Office Files. Psychological Strategy Board Files. Harry S. Truman Presidential Library. Independence, Mo.

U.S. President's Committee on Information Activities Abroad (Sprague Committee). Dwight D. Eisenhower Presidential Library. Abilene, Kans.

U.S. State Department. Foreign Relations of the United States. Eisenhower Administration. Vol. 10. Pt. 1. *Eastern Europe Region, Soviet Union, Cyprus.*

———. Foreign Relations of the United States. Johnson Administration. Vol. 34. *Energy, Diplomacy, and Global Issues.*

———. Foreign Relations of the United States. Kennedy Administration. Vol. 25. *Organization of Foreign Policy: Information Policy; United Nations; Scientific Matters.*

Washburn, Abbott. Oral History (January 1968.) Dwight D. Eisenhower Presidential Library. Abilene, Kans.

White, Lee C. Papers. John F. Kennedy Presidential Library. Boston, Mass.

Published Sources

Abbas, Ackbar. *Hong Kong: Culture and the Politics of Disappearance.* Minneapolis: University of Minnesota Press. 1997.

Barth, J. L., with C. S. Dyer and E. G. Stassinopolis. "Space, Atmospheric, and Terrestrial Radiation Environments." *IEEE Transactions on Nuclear Science* 50, no. 3 (June 2003): 466–82.

Bergaust, Erik, and William Beller. *Satellite!* New York: Hanover House. 1956.

Berghahn, Volker R. *America and the Intellectual Cold Wars in Europe.* Princeton, N.J.: Princeton University Press. 2001.

Bernhard, Nancy E. *U.S. Television News and Cold War Propaganda, 1947–1960.* Cambridge: Cambridge University Press. 1999.

Bird, William L. *Better Living: Advertising, Media, and the New Vocabulary of Business Leadership, 1935–1955.* Evanston, Ill.: Northwestern University Press. 1999.

Callahan, David, and Fred I. Greenstein. "The Reluctant Racer: Eisenhower and U.S. Space Policy." In *Spaceflight and the Myth of Presidential Leadership.* Edited by Roger D. Launius and Howard E. McCurdy. Urbana: University of Illinois Press. 1997.

Clarke, Arthur. *Voice Across the Sea.* New York: Harper and Row. 1958.

Comor, Edward. *Communication, Commerce, and Power: The Political Economy of America and the Direct Broadcast Satellite, 1960–2000.* London: Macmillan. 1998.

Congressional Record. 81st Cong., 2nd sess., 1950. Vol. 96, pt. 110.

Conway, Flo, and Jim Siegelman. *Dark Hero of the Information Age: In Search of Norbert Wiener, the Father of Cybernetics.* New York: Basic Books. 2005.

Crane, Rhonda J. *The Politics of International Standards: France and the Color TV War.* Norwood, N.J.: Ablex. 1979.

Curtin, Michael. *Redeeming the Wasteland: Television Documentaries and Cold War Politics.* New Brunswick, N.J.: Rutgers University Press. 1995.

Day, Dwayne A., with John M. Logsdon and Brian Latell, eds. *Eye in the Sky: The Story of the Corona Spy Satellites.* Washington, D.C.: Smithsonian Institution Press. 1998.

Defense Threat Reduction Agency. *Twenty-First Century Threat Reduction.* Report. 30 November 2001. http://www.wslfweb.org/docs/dtraasco/nuclearstudies.pdf.

Der Derian, James. *Virtuous War: Mapping the Military-Industrial-Military-Entertainment Network.* Boulder: Westview. 2001.

Desjardins, Mary. *Recycled Stars: Female Stardom in the Age of Television and Video.* Durham, N.C.: Duke University Press. Forthcoming.

Dickson, Paul. *Sputnik: The Shock of the Century.* New York: Walker. 2001.

Dizard, Wilson. *Digital Diplomacy: U.S. Foreign Policy in the Information Age.* Westport, Conn.: Praeger/CSIS. 2001.

———. *Inventing Public Diplomacy: The Story of the U.S. Information Agency.* Boulder: Lynne Reinner. 2004.

Drummond, Phillip, and Richard Paterson, eds. *Television in Transition.* London: BFI. 1985.

Drummond, Phillip, Richard Paterson, and Janet Willis, eds. *National Identity and Europe: The Television Revolution.* London: BFI. 1993.

DuPont, Daniel. "Nuclear Explosions in Orbit." *Scientific American* 290, no. 6 (June 2004): 100–107.

Early, James. "Telstar I—Dawn of a New Age." *SMEC Vintage Electrics* 2 (1990): 67–84. http://www.smecc.org/james_early___telstar.htm.

Edwards, Paul. *The Closed World: Computers and the Politics of Discourse in Cold War America.* Cambridge, Mass.: MIT Press. 1996.

Elsner, Monika et al. "The Early History of German Television: The Slow Development of a Fast Medium." *Historical Journal of Film Radio and Television* 10, no. 2 (1990): 193–219.

Enden, Raundo, Eino Lytytinen, Timo Vihavainen, Raimo Salokangas, and Kari Ilomen, *Yleisradio 1926–1996: A History of Broadcasting in Finland.* Helsinki: WSOY. 1996.

Erlichigoity, Fernando. *Planet Management: Limits to Growth, Computer Simulations, and the Emergence of Global Spaces.* Evanston, Ill.: Northwestern University Press. 1999.

Ezell, Edward Clinton, and Linda Neuman Ezell. *The Partnership: A History of the Apollo-Soyuz Test Project.* NASA SP-4209, NASA History Series. Washington, D.C.: Government Printing Office. 1978. http://www.hq.nasa.gov/office/pao/History/SP-4209/ch2-3.htm#explanation2.

Fehrenbach, Heide. *Cinema in Democratizing Germany: Reconstructing National Identity After Hitler.* Chapel Hill: University of North Carolina Press. 1995.

Fekete, Ann Freshman. "Television in East and West Germany." *Television Opportunities Newsletter.* July–August 1953.

Foucault, Michel. "The Discourse on Language." 1970 College de France lecture. Translated by Rupert Sawyer in Foucault, *The Archeology of Knowledge.* New York: Tavistock. 1972.

Geniow-Hecht, Jessica. *Transmission Impossible: American Journalism as Cultural Diplomacy in Postwar Germany 1945–1955.* Baton Rouge: Louisiana State University Press. 1999.

Gerovitch, Slava. "'Mathematical Machines' of the Cold War: Soviet Computing, American Cybernetics and Ideological Disputes in the Early 1950s." *Social Studies of Science* 31/2 (April 2001): 253–87.

———. "'Russian Scandals': Soviet Readings of American Cybernetics in the Early Years of the Cold War." *The Russian Review* 60 (October 2001): 545–68.

———. *From Newspeak to Cyberspeak: A History of Soviet Cybernetics.* Cambridge, Mass.: MIT Press. 2002.

Gimbel, John. *Science, Technology, and Reparations: Exploitation and Plunder in Postwar Germany.* Stanford, Calif.: Stanford University Press. 1990.

Glander, Timothy. *Origins of Mass Communications Research During the American Cold War: Educational Effects and Contemporary Implications.* Mahwah, N.J.: Earlbaum. 2000.

Glover, Daniel R. "NASA Experimental Communication Satellites, 1958–1995." In Andrew J Butrica, ed. *Beyond the Ionosphere: Fifty Years of Satellite Communications.* NASA SP-4217, NASA History Series. Washington, D.C.: Government Printing Office. 1997. http://history.nasa.gov/SP-4217/sp4217.htm.

Gould, Jack. "Television Station WPIX has Premiere." *New York Times.* 20 June 1948.

Graham, Loren. *What Have We Learned About Science and Technology From the Russian Experience?* Stanford, Calif.: Stanford University Press. 1998.

Haddow, Robert. *Pavilions of Plenty: Exhibiting American Culture Abroad in the 1950s.* Washington, D.C.: Smithsonian Institution Press. 1997.

Harford, James. *Korolev.* New York: John Wiley and Sons. 1997.

Hempel, Manfred. "German Television Pioneers and the Conflict Between Public Programming and Wonder Weapons." *Historical Journal of Film Radio and Television* 10, no. 2 (1990): 123–62.

Hixson, Walter. *Parting the Curtain: Propaganda, Culture, and the Cold War 1945–1961.* New York: Palgrave. 1997.

Hoff, Peter. "German Television (1935–1944) as a Subject and Medium of National Socialist Propaganda." *Historical Journal of Film Radio and Television* 10, no. 3 (1990): 227–40.

Jones-Imhotep, Edward. "Disciplining Technology: Electronic Reliability, Cold-War Military Culture and the Topside Ionogram." *History and Technology* 17 (2000): 125–75.

Kerry, Richard. *The Star-Spangled Mirror: America's Image of Itself and the World.* Savage, Md.: Rowman and Littlefield. 1990.

Kohntopp, Kerstin, and Siegfried Ziclinksi. "*Der Deutsche Rundfunk* and Television: an Introduction and Bibliography of Television-Related Articles, 1923–1941." *Historical Journal of Film Radio and Television* 10, no. 3 (1990): 221–25.

Kotkin, Stephen. *Magnetic Mountain: Stalinism as a Civilization.* Berkeley: University of California Press. 1995.

Kuklick, Bruce. *Blind Oracles: Intellectuals and War from Kennan to Kissinger.* Princeton, N.J.: Princeton University Press. 2006.

LaFeber, Walter. "Technology and U.S. Foreign Relations." *Diplomatic History* 24, no. 1 (Winter 2000): 1–19.

Light, Jen. *From Warfare to Welfare: Defense Intellectuals and Urban Problems in Cold War America.* Baltimore, Md.: Johns Hopkins University Press. 2003.

Logsdon, John, ed. *Exploring the Unknown: Selected Documents in the History of the U.S. Civilian Space Program.* Washington, D.C.: National Aeronautics and Space Administration. 1998. Microfilm.

Marling, Karal Ann. *As Seen on TV: The Visual Culture of Everyday Life in the 1950s.* Cambridge, Mass.: Harvard University Press. 1994.

Martin, Donald. *Communication Satellites.* 4th ed. Los Angeles: Aerospace Press and American Institute of Aeronautics and Astronautics. 2000.

Mayers, David. *The Ambassadors and America's Soviet Policy.* New York: Oxford University Press. 1995.

Needell, Allan A. "Project Troy and the Cold War Annexation of the Social Sciences." In Christopher Simpson, ed. *Universities Under Siege: Money and Politics in the Social Sciences During the Cold War.* New York: New Press. 1998.

Nelson, Michael. *War of the Black Heavens: The Battles of Western Broadcasting in the Cold War.* Syracuse, N.Y.: Syracuse University Press. 1997.

Nielsen, Waldemar. *Inside American Philanthropy: the Dramas of Donorship.* Norman: University of Oklahoma Press. 1996.

Noam, Eli. *Television in Europe.* Oxford: Oxford University Press. 1991.

Osgood, Kenneth. *Total Cold War: Eisenhower's Secret Propaganda Battle at Home and Abroad.* Lawrence: University of Kansas Press. 2006.

Parks, Lisa. *Cultures in Orbit: Satellites and the Televisual.* Durham, N.C.: Duke University Press. 2005.

Partner, Simon. *Assembled in Japan: Electrical Goods and the Making of the Japanese Consumer.* Berkeley: University of California Press. 1999.

Pierce, John Robinson. "Communication Satellites." *Scientific American* 205 (October 1961): 90–102.

Ploman, Edward W. *Space, Earth and Communication.* Westport, Conn.: Greenwood Press. 1984.

Ponomarkeno, Maria. "Out of the Kitchen: Khrushchev's 1959 Visit to the United States." MA thesis, University of Chicago. 2005.

Price, Monroe. *Television, the Public Sphere, and National Identity.* Oxford: Oxford University Press. 1995.

"RAMAC and Model C on Moscow Mission." *IBM World Trade News.* July 1959.

Rawnsley, Gary, ed. *Cold War Propaganda in the 1950s.* London: Macmillan. 1999.

Richelson, Jeffrey T. *The Wizards of Langley: Inside the CIA's Directorate of Science and Technology.* Boulder: Westview. 2001.

Roundtable on "The American Occupation of Germany in Cultural Perspective." *Diplomatic History* 23, no. 1 (Winter 1999):1–77.

Saunders, Frances Stonor. *The Cultural Cold War: The CIA and the World of Arts and Letters.* New York: New Press. 1999.

"Scientists Set Transmission Record." *Northwestern University Observer.* 5 December 2002.

Schivelbusch, Wolfgang. *In A Cold Crater: Cultural and Intellectual Life in Berlin, 1945–1948.* Translated by Kelly Barry. Berkeley: University of California Press. 1998.

Schwoch, James. "Global Dialogues, Paradigmatic Shifts, and Complexity: Emergent Contours of Theory and Praxis in Telecommunications Policy." *Emergences: Journal for the Study of Media and Composite Cultures* 11, no. 1 (May 2001): 133–52.

———. *The American Radio Industry and Its Latin American Activities, 1900–1939.* Urbana: University of Illinois Press. 1990.

Shulman, Holly Cowan. *The Voice of America: Propaganda and Democracy, 1941–1945.* Madison: University of Wisconsin Press. 1990.

Simpson, Christopher. *Science of Coercion: Communication Research and Psychological Warfare, 1945–1960.* New York: Oxford University Press. 1994.

Slack, Edward. "A Brief History of Satellite Communications." *Pacific Telecommunications Review* 22, no. 3 (2001): 7–20.

Smith, Anthony ed. *Television: An International History.* 2nd ed. Oxford: Oxford University Press. 1998.

Sproule, J. Michael. *Propaganda and Democracy: The American Experience of Media and Mass Persuasion.* Cambridge: Cambridge University Press. 1997.

Suri, Jeremi. *Power and Protest: Global Revolution and the Rise of Détente.* Cambridge, Mass.: Harvard University Press. 2003.

Tracey, Michael. *The Decline and Fall of Public Service Broadcasting.* Oxford: Oxford University Press. 1998.

"Treaty Banning Nuclear Weapons Tests in the Atmosphere, in Outer Space and Underwater." 10 October 1963, *United States Treaties and Other International Agreements* 14, pt. 2.

Uricchio, William. "Introduction to the History of German Television, 1935–1944." *Historical Journal of Film Radio and Television* 10, no. 3 (1990): 115–22.

Von Eschen, Penny. *Satchmo Blows Up the World: Jazz Ambassadors Play the Cold War.* Cambridge: Harvard University Press. 2004.

Wagnleitner, Reinhold. *Coca-Colonization and the Cold War: The Cultural Mission of the United States in Austria After the Second World War.* Chapel Hill: University of North Carolina Press. 1994.

Wang, Jessica. *American Science in an Age of Anxiety: Scientists, Anticommunism, and the Cold War.* Chapel Hill: University of North Carolina Press. 1999.

Whalen, David J. "Billion Dollar Technology: A Short Historical Overview of the Origins of Communications Satellite Technology, 1945–1965." In Andrew J Butrica, ed. *Beyond the Ionosphere: Fifty Years of Satellite Communications.* NASA SP-4217, NASA History Series. Washington, D.C.: Government Printing Office, 1997.

———. *The Origins of Satellite Communications, 1945–1965.* Washington, D.C.: Smithsonian Institution Press. 2002.

Williams, Arthur. *Broadcasting and Democracy in West Germany.* Philadelphia: Temple University Press. 1976.

Winkler, Jonathan. "Wiring the World: U.S. Foreign Policy and Global Strategic Communications, 1914–1921." PhD diss., Yale University. 2004.

Index

JAMES SCHWOCH is an associate professor of Media, Technology, and Society at Northwestern University. He is the coeditor of *Questions of Method in Cultural Studies* and *Writing Media Histories: Nordic Views.* He is also the coauthor of *Media Knowledge: Readings in Popular Culture, Pedagogy, and Critical Citizenship* and the author of *The American Radio Industry and Its Latin American Activities, 1900–1939.*

The University of Illinois Press
is a founding member of the
Association of American University Presses.

―――――――――――――――――――

Composed in 10.5/13 Adobe Minion Pro
by Jim Proefrock
at the University of Illinois Press
Manufactured by Sheridan Books, Inc.

University of Illinois Press
1325 South Oak Street
Champaign, IL 61820-6903
www.press.uillinois.edu